Ayn Rand and *Song of Russia*

Communism and Anti-Communism in 1940s Hollywood

Robert Mayhew

THE SCARECROW PRESS, INC.
Lanham, Maryland • Toronto • Oxford
2005

SCARECROW PRESS, INC.

Published in the United States of America
by Scarecrow Press, Inc.
A wholly owned subsidiary of
The Rowman & Littlefield Publishing Group, Inc.
4501 Forbes Boulevard, Suite 200, Lanham, Maryland 20706
www.scarecrowpress.com

PO Box 317
Oxford
OX2 9RU, UK

British Library Cataloguing in Publication Information Available

Library of Congress Cataloging-in-Publication Data

Mayhew, Robert.
  Ayn Rand and Song of Russia : Communism and anti-Communism in 1940s
Hollywood / Robert Mayhew.
    p. cm.
  Includes bibliographical references and index.
  ISBN 0-8108-5276-4 (alk. paper)
  1. Song of Russia (Motion picture) 2. Rand, Ayn. 3. United States. Congress. House.
Committee on Un-American Activities. 4. Communism and motion pictures—United
States. I. Title.
PN1997.S63335M39 2005
791.43'72—dc22

                                                                            2004011944

⊗™ The paper used in this publication meets the minimum requirements of
American National Standard for Information Sciences—Permanence of Paper for
Printed Library Materials, ANSI/NISO Z39.48-1992.

In memory of the Lubyanka Thousand—
the over one thousand writers
murdered in the Soviet Union
during the period the Hollywood Ten
supported Stalin—and to Ayn Rand,
who made it out.

Contents

~

Acknowledgments

I wish to thank Leonard Peikoff for permission to use previously unpublished materials of Ayn Rand. Thanks also to Jeff Britting, archivist (and my sherpa) at the Ayn Rand Archives, for his help in guiding me through mountains of material on Ayn Rand, and for his enthusiasm and encouragement. Michael Berliner answered a number of questions about Ayn Rand's life, and chapter 4 is much better as a result. A version of chapter 8 appeared as an article in *The Intellectual Activist*; editor Rob Tracinski made a number of suggestions that improved that chapter. I am extremely grateful to Tore Boeckmann and Shoshana Milgram, who each read through a draft of the entire book, and made numerous useful comments. Barbara Hall and her staff at the Margaret Herrick Library in Los Angeles were extremely helpful in guiding a stranger to film archives through the many treatments, outlines, screenplays, etc., in the *Song of Russia* file. Many thanks to Richard Collins, co-screenwriter of *Song of Russia*, who was very generous with his time, granting me three interviews. Seton Hall University and the Ayn Rand Institute both awarded me travel grants that made possible two trips to California to work at the Ayn Rand Archives and the Margaret Herrick Library. Further, some of this book was written in spring 2000, while I was on sabbatical leave; my thanks to Seton Hall for its continued support of my research. Special thanks are due the Charles Sures Memorial Scholarship Fund (of the Ayn Rand Institute) for two grants which enabled me to focus my research time on this project.

Much of this book deals with Stalin's Russia, and with the Hollywood Communists who supported her. My wife, Estelle, has heard me talk about some depressing topics during the past few years. Many thanks for her patience and support.

~

A Note on the Hollywood Ten
and the Lubyanka Thousand

Throughout this book, I refer to the Hollywood Ten, that is, the ten "unfriendly" witnesses at the October 1947 HUAC hearings in Washington, D.C. (who later went to jail for contempt of Congress). Because I often discuss (and criticize) them as one group, I should point out that although there were subtle differences among them—for example, in the degree to which they remained Communist in the years following the death of Stalin—the only significant exception is Edward Dmytryk, who fully repudiated his Communist past when he broke with the Party. Please keep this exception in mind when I speak critically of the Hollywood Ten.

In the dedication, I refer to the Lubyanka Thousand. The Lubyanka was the infamous Moscow headquarters of the Soviet secret police (whatever they called themselves: Cheka, GPU, NKVD, KGB). Many innocent people were imprisoned, tortured, and killed there. On the Lubyanka Thousand— the writers who perished in the Soviet Union under Stalin—see chapter 6 of this book, under "Culture," or for a fuller account, Vitaly Shentalinsky's *Arrested Voices: Resurrecting the Disappeared Writers of the Soviet Regime* (New York: Free Press, 1996).

~

Introduction

At a *bon voyage* party for Ayn Rand in January 1926, before she left Russia for the United States, a gentleman approached her and said: "When you get there, tell them that Russia is a huge cemetery and that we are all dying."[1] For much of her life, Ayn Rand told us.

She did so when, in the 1930s, she gave anti-Soviet speeches to a Hollywood becoming increasingly enamored of the Soviet Union. And she did so in her first novel, *We the Living*, which ripped the leftist veil off the Soviet dictatorship and its hostility to human life. Toward the end of that novel, the heroine—who wants desperately to escape Russia—promises a relative: "I'll tell them about everything . . . over there . . . where I'm going . . . I'll tell them about everything . . . it's like an S.O.S. . . . And maybe . . . someone . . . somewhere . . . will understand."[2]

After achieving success with her next novel, *The Fountainhead*, Rand continued to send out this S.O.S. about the misery of Soviet "life," hoping that someone, somewhere, would hear it. In October 1947, over twenty years after leaving Russia, she went to Washington, D.C., to testify before the House Un-American Activities Committee (HUAC), then investigating Communist infiltration into the motion picture industry—an industry in which she had worked for many years. "My coming here is not a patriotic duty," she told a reporter in Washington at the time, "so much as it is something I wanted to do, part of what I'm trying to say."[3] Part of what she was "trying to say" was that dictatorship—and at the time, that meant the Soviet Union and Communism most of all—is evil, dangerous, and contrary to the interests and fundamental principles of America.

Unfortunately, and contrary to what they had led her to expect, the HUAC asked Rand solely about the film *Song of Russia* (MGM, 1944).

This book is about *Song of Russia*, and Ayn Rand's HUAC testimony on it. In part 1, I present a synopsis of *Song of Russia* (chapter 1), then discuss how it was made (chapter 2) and how it was received after its release (chapter 3). In part 2, I look at Rand's life (chapter 4), discuss her opinion of the HUAC (chapter 5), analyze her HUAC testimony (chapters 6 and 7), and finally, discuss how her testimony was—and continues to be—treated by commentators (chapter 8). There is a brief conclusion.

Why focus on *Song of Russia*, given its quality—it is a mediocre film—and Rand's opinion of it as obvious propaganda and thus unimportant? Because *Song of Russia* is superb for the case study undertaken in this book. It is a pro-Soviet film, made by a conservative studio head (Louis B. Mayer), starring a conservative actor (Robert Taylor), and written predominantly by members of the U.S. Communist Party. But most of all, it is the film Rand commented on in her HUAC testimony.

Ayn Rand is uniquely qualified as a commentator on Hollywood Communism. She was born in Russia in 1905, witnessed the revolution in 1917, and remained there until 1926. In Russia she heard firsthand what Communists had to say and experienced firsthand what they do when in power. She felt the terror of living under Communism; for example, she was "purged" from the University of Leningrad along with other non-Communist students, genuine victims of a Communist blacklist. In the United States, she lived in Hollywood from September 1926 to November 1934, and again from December 1943 to October 1951, working much of that time as a screenwriter. During her Hollywood periods—and especially the latter—she encountered and fought against Hollywood Communism. Finally, at the time she was called to testify in Washington, she was maturing as an original philosopher, and especially as a moral and political philosopher. As a result, she had a lot to say that was not said elsewhere, about fundamental issues that went well beyond *Song of Russia*, including the nature and function of the HUAC, whether the hearings violated freedom of speech, the nature and propriety of blacklists, and so on.

An analysis of the making of *Song of Russia*, its nature and reception, and Ayn Rand's comments on it provides us with a focused look at Communism in Hollywood *and* a unique philosopher's views on Hollywood Communism. This case study supports an appraisal quite different from the standard picture of Hollywood Communism, the 1947 HUAC hearings, and how we ought to evaluate the friendly witnesses (including Rand) who cooperated with the HUAC and the unfriendly witnesses (the Hollywood Ten) who did not.

According to this standard picture of the 1947 HUAC hearings—as found, for example, in *Tender Comrades*, a collection of interviews of Hollywood leftists, published fifty years after the these hearings[4]—whatever Ayn Rand's intentions, she collaborated with a Nazi-like government organization in one of the worst periods of American history. In this view, the HUAC was a group of power-hungry fascists who subjected the heroic Hollywood Communists and their sympathizers—who were humane and progressive—to nothing short of an inquisition. This was—as Lillian Hellman dubbed it—Scoundrel Time. Similarly, Norman Mailer calls this period "that squalid time when the witch-hunt was on in Hollywood." And according to Hollywood leftist Walter Bernstein, the HUAC represented "the closest thing to Nazis holding positions of influence within the United States."[5] This was a time—we have heard endlessly—of witch hunts, red-baiting, and anti-Communist paranoia, when snitches named names to save their necks, and innocent victims lost their livelihood, while the HUAC trampled on the First Amendment.

In light of who the Hollywood Communists actually were, who and what they in fact supported, and what really happened at the 1947 HUAC hearings and after, the standard picture is utter nonsense.

This case study should aid in correcting the false picture that has been painted of that era and of the Communists who worked in Hollywood in the 1940s. A proper understanding of this period in American history begins with Kenneth Billingsley's *Hollywood Party*,[6] but much more needs to be said.

In 1944, George Orwell complained:

England is lacking . . . in what one might call [Soviet] concentration-camp literature. The special world created by secret police forces, censorship of opinion, torture and frame-up trials is, of course, known about and to some extent disapproved of, but it has made very little emotional impact. One result of this is that there exists in England almost no literature of disillusionment about the Soviet Union.[7]

This captures well another reason for writing this book. Sixty years after Orwell wrote these lines, the same can be said of the Left in the United States, and certainly of Hollywood and the movies it makes. There is disapproval of the former Soviet Union and a grudging admittance that, well, yes, the Soviets did violate human rights. But the disapproval is perfunctory, and certainly not passionate. The "never again" attitude properly surrounding the Holocaust, which has contributed to the appearance of so many films on the Nazis and the horrors they committed, is nowhere in evidence if one looks at Hollywood's history of (not) presenting the Soviet Union and Communist atrocities. Instead of "never again" (and the implication: "never forget"), the attitude is, "Let's put this behind us."[8]

It is my hope that this book will help to open Hollywood's eyes to its unconscionable neglect to tell the truth about the Soviet Union—to do what *Song of Russia* claimed to do, but did not. In Europe—where Communism has always been taken more seriously than in the United States—the film industries are beginning to make movies that accurately portray the Soviet Union and Eastern Europe (for example, the 1994 Russian film *Burnt by the Sun*, and the 1999 French film *East-West*). Meanwhile, Hollywood remains reactionary; the industry dares say nothing that might suggest the truth: that what the Hollywood Communists supported for all those years was a monstrous evil.

Finally, I want to defend Ayn Rand and her much-maligned HUAC testimony. It hardly seems possible, but in reaction to her attempts to tell Americans about the horrors of the Soviet Union—in her HUAC testimony and elsewhere—she has received ridicule and scorn, and she has received it from people whose raison d'être, politically, is a supposed concern for the suffering of humanity. This book makes clear that Rand's HUAC testimony and her evaluation of the HUAC hearings are correct.

A woman writer, confined to the infamous Siberian gulag, Kolyma, wrote on the back of an envelope:

> In honor of the slain one stays silent
> Or talks at the top of one's voice.[9]

In the fifty years since the HUAC hearings, the Hollywood Communists and their sympathizers have remained silent about those slain in the Soviet Union they supported; but their silence has nothing to do with honor. They have, however, been complaining vigorously and loudly about the supposedly brutal treatment they received in the 1940s and after for their devotion to the Soviet Union. In honor of the slain, and out of disgust for the Hollywood Communists and their undeserved status as victims, Ayn Rand "talked at the top of her voice." But she died over twenty years ago. I wrote this book to help to ensure that her voice will continue to be heard, and so that what the Hollywood Communists did—what they supported—will not be forgotten.

Notes

1. Quoted in Leonard Peikoff's foreword to the sixtieth anniversary edition of Ayn Rand, *We the Living* (New York: Signet, 1996; original ed., Macmillan, 1936; rev. ed., Random House, 1959), v.

2. Rand, *We the Living*, 451 (ellipses in original).

3. Mary McGrory, "Ayn Rand, Russian-Born Authoress, Says She's Glorifying Capitalist in New Novel," *Washington Star*, November 2, 1947.

4. Patrick McGilligan and Paul Buhle, eds., *Tender Comrades: A Backstory of the Hollywood Blacklist* (New York: St. Martin's Griffin, 1997).

5. Lillian Hellman, *Scoundrel Time* (Boston: Little Brown, 1976); Mailer's quote is from his cover blurb for *Tender Comrades*; Bernstein's is found in McGilligan and Buhle, *Tender Comrades*, 48.

6. Kenneth Lloyd Billingsley, *Hollywood Party: How Communism Seduced the American Film Industry in the 1930s and 1940s* (Rocklin, CA: Prima, 1998).

7. George Orwell, "Arthur Koestler" (typescript dated September 11, 1944), in George Orwell, *Essays*, selected and introduced by John Carey (New York: Everyman Library, 2002), 739.

8. On this attitude among revisionist historians of American Communism, see John Earl Haynes and Harvey Klehr, *In Denial: Historians, Communism and Espionage* (San Francisco: Encounter Books, 2003), 85–87.

9. Vitaly Shentalinsky, *Arrested Voices: Resurrecting the Disappeared Writers of the Soviet Regime*, trans. John Crowfoot (New York: Free Press, 1996), 284.

PART ONE

DISTORTING FACTS: SONG OF RUSSIA

~

CHAPTER ONE

Song of Russia: A Synopsis

Song of Russia (MGM, 1944) is today relatively unknown and inaccessible—
it is not available on video or DVD, and rarely appears on television—and so
a detailed synopsis of the film is necessary.[1] Such a synopsis is needed to understand fully the history of the creation of the film, as well as Ayn Rand's
HUAC testimony.

The opening credits roll to the sound of Tschaikovsky's Piano Concerto No. 1.
    The film opens in New York City. At "Manhattan Hall"—its name in
bright lights—famed American conductor John Meredith (Robert Taylor) is
about to perform a tribute to Russia. It is most likely sometime in 1942.
    The announcer tells us that fate sent John Meredith to Russia in 1941,
where "he heard and saw and felt and suffered the appalling horrors of the
Nazi invasion,"[2] and the awful months that followed. Meredith takes the
stage. The announcer continues: This experience gave Meredith a deeper
understanding of Russian composers. As he holds the baton, "his thoughts
must inevitably be carried back to his intense and dramatic experience" in
wartime Russia. Meredith leads the orchestra in the American national anthem. His thoughts do go back to Russia.
    There is a flashback to Meredith's arrival in Russia. His plane has landed,
and a Russian band plays the American national anthem—there has been no
break in the music since before the flashback—while a cheerful crowd (despite the grim weather) waits for Meredith to disembark. Amid the sea of um-
brellas is a Soviet flag, with hammer and sickle. In the background, a sign

reads "Mockau" (Moscow). During the national anthem, we see portraits of Lenin and Stalin. A radio announcer informs the crowd that John Meredith has arrived. We learn that he is on a concert tour of Russia.

Petrov (Felix Bressart), of the Central Art Committee of the Government, greets Meredith "on behalf of the 190 million citizens." He ends his greeting with: "All hail the cultural achievements of our free people." While Petrov speaks, an attractive young lady with medium-length dark hair, dark eyes, and an intense, bright smile, presses forward, anxious to speak to Meredith. But she is blocked. A bit later, moving slowly through a crowd, with the persistent girl following, members of the press ask Meredith for an interview: "What are your impressions of Moscow?" "Have you any statement for *Pravda*, please?"

Next, Meredith is settled in and refreshed, practicing with an orchestra a selection from Tschaikovsky's *Nutcracker*. A bit later, as he discusses his schedule with his business manager, Hank Higgins (Robert Benchley), the young Russian woman—Nadya Stepanova (Susan Peters)—finally gets Meredith's attention by playing Tschaikovsky on the piano.

John: "You're wonderful. Who are you?"
Nadya: "I want to talk to you."
John: "Okay."

Nadya has come from a small village, Tschaikowskoye (named after Tschaikovsky), just to talk to Meredith.[3] She asks if he could perform at their music festival, which they hold every year after the harvest. Such decisions aren't made on an empty stomach, and besides, John likes what he sees: "How about dinner?"

He takes her to an opulent, crowded restaurant, with brilliant chandeliers and a band playing lively music. The crowd is cheerful and smiling. John's presence is noticed, and a young lady asks for his autograph. A waiter arrives, and Nadya orders a vast array of Russian foods, including zakuski, borscht, pirojki, lososina, beef stroganoff, cutlets Pojarski, and shashlik. John looks around thoughtfully, and comments: "I can't get over it. Everybody seems to be having such a good time. . . . I always thought Russians were a sad, melancholy people, sitting around brooding about their souls. This is such a surprise." To Nadya, he adds: "You're a surprise, too. . . . If I didn't know that I met you in Moscow, you might be an American girl." She replies: "But I've never even met an American before."

Nadya gets down to business, and asks John whether he'll come to Tschaikowskoye for their festival. He promises to try to arrange it. In the meantime, they'll see Moscow together, which they do the following day.

A montage of Moscow highlights, set to triumphant Russian music, flashes past us, introducing us to the city. Trolleys shoot past, and buses and an endless stream of cars, shiny and fast moving. John holds up a brochure on the famous Moscow subway; next, the couple is traveling on it, in the company of smiling Red Army soldiers. With a shot of a statue of Stalin, we move from the subway to smiling children in the park, to a soccer stadium full of fans, to an Olympic-size swimming pool. Next, John and Nadya are on a hydroplane, sitting comfortably and sipping drinks. Moscow is a thriving, prosperous city.

Cut to a ballroom at night. John has taken Nadya dancing. "It's all arranged," he tells her. "I'm coming to your village in August." She asks him why he wanted to come to Russia. He says he has been interested in Russian music since he was fourteen years old, when he first heard Tschaikovsky's Symphony Pathetique. Later, at dinner—"the most romantic spot in the whole city"—they listen to a melancholy song, "And Russia Is Her Name" (Yip Harburg's lyrics set to the melody of Jerome Kern's "Lyrical Foxtrot"):

> She stood beside my plow, she kissed away my tears,
> And warmed my empty hands through all the empty years,
> And when she smiled, the heartbreak vanished and the daybreak came,
> And she is still my own, and Russia is her name.

Throughout the day, with every glance, gesture, smile, and touch, it becomes obvious that John and Nadya are in love. "Tell me about yourself," he asks. "I'm just an ordinary Russian girl from a little village," she replies. Later, embracing after a long kiss, they declare their love for each other. But there is a problem, she says: "We have serious differences—socially, culturally." John sees no problem.

In the next scene, John conducts Tschaikovsky's Piano Concerto No. 1, as Nadya, smiling, watches with great admiration from the balcony. But her smile fades to a frown, and when he looks up at the conclusion of the piece, she is gone.

The story moves from town to country—from Moscow to Tschaikowskoye.

In the village center, we see bustling, busy townspeople; the church, with two onion shaped domes, is prominent; there is a row of houses in good condition. The screen is next filled with fields of wheat waving in the wind. Peasants are working the fields. We move in on them. Their clothes and faces are clean. Nadya and another girl—both attractive and smiling—are working on the back of a tractor, driven by Nadya's father, Stepanov (Michael Checkhov). In the background, there are a couple of other tractors and a couple of horses. Tschaikowskoye is a thriving, prosperous village.

A twelve-year-old boy named Peter (Darryl Hickman) drives up in a car to tell Nadya, with great excitement, that John Meredith will be arriving in Tschaikowskoye on the 3:00 P.M. train! (John cut his tour short, and so is arriving in May instead of August.) She does not look pleased. She can't make the train, she says, for she has work to do.

The train arrives on time; John is met by the head of the music school, Alexander Meschkov (Vladimir Sokoloff), a smiling crowd, and a student band. Everyone, young and old, appears clean, healthy, and happy—and excited at the arrival of the famous American musician. Nadya's father invites John to stay at their house, and he accepts. A bit later he meets some of the Stepanovs' neighbors, seated around a radio. Boris (John Hodiak), with a wide smile, tells John: "We grow many fine things in our country, but the finest crop of all is this," indicating his son Peter with a gentle pat on the back.

John hears the peasants returning from the fields, singing cheerfully. He and Nadya finally see each other. Nadya is cool to "Mr. Meredith." He tells Nadya's sister: "In my country, that's known as the brush-off."

At night, outside of the Stepanov's modest but well-kept house, a light is burning bright inside, and with three neighborhood children, we peek through the window to see John and the Stepanovs having dinner. "Mr. Meredith," Stepanov declares, "here you are at a simple, peasant farm table, where we have nothing to offer you but our company, and the country food we eat ourselves." The successful, cosmopolitan American is obviously impressed at the abundance of food and drink at an average peasant meal.

Stepanov changes the subject to an object of great pride: "Our tractor is a beauty." One assumes he owns it; he has named it Golubchuk (Darling). John is then given a tour of the farm and their grain. Agriculturally, things are going well.

In the farm's loft, at their first chance to be alone, John confronts Nadya and asks her why she left. Nadya tells him that *he* is moved by emotion—for him, "I love you" is sufficient motivation. *She*, however, is moved by reason—she is realistic. The reason she left him in Moscow, she explains, is that there are thousands of miles between them: He belongs in a concert hall, she in a Russian village. John responds by proposing to her. Her answer: "I have a great responsibility, to my family and to my village, and to the way in which I've lived. I don't quite see how I can build a life with you, and then also help to build a better and better life for my country." She has to think it over.

The next day, Peter drives John around the farmland, explaining the Russian system of civil defense, in which everyone takes part. They drive toward a group of men and women, all neat and smiling, who—young and old—are practicing civil defense. Nadya is behind a machine gun, honing her skills. There is singing in the background.

We cut to the next scene—two domes of a Russian Orthodox church—and learn of Nadya's decision. A priest marries John and Nadya, according to traditional Orthodox customs. At the wedding feast, there is plenty of food, chocolate cake, vodka, wine, and good cheer. The father toasts the couple: "To your happiness, to the happiness of your great country, to the happiness of our great country," to which the priest adds: "To Nadya and John, God bless you both."

Hank, John's manager, drunkenly voices the only objection to the marriage. He tells Stepanov that he just doesn't see it: "He's an American. It's unpatriotic." "You'll see it, you'll see it," Stepanov responds, pouring him another shot of vodka.

Peter congratulates the newlyweds. John tells him he has a lot of ability; Peter replies: "But I also have the opportunity. That's very important."

John and Nadya leave Tschaikowskoye and he resumes his tour. We are shown a montage of the tour—John conducting, Nadya gazing proudly from the wings or a balcony—and it is a big success. Next, the couple is at home, having a lazy moment alone; lying beside each other on the floor, she asks him to tell her about America.

John: It's wonderful.
Nadya: What makes it wonderful?
John: I don't know.

Nadya asks what she'll do in America. Practice, study, and perform, John says. This gives him an idea: She'll be soloist at his next performance of Tschaikovsky's Piano Concerto No. 1. A bit later, she is doing just that, with the performance broadcast over the radio.

We move slowly from Nadya to John to the radio microphone, then to the clouds outside in the night sky, then to a group of familiar characters gathered around a radio in Tschaikowskoye. A girl asks Stepanov who else is listening to Nadya's performance. He replies: "Everybody who loves music"— millions of people, "from the Eastern Pacific to the Western frontier." We take off again, moving slowly from tranquil waters shimmering in the moonlight, to tall evergreen forests, to the Western border, all the while Tschaikovsky playing in the background. A couple of soldiers are standing guard; others are in the guardhouse, smiling while they listen to Nadya play over the radio. This peaceful setting is soon replaced by a German headquarters—in Poland, presumably, near the Soviet border. There is an abrupt change in music: Tschaikovsky is replaced by German military music.

A German officer is handed an envelope and reads it. A serious look appears on his face. Behind him, we see first a picture of Adolf Hitler, and then a calendar: it is June 21, 1941. Cut to the German Army preparing for an invasion. Cut back to the Russian border: It's early morning, a day as beautiful as the night was peaceful. Three smiling soldiers emerge from the guardhouse—suddenly, there's a huge explosion, and the three soldiers collapse.

In rapid succession, we see footage of German troops attacking; footage of the Russian response; a surprising number of troops and artillery vehicles flowing through or out of Tschaikowskoye; John and Nadya anxiously waiting—in a spacious, modern-looking apartment or hotel room—for word from Nadya's family.

Nadya can't wait any longer; she says she must go to her village to help, while John does his part by staying on tour. "We are each of us an individual with individual abilities," she says. John convinces her to stay with him—until they hear a man and arguments much more persuasive than his wife and her appeal to independent ability. Stalin addresses the nation.[4]

The radio announcer introduces him: "Our commander in chief, Comrade Stalin." Stalin says: "The enemy is cruel and implacable. He's out to seize our land, watered with our sweat; to seize our grain and oil, secured by our labor." During the speech, we see fields full of wheat, grain spilling out from a conveyer belt, an abundant flow of oil. Stalin continues: "Thus the issue is one of life and death for the peoples of the Soviet Union—whether they shall remain free, or fall into slavery." Stalin reassures them that they have allies in the United States and Europe, and he advises them to use the "scorched earth" policy, if forced to give up their villages and farms. He refers briefly to collective farmers, who, he says, "must drive off all of their cattle, and turn over their grain for transport to the rear."

Stalin's speech convinces John that Nadya was right; she should go to Tschaikowskoye, while he continues on tour.

In the next scene, Nadya says goodbye to Hank, who calls her a fool for going, when she and John could instead be leaving for the United States and safety. But he adds:

> I come from a small town, too. A little place in New England called Lexington. A lot of fools, like you, fought for that once—died for it, right there on the Village Green. Some day you'll see my town, you and John, I'm sure of it. It'll still be there because, back home, we have a lot of fools like you.

John puts her on the train to Tschaikowskoye. Tschaikowskoye is abuzz with military activity and preparation. Troops, soldiers in motorcycles with sidecars, jeeps, and trucks fill the village center.

Nadya, with a bottle and rag in one hand and a piece of chalk in the other, demonstrates to a classroom full of attentive children how to make a Molotov cocktail. On the blackboard behind her is a drawing of a tank. A Molotov cocktail, she explains, is "very useful in setting fire to enemy tanks. It was first used by the people of Spain in fighting the invasion of their country."

Meschkov interrupts the class with news from the front. The Nazis are getting too close. "All children under the age of twelve must be evacuated from this region at once." Peter, looking concerned, politely asks whether this order includes children who *are* twelve. With great relief, a big smile, and a thank you, he learns that he doesn't have to leave—he can stay and fight. As the children file out, Meschkov reassures them that they will be back: "The music—the culture—we've been building here will never die."

Alone with Boris, Nadya learns that since the region is under martial law, the festival is canceled and John will not be given a pass to travel to Tschaikowskoye. In the two-minute phone call she and John are allowed, she is unwilling to tell him the bad news.

Next, John is in Moscow conducting the final concert of his tour in a hall filled with doctors, nurses, and wounded soldiers. After the ovation, he addresses the audience: "Before I came to Russia, I knew your country only through its music. Now, thanks to this tour, I've been able to meet you, to talk to you, to get to know you—in fact, to marry you." He's interrupted by an air raid alarm. Rows of people file in an orderly fashion into the subway via the escalators. Here, John finally learns (from Hank) that he cannot travel to Tschaikowskoye. But later, Hank manages to get a pass for John, and they say their good-byes at the station.

The train is full of soldiers singing, strumming guitars, playing cards. Suddenly, German planes attack, and fighting ensues. A bridge that they're approaching is blown up, but the train stops in time and everyone bails out. John continues on foot, in the rain.

Meanwhile, back in Tschaikowskoye, an assembly of villagers meets to decide their fate—that is, what should be done with their wheat in the face of the approaching Nazis: scorch the earth, or wait and see what happens. Nadya offers a third possibility: start threshing the grain at once, and transport it away from the Germans; but be prepared at a moment's notice to burn everything, "as our commander in chief told us."

John hitches a ride by truck. The truck driver says her best friend is an American from Detroit—"this truck." She continues: "Some day, after we've beaten the Nazis, I'm going to go to Detroit, and shake hands with the fellows who built it." They encounter another bridge that's out; John is back on foot. A bit later he runs into a wounded Russian soldier, who confirms John's identity, not by checking his papers—"papers can be forged"—but by quizzing him about the location and program of his last concert. It turns out the soldier was there. John asks: "How come they let you come back here in this condition?" The soldier responds that when he heard the Nazis were getting close to his village, he begged the doctors to release him.

> Soldier: I still have two hands; my eyes too are as good as ever. I still can shoot.
> John: I wish I could see your face. . . . I'd like to remember what courage looks like.
> Soldier: There's nothing so brave about it. Thousands of others are doing the same thing.
> John: That's what so incredible. You never give up.
> Soldier: What's so incredible about it? Can you give up your mother's love? Can you forget the way she sang to you? The way she nursed you? Give up our land—how can we? It's our mother.

They walk for a bit longer, and then the soldier points him in the direction of Tschaikowskoye. John says: "I'd like to shake your hand, soldier."

In the next scene, guards bring John before an officer of the Red Army, whose desk is in a rundown, battle-beaten shack. John's pass says Smolensk, which is twenty miles from Tschaikowskoye. If the pass indicates Smolensk, the officer says, John must go to Smolensk. John pleads with him, asking whether he knows what it's like being separated from his wife, with the Germans closing in. The officer *does* know; he tells John that the Nazis killed his wife the previous night. He allows John to go to Tschaikowskoye.

Nearly there, John encounters a worn-out, war-torn, distraught, and beaten row of troops shuffling slowly away from Tschaikowskoye. A limping soldier tells John the village was shelled all night.

Tschaikowskoye is in shambles. The church and most of the houses are barely standing. Roofs are torn and twisted; planks, strips of metal, and debris clutter what was a clean village center. A few people slowly load refuse onto carts.

John begins his search for Nadya. Her house looks badly broken and abandoned. Her father's dead body lies next to the tractor, which is now a wreck. The music school is in bad shape as well. Before it, the delirious schoolmaster rambles on, holding a broken violin. He says to John: "Look what they've done to our music."

All day and into the night, John searches the fields for Nadya, while the peasants are hard at work, burning their grain, sweat covering their bodies. Working hard and at such an awful task, they cannot concern themselves with John's search for his wife.

After many hours—the sun has already risen—John finds her, walking back to town with a group of villagers. John and Nadya run to each other and embrace. In the distance, Peter waves and runs toward them. But before he reaches them, a German plane guns the boy down, and he dies. The priest, who is with Boris (the boy's father), makes the sign of the cross over Peter's body.

John wants to stay and fight the Germans, but Boris tells him: "It would be a great honor. But I'm afraid that it is not the right way. . . , because there is so much more that you can do. You can go back to your country and tell them what you have seen here. . . . This is the greatest thing that you can do." Nadya must go too, he says, to help her husband tell the American people "that we will hold on; that millions like your father, and my son, are not sacrificing their lives in vain"—that the Germans will never conquer Russia.

The film ends where it began: John Meredith in New York City, conducting Tschaikovsky's Piano Concerto No. 1—the soloist, his wife Nadya. While they play, we can still hear Boris' plea: "We will feel you fighting side by side with us, all soldiers in the same army. Fighting to bring a new light to our children, for that great day when the whole world will ring with a new song of freedom; for you will bring our great countries closer together, in the fight for all humanity."

Close up of Nadya.

The End.

This synopsis makes clear that *Song of Russia* is a work of propaganda. A fuller defense and discussion of this appraisal can be found in chapters 6 and 7. We turn now to how this propagandistic film came to be.

Notes

1. *Song of Russia* is occasionally shown on the cable station Turner Classic Movies.

2. Passages quoted in this chapter are from the film.

3. So far as I can tell, Tschaikowskoye is a fictitious village. We are told that it is 20 miles from Smolensk, which is about 250 miles west of Moscow, and which was overtaken by the Nazi invasion in 1941. In the western Urals, there is a village called Tschaikovsky near the town of Votkinsk, the birthplace of the composer. In Votkinsk, there is a Tschaikovsky museum-estate; but being nearly 700 miles to the *east* of Moscow, this cannot be the Tschaikowskoye of *Song of Russia*.

4. I was unable to discover the name of the actor who played Stalin.

CHAPTER TWO

~

The Making of *Song of Russia*

Since MGM production files are out of the hands of scholars, a full production history of *Song of Russia* is currently impossible. Without such records, I have had to rely on (1) the many versions of treatments, screenplays, outlines, notes, etc., for what would eventually be called *Song of Russia*; (2) the Office of War Information files on *Song of Russia*; (3) correspondence between MGM and the Hays Office on *Song of Russia*; and (4) the HUAC testimonies of Louis B. Mayer, Robert Taylor, and Richard Collins and interviews with people connected with the making of this film. The first source is the most reliable and important; the second and third are next in order of reliability. Because of the limitations of the fourth—recollections from politically charged contexts, in some cases over fifty years after the film's release—they are relied on only when other evidence is unavailable, though they have proved to be useful.

Getting Started

During most of his adult life, Louis B. Mayer was head of Metro-Goldwyn-Mayer. He was politically conservative, but not a political animal. What mattered most to him was MGM. Although he made anti-Communist statements in his 1947 HUAC testimony, for the most part he had an apolitical attitude toward his studio. Biographer Charles Higham writes that Mayer "allowed for a wide range of political opinion. He nourished Communists and fascists alike; if they could do a good job, and didn't blow up the studio, they were all right with him."[1] For example, when Mayer discovered that one of his top directors, Jules Dassin, was a member of the Communist Party, he didn't fire him; rather, he tried to persuade him to quit the Party. Richard Collins explains:

> [Mayer] didn't approve of [Communism] as a political philosophy or movement. But I think he hated to lose a good director, and that's why he talked to Dassin. He hated to lose him, partly because of money, but also because of his own self-esteem and *amour propre*—that he was a man who ran a great studio and that the people in it were talented. . . . He didn't want to lose any part of it.[2]

A further indication of, or reason for, this apolitical attitude was the desire to avoid trouble. As Eddie Mannix, an executive producer at MGM, once put it: "Metro doesn't want to make controversial subjects."[3]

In the spring of 1942, World War II was raging, the United States was in the war, Hitler and Stalin were no longer allies—and the story that was to become *Song of Russia* was sent to MGM. The first version of the treatment, "Scorched Earth," is dated March 31, 1942 (MHL f.2915).[4] This fits Mayer's HUAC testimony: "It was in April of 1942 that the story for Song of Russia came to our attention."[5]

Around this time, one of MGM's producers, Joe Pasternak, was finishing up the wartime musical *Thousands Cheer* (1943). Paul Jarrico and Richard Collins had written the screenplay. Happy with the success of this film, Mayer decided Pasternak should make another wartime musical with the same team, so he assigned them to "Scorched Earth." Perhaps to contribute to the film's authenticity, Mayer asked Russian-born Gregory Ratoff to direct.

The team working on the "Scorched Earth"/"Song of Russia" project was a strange mix. The producer, Joe Pasternak, was Hungarian—and anti-Communist, according to Higham, though Richard Collins does not recall him being very political.[6] Collins tells the following story, which reveals something about director Gregory Ratoff's attitude toward the Soviets:

> I remember . . . there was a Russian hunchback who came [from the Soviet Union] with a group to buy motion picture equipment. As he was from the Soviet Union, I got to know him. I remember that I got some film on what was then called Leningrad, and I was watching it with the director, Gregory Ratoff, who was a White Russian [and born in St. Petersburg]. We went into the projection room, and when St. Petersburg came on, Ratoff said "St. Petersburg," and the Russians said "Leningrad." And later when St. Petersburg appeared again, they said "Leningrad" and he said "St. Petersburg." . . . But I doubt if

[politics] entered into his mind [while making *Song of Russia*]. I think he figured it was a big MGM movie and musical, "It can't do me any harm. I'll do it." The only political thing was that there was . . . a certain edge to him when he kept saying "St. Petersburg." As far as he was concerned, it was St. Petersburg originally and forever. . . . Everything about him was really from another regime; he didn't believe in what was happening [in Russia]. But it was not on his agenda, which was to survive and tell stories and sell them and be charming and so on.[7]

In contrast to the director, the producer, and the head of MGM, consider the writers on this project. First, of the three men who wrote the original story "Scorched Earth" (Leo Mittler, Viktor Trivas, and Guy Endore), at least two were members of the U.S. Communist Party. Richard Collins confirmed that Trivas and Endore were both in the Party, though he did not know whether Mittler was a member.[8] Mittler was a member of the Writers Mobilization for Defense, described by the FBI as a Hollywood Communist front organization. Further, the FBI regarded him as "an associate of reported German Communist sympathizers in Hollywood."[9] Mittler and Trivas had strong ties to the left in Weimar Germany and had emigrated once the Nazis came to power in 1933. By 1941, both were in California.[10]

The two men assigned to write the screenplay, Jarrico and Collins, were also members of the Communist Party. Jarrico eventually left the Party in the 1950s, though he would defend his political past, for the most part, to the end of his life. But in the late 1940s, Collins became disillusioned with both the Party and the Soviet Union; and he found it increasingly more difficult to find work (more on that in chapter 5). As a consequence, he cooperated with the HUAC during their 1951 hearings.[11]

Further, the majority of other writers who would contribute in one way or another to the screenplay were members of the Party: John Wexley, Guy Trosper, Michael Blankfort, Boris Ingster, Paul Trivers, and Anna Louise Strong.[12] In 1935, Strong had written *I Changed Worlds*, which heaped praise on the Soviet Union, and some years after the release of *Song of Russia*, the *People's Daily World* called her "one of the best informed living Americans on the Soviet Union."[13] It was probably her reputation as an "expert" on the Soviet Union that led the studio to make her an uncredited technical advisor on the film.[14] Finally, the lyrics to the song "And Russia Is Her Name" were penned by the then Communist Party member E. Y. (Yip) Harburg.

Edgar G. Ulmer, in an interview with Peter Bogdanovich, claims that he wrote a screenplay called "The Hostages," which he describes as "the script used for *Song of Russia*, which was produced by Pandro S. Berman [sic] at

Metro." I encountered nothing in the files on *Song of Russia* that supports this claim, and conclude that Ulmer must be confusing *Song of Russia* with some other film.[15] Paul Buhle and Dave Wagner, in *Radical Hollywood*, present a cluster of errors regarding the writing credits for *Song of Russia*. For example, at one point they claim that Lester Cole was a contributing writer. I have come across no evidence for such a contribution, and they provide none.[16]

When I asked Collins how he and Jarrico felt about the project, he said: "We were just assigned to it, as a team. We didn't ask for it. They just gave it to us. . . . And I guess as good Comrades we felt wonderful. We thought this was a great opportunity."[17] At the 1951 HUAC hearings, Frank Tavenner asked Collins: "Was the writing of this screenplay influenced by the membership of yourself and Jarrico in the Communist Party?" Collins replied:

> Well, I suppose it could have been to some degree, in that we probably knew more about the country than one would know if you had never read anything about it or looked at anything about it. We had seen Soviet films and read material about the Soviet Union, and I imagine we had a certain amount of knowledge about it. Nothing first-hand, but at least second- or third-hand. But in terms of what we said in the picture I doubt if it had anything to do with our being Communists except that we were pleased with . . . the assignment.[18]

Recently asked about the Party's interest in the film, Collins said that he didn't remember any specific discussions with the Party about *Song of Russia*, "except that it was a good assignment. I don't think anybody in the Party read the script and said you should do this or that. It was enough that Jarrico and I were doing it. They figured that it was in good hands."[19]

Metro-Goldwyn-Mayer and the Office of War Information

Aside from any special reasons the Communists involved may have had for wanting to work on the project, and besides the obvious and understandable desire on the part of MGM to make money, did Mayer have any other reasons for making this film? In his HUAC testimony, trying to recall why he pursued this project, Mayer said that Pasternak wanted "to make a picture with Tschaikowsky's music and it would have to be laid in Russia. That is how it all got started." A bit later he said that it "seemed a good medium of entertainment and at the same time offered an opportunity for a pat on the back for our then ally, Russia. It also offered an opportunity to use the music of Tschaikowsky."[20] When I first asked Collins about Mayer's attitude toward making *Song of Russia*, he laughed and said: "He wanted to make a musical!"[21] John Wexley, who worked on the script for four weeks toward the end of the project, remembers Mayer telling him: "Each studio is asked to make some kind of contribution to the war. This is a very reluctant contribution."[22] So it is possible that Mayer's initial purpose was entertainment, but that not long after taking on the project, it became MGM's reluctant pat on Russia's back.

The crucial question is, each studio was asked *by whom?* The answer is the government under Franklin Delano Roosevelt's administration, and particularly, the Office of War Information (OWI).

As part of his prepared statement for the HUAC, Louis B. Mayer said:

> There were a number of representatives of the Government who made periodical visits to the studios during the war. They discussed with us from time to time the types of pictures which they felt might assist the war effort. They were coordinators and at no time did they attempt to tell us what we should or should not do. We made our own decisions on production.[23]

Later he had the following exchange with Congressman Smith, which stays pretty close to his prepared statement:

> Smith: Did a Government representative ever come to you, Mr. Mayer, about the making of [*Song of Russia*]?
> Mayer: I don't recall anybody coming about the making of it. I think I told them about it or discussed it with them. So much happened in that period, coming and going. They had an office out there—War Information, I think they called themselves.[24]

HUAC counsel Stripling was not willing to drop the issue, and Mayer in his reply is less confident:

> Stripling: Was this picture made at the request of the Government?
> Mayer: I had originally thought it was. I tried to think it out as to who, and it is just blank to me. I have come to the conclusion, by talking to Mr. Cates, who was executive in charge of the producer who made it, and talking to the producer—he claimed that, when he started with me, he would like to make a picture with Tschaikowsky's music and it would have to be laid in Russia. That is how it all got started. This story Scorched Earth was dug up as the premise on which we would be able to use that music. I recall talking to some of the men that were in the liaison office between the Government and ourselves about the picture when we were going to make it. I know they liked the idea that we were going to make it because they did want a pat on Russia's back, to keep them fighting.[25]

As we have seen, Mayer eventually arrived at the position that the sole purpose of the film, *originally*, was entertainment and Tschaikowsky. Helping Russia later became another purpose—one supported by the OWI. But Mayer has introduced some confusion about who made first contact, MGM or the OWI.

We find a similar lack of clarity in the testimony of Robert Taylor. At the 1947 HUAC hearings, Stripling asked the same question he had asked Mayer:

> Stripling: [I]n connection with the production of Song of Russia, do you know whether or not it was made at the suggestion of a representative of the Government?
>
> Taylor: I do not believe that it was made at the suggestion of a Government representative; no, sir. I think the script was written and prepared long before any representative of the Government became involved in it in any way.
>
> Stripling: Were you ever present at any meeting at which a representative of the Government was present and this picture was discussed?
>
> Taylor: Yes, sir; in Mr. L.B. Mayer's office. One day I was called to meet Mr. [Lowell] Mellett [of the OWI] whom I met in the company of Mr. Mayer and, as I recall, the Song of Russia was discussed briefly. I don't think we were together more than five minutes.
>
> It was disclosed at that time that the Government was interested in the picture being made and also pictures of that nature being made by other studios as well. As I say, it was to strengthen the feeling of the American people toward the Russian people at that time.[26]

As with Mayer, there is an almost nervous eagerness to disabuse the committee of the idea that the government first approached MGM and then forced them to make a film. On the other hand, we see in both testimonies the idea that there was certainly a great deal of interest in, and many dealings with, MGM on the part of the OWI.

The statements of the two screenwriters—many years after the film was made—are divided on whether the government exerted any pressure on MGM to make *Song of Russia*. Paul Jarrico said: "Hollywood was more than willing to do war films, but it took a lot of pressure by Roosevelt and the OWI to get the major studios to celebrate our alliance with Russia."[27] Richard Collins recalls the situation differently:

> It was not like the other picture, Mission to Moscow. . . . That film was asked for. As I understand it, the State Department said to Warner Brothers, "We'd like you to do this," and that's why they did it. But I don't think the State Department said to Mayer, "We'd like you to make this pro-Soviet film." . . . I don't think there was that kind of pressure to make it, or I think we would have

heard about it, just as we heard about [government pressure in the case of] *Mission to Moscow*.[28]

Before coming to any conclusions about who contacted whom, and in either case, what role the OWI may have played in making *Song of Russia*, consider the creation and nature of the OWI.[29]

By 1940, if not earlier, FDR was ready to put a lot of pressure on the film industry to make movies to support the Armed Forces. As Koppes and Black report in *Hollywood Goes to War*:

> In August [1940] FDR asked Nicholas Schlenk, president of Loew's (parent of MGM), to make a film on defense and foreign policy. By mid-October *Eyes of the Navy*, a two-reeler which a studio executive promised would win the president thousands of votes, graced neighborhood movie houses. Schenk's interest may have been personal as well as patriotic. His brother Joseph, head of Twentieth Century-Fox, was convicted of income tax evasion. President Roosevelt asked Attorney General Robert Jackson to let the studio chief off with a fine, and so did Roosevelt's son James, to whom Joseph Schenck had lent $50,000.[30]

In February 1941, in a message to the annual Academy Awards banquet, FDR thanked the industry for its "splendid cooperation."[31] But although they had toed the line, they apparently had not done enough. In April 1942, presidential assistant Lowell Mellett—who had "picked up the nickname 'white rabbit'" for his lack of "a forceful personality"[32]—set up a propaganda office in Hollywood, headed by Mellett's protégé, Nelson Poynter. This would soon become a branch of the Bureau of Motion Pictures (headed by Mellett), which was in turn part of the Domestic Branch of the Office of War Information. The OWI was created on June 13, 1942, replacing a hodgepodge of existing propaganda agencies.[33] Initially, there was outrage on the part of the studios—for example, one studio head said: "We don't want people whom we would not employ, because they are not qualified through experience and training, telling us what to do"[34]—but it did not last.

Nelson Poynter sometimes attended fifteen story conferences a week. In June 1942, two months after MGM acquired "Scorched Earth," he had a long meeting with Executive Producer Eddie Mannix of MGM, "in which he urged him to make fewer combat films and more on the war issues."[35] That same month he addressed a Hollywood writers' group, where he praised the pro-British *Mrs. Miniver* (MGM, 1942), and added that what was needed was "a *Mrs. Miniver* of China or Russia, making clear to our people our common interest with the Russians and Chinese in this struggle."[36] He got what he asked for in MGM's *Song of Russia*.

During that summer, the OWI issued the "Government Information Manual for the Motion Picture Industry." The manual asked filmmakers to consider, for each film they were (thinking of) making, seven questions:

1. Will this picture help win the war?
2. What war information problem does it seek to clarify, dramatize, or interpret?
3. If it is an "escape" picture, will it harm the war effort by creating a false picture of America, her allies, or the world we live in?
4. Does it merely use the war as the basis for a profitable picture, contributing nothing of real significance to the war effort and possibly lessening the effect of other pictures of more importance?
5. Does it contribute something new to our understanding of the world conflict and the various forces involved, or has the subject already been adequately covered?
6. When the picture reaches its maximum circulation on the screen, will it reflect conditions as they are and fill a need current at that time, or will it be outdated?
7. Does the picture tell the truth, or will the young people of today have reason to say they were misled by propaganda?[37]

Judging from the OWI reviews of the pro-Soviet films *Mission to Moscow*, *North Star*, and *Song of Russia*, it is not hard to understand why truth is at the bottom of the list. (More on the OWI review of *Song of Russia* later.)

Much of the OWI manual—and many of their reviews of films—were themselves propaganda, in many cases extreme pro-New Deal propaganda, and in some cases pro-Soviet. Here is an example of the former:

> [Executive Producer Eddie] Mannix "yelled and screamed," Poynter said, and charged that OWI was trying to force the studio to make [King Vidor's "America" into] a "new deal picture." "Metro doesn't want to make controversial subjects," the MGM executive said. Poynter defended himself by saying he didn't think the "continued growth of democracy" was controversial.[38]

In other words, Poynter believed that since the New Deal and its underlying philosophical assumptions are, as he sees it, obviously correct, the studios should not complain about having them forced down their throats.

The OWI took the same attitude on other issues. For example, how should films treat the Soviet Union, given its vast differences with the United States? The "Government Information Manual for the Motion Picture Industry" states—and recall that this is supposed to be policy accepted by the industry without serious objections, as obviously correct as New Deal democracy was to Nelson Poynter—that "The Allies were *ipso facto* democracies." This includes the Soviet Union, a fact which, again, is not subject to any objections. But the OWI realized that this level of absurdity might raise a question, and they were ready for it. The manual reads: "Yes, we Americans reject communism. *But we do not reject our Russian ally.*"[39] This approach to the Russians—widespread at the time, and defended in some circles until the fall of Soviet Communism—is too bizarre to take seriously. Using the same "logic," we could just as easily have allied ourselves with the Nazis to put an end to Stalin's destruction of human life, arguing: "Yes, we Americans reject Nazism. *But we do not reject our German ally.*"

In Ayn Rand's *Atlas Shrugged*, a power-lusting villain, Wesley Mouch—who, like Lowell Mellett, was not "a forceful personality"—failed at business, and so went into government as a lowly bureaucrat, only to rise to become commissar of the entire economy. Confronted with each new disaster, he demands "wider powers."[40] Mellett, sensing that the OWI was not doing all that it could to make the best movies possible for the war effort, demanded wider powers. "In the late summer of 1942 the Censorship Bureau's New York Board of Review, which scrutinized newsreels, issued a stringent supplement" to the tough line already taken by the Office of Censorship. In the fall of that year, Mellett urged that these same standards be applied to feature-length films.[41] In September 1942, he pushed for "the Office of Censorship to bar bad [to the OWI] pictures from export,"[42] thereby depriving any studio that made "bad" films of possibly huge profits. And on December 9, 1942, he proclaimed to the studio heads in Hollywood:

> For the benefit of both your studio and the Office of War Information it would be advisable to establish a routine procedure whereby our Hollywood office would receive copies of studio treatments or synopses of all stories which you contemplate producing and of the finished scripts. This will enable us to make suggestions as to the war content of motion pictures at a stage when it is easy and inexpensive to make any changes which might be recommended.[43]

Again, there was outrage on the part of the studios, followed by capitulation. By early 1943, all of the major studios, with the exception of Paramount, were regularly submitting screenplays to the OWI.[44]

The OWI was created on June 13, 1942. Nelson Poynter asked for less combative movies that same month. By this time, MGM already had the original story "Scorched Earth." According to the OWI files on *Song of*

Russia, the first record of any contact is a review by an OWI staff member, dated December 18, 1942, of a version of the Collins-Jarrico screenplay (MHL f.2928–29). So MGM did not make "Scorched Earth" into a film as a result of OWI influence. But the OWI certainly could have influenced the *direction* the story's evolution took. For example, as we shall see in the next section, as the story progresses, it becomes less focused on combat. This may have been owing to the OWI's influence.

Work on the screenplay had begun before the OWI got involved. But after MGM began work on the film, the OWI "encouraged" them to complete the project—according to the OWI's specifications.

But what was this *encouragement*? There's the rub. The government's "encouragement" consisted of a high degree of pressure—not simply to make the movie, but to make it the kind of movie that the OWI thought best. For it certainly did not do a studio any good to oppose the OWI's wishes, and the government actively and enthusiastically approved of this film and wanted it to be made according to its specifications. Clearly, the Left is capable of censorship and the violation of the freedom of expression—an issue we shall return to in chapter 5.

As an indication of the power of the OWI, and the need to get their approval, consider a December 24, 1942, letter from Maurice Revnes (MGM) to Lowell Mellett, written at the suggestion of Nelson Poynter. Revnes writes that the "studio feels that it will be a contribution to the war effort," but shortly thereafter, he gets to the main reason for his letter: a request that "an effort would be made to secure the temporary release of Lieut. Emmett (Van) Haflin [sic, Heflin] who would, if released, play the star role."[45] (More on the OWI and its influence over content and casting later in this chapter.)

Recently declassified documents reveal that the OWI was riddled with Communist agents; but apparently no such agents worked in the Hollywood division.[46] This need not have been owing to a lack of interest in Hollywood films on the part of the Soviets. Perhaps the Communists saw that they had no need to have agents there, for as we shall see, the New Dealers reviewing films for the OWI followed a line that was virtually indistinguishable from the Soviets.

From "Scorched Earth" to *Song of Russia*: The Evolution of the Screenplay

The writers working on this project had to travel some distance between the original story, "Scorched Earth," and the film *Song of Russia*. What steps were made, and why? This section does not cover the entire history but merely presents the changing versions of the major treatments and screenplays, with an emphasis on structure and action. Later I turn to the "contributions" of the Hays Office and the Office of War Information, and to the removal of propaganda.

Treatment (SCORCHED EARTH) by Leo Mittler, Viktor Trivas and
Guy Endore; no date (copied 3/31/42); 59 pages and 55 pages [two copies,
original and retyped version] (f.2915)

This treatment was received by MGM in April 1942. The story begins in the village of Tschaikowskoe. An American conductor, Fredric Cavanaugh (the proto John Meredith), is a former pupil of Meschkov, a music teacher, and is traveling in Russia with his teenage brother. Meschkov's daughter, Sonya (the proto Nadya Stepanov), is a singer. Fredric and Sonya meet in her village and become interested in one another.

Music is central to village life—even more so than in the final version. There is a Tschaikowsky museum, as well as a music school. Everyone is patriotic and prepared for war. Meschkov's house is two stories high, and food is clearly no problem for these villagers. The treatment reads: "The table groans with food, mounds of kasha, vegetables, and roast fowl, cucumber salad and sour cream, caviar and shashlik still hot on the spit. Only people who can look back on times when there was famine, can lay away such enormous portions." Fredric must go to Moscow; but when the Germans attack Russia, he returns to Sonya's village to be with her and to help in the fight. They declare their love for each other; he proposes and she accepts. The wedding ceremony is performed by a commissar; there is no sign of religion anywhere.

In this version of the story, there is much greater emphasis on guerrilla preparations and on the Germans and their treatment of the Russians. The guerrillas (including Fredric and Sonya) prepare to fight, for the Germans are getting close. The Germans attack Tschaikowskoe, killing and capturing many. Fredric is captured, but the Germans promise to release him if he swears to remain neutral. (There are a number of references to American isolationism and neutrality.) He swears—understandably with no intention of keeping his word. The guerrillas fight on, with Sonya taking part in raids on the Germans. The Germans find the marriage certificate of Sonya and Fredric and conclude that if they watch Fredric closely, they will eventually capture Sonya.

The guerrillas adopt a policy of scorched earth: Whatever can be of use to the Nazis must be destroyed, even the music school.

Toward the end of the story, Sonya and Fredric—who is no longer neutral—are reunited. The Nazi mistreatment of the villagers continues; significantly, Sonya's father is killed. Hitler speaks over the radio, announcing that Russia is a defeated nation. It becomes clear to the Russians that the Germans will loot and destroy Russian culture. Fredric and Sonya are captured and sentenced to hang. Word gets to the guerrillas, and in an eleventh-hour rescue, Fredric and Sonya are saved. There is work to be done: The guerrillas (and Russia generally) need to be helped.

The basic structure of this version of the story (and some subsequent revisions) is as follows:

1. An American conductor and a Russian singer fall in love in a wonderful Russian village.
2. Germany attacks Russia, and the Russians fight back.
3. The couple stays together, in Russia, in the midst of guerrilla warfare against the Germans. The war threatens their relationship.
4. It is made clear that no one should remain neutral; everyone must fight the Nazis.

There are about ten more versions or outlines or revisions of this treatment before Jarrico and Collins begin working on it. What follows are the highlights.

Outline (SCORCHED EARTH) by Leo Mittler and Viktor Trivas; no date (copied 5/12/42); 11 pages (f.2916)

In this outline, Sonya the singer has become Natasha the pianist, and Fredric (still a conductor) has become Michael. There is now a romantic conflict involving Natasha, Michael, and Boris (an engineer and civil defense instructor), with Natasha torn over whether to choose Michael or Boris. Her main obstacle to a relationship with Boris is that in his view, she represents art for art's sake, whereas he—as a good Marxist—believes art must serve political aims (here, the war effort). Romantically, she chooses Boris, but she goes to Moscow with Michael to perform in a concert. (We here have the first mention of Tschaikowsky's First Piano Concerto.)

The Germans attack Russia, so Natasha and Michael immediately return to Tschaikowskoe. Boris cannot forgive her for "leaving her post." With the Germans closing in, Boris urges a policy of scorched earth. Natasha comes to see that Boris is right, not just about scorched earth, but about the role of an artist. Michael—a neutral American—is captured by the Germans but is later rescued by Boris. No longer neutral, Michael leads a daring mission against the Germans. The guerrillas (including Michael), with the help of the Red Army, defeat the Germans. The villagers must rebuild Tschaikowskoe—and Russian culture.

Treatment (SCORCHED EARTH) by Guy Trosper and Irmgard von Cube; 6/8/42, through 6/29/42; approximately 150 pages [original; revised; also three-page section by Guy Trosper, June 17, 1942] (f.2917)
In this treatment, the hero is for the first time called John Meredith. The heroine is now a singer named Sonia Meschkov. We get our first hint of religion in the village: "Tschaikowskoe is a fascinating blend of old Russia and new. There is a church, with onion-shaped towers. And then there is the small but modern administration building of the collective farm." Hitler's speech has been replaced by Stalin's famous "scorched earth" speech, which appears in the film. There is the same emphasis on guerrilla fighting, but in this version, Boris' son, Peter, dies (though not as he does in the film), and the Tschaikowsky museum is destroyed.

John proves to be a useful guerrilla, and as a result there is a 100,000 ruble reward for his capture. A German officer tells the villagers to turn Meredith in, or the slaughter will continue. Instead, the guerrillas attack and Boris is fatally wounded. His last words are: "All that is left is the Museum, which the Russians will preserve as the Germans left it, in ruins, a memorial to Fascist culture." But Tschaikowskoe is not destroyed spiritually: "It will rise again, like Phoenix, to attest to the world that the spirit of all Russians, of free people on all the face of the earth, and the spirit of Tschaikowsky, cannot be destroyed."

Guerrilla anecdotes from Anna Louise Strong; 7/6/42 (copied 9/21/42); 16 pages and 24 pages [two copies, original and retyped version] (f.2919)
This is a collection of accounts of purportedly actual events from the German–Russian war that Strong thought might be successfully incorporated into the story. (Jarrico and Collins later call them "WONDERFUL."[47]) I mention only one, since it may have influenced the final product: "A 'Peter' Incident ?" This account of a thirteen-year-old boy machine-gunned by Germans while running toward the Red Army could be the source of Peter's death scene in the final version.

Composite script of treatment (SCORCHED EARTH) by Anna Louise Strong and Guy Trosper; 7/7/42, through 7/23/42; approximately 190 pages [also four-page new sequence arrangement by Anna Louis Strong, July 19, 1942] (f.2920)
This treatment basically follows the earlier versions. Thematically, the emphasis is still on the rejection of American neutrality, but it is worth

mentioning, because it introduces an important conflict that survives to the final version: Should Sonja (later, Nadya) go to America with John—remain with the man she loves, and escape the dangers of war—or stay in Russia and fight? In this version, John tells her he is going to America and asks her to come with him.

> Sonya: America! But I thought—you're coming back—
> John: I'm a neutral, darling. I couldn't stay here.
> Sonya: No—I suppose not—

But in the end, John sees the light, rejects neutrality, and stays.

There followed a number of revisions that need not be covered here, though some are considered later, when the removal of propaganda from the screenplay is discussed.

Interlude: The Jarrico–Collins Collaboration

Before turning to the first version of "Scorched Earth" by Paul Jarrico and Richard Collins, it is necessary to describe the controversy over the nature of their respective contributions to Song of Russia.

When I first interviewed Richard Collins, I asked him what he and Jarrico each contributed to the screenplay. He replied:

> Sometimes I'd write the scene and he'd re-write it or he'd write the scene and I'd say, "Well, wait a minute;" something like that. But we were in separate offices. We had the same secretary, who happened to be in my office. As I remember it, I think I liked his dialogue. I thought it was excellent or good at least. I think structure was my strength, and dialogue was Jarrico's.[48]

Sometime after this interview, I read the oral history Tender Comrades, in which Jarrico—reversing his role as champion of the uncredited blacklisted screenwriter—paints a radically different picture:

> Pasternak . . . asked Jarrico and Collins, who'd just done a successful musical for him, to do the screenplay, and at least one of them jumped at the chance. I knocked myself out to do it fast—the Battle of Stalingrad was raging—but Collins seemed to be dragging his feet. . . . When we finished the script, Collins said to me, shamefaced, "Look, I've done ten percent; you've done ninety percent. I don't deserve credit." I turned the offer down. "We were hired as a team," I said, "and we'll take credit as a team. But I don't think we ought to work together again."[49]

Given the adage, "the one who repeats an insult is the one who insults me," I was reluctant to mention this story to Collins. But I decided that since Jarrico's version was part of the historical record, Collins's reply—should he wish to give one—should be as well. So I suggested he read the interview in *Tender Comrades*. He was pleased that I alerted him to it, and when I asked whether Jarrico's account was accurate, he replied:

> No. In the first place, we were both deeply involved in the CPUSA at that point, and so there was no reason why I would drag my heels on the script—he said he had to write all of it! No, because at that time, we were both gung ho about the Soviet Union. . . . Jarrico, and Lardner in his book [*I'd Hate Myself in the Morning*]—their anger with the so-called "friendly witnesses" is so large that they tend to get off the track. . . .[50] I don't remember saying to Jarrico at the end of the writing that he wrote it all, therefore he should get sole credit. That was really very sweet of him! Jarrico had the grace to say no! . . . At that time, I had no reason not to write the script with Jarrico, any more than any other script I wrote. He allowed his present and my present positions to influence what [he thought] we both did fifty years before. . . . This is the basic communist position: 'We have the right to lie, because we are the future—we're the good guys.' I don't think they said that to themselves, but I think that's what got through. Because [Jarrico's story] is a fairy tale.[51]

Since I have encountered no evidence supporting Jarrico's version—and since the Communist position on the right to lie is as Collins describes it (more on that in later chapters)—I continue under the assumption that the *Song of Russia* screenplay was a joint Jarrico–Collins effort.

Notes ("An American Visits the U.S.S.R.") by Paul Jarrico and Richard Collins; 8/31/42; 11 pages (f.2923)

We immediately see in these notes changes in the direction of the final version. For example, the story begins at the Moscow airport, with the head of the "Society of Cultural Relations" greeting John. While in Moscow, there is an emphasis on its prosperity.

After three brief reviews of past treatments, Jarrico and Collins present a sketch of the possible structure for the story:[52]

1. Moscow at peace: John arrives in Moscow, and is pursued by a young Russian woman (Sonya Meschkov, who now plays the piccolo!). Their relationship is superficial: it does not yet evolve into a genuine romance. In fact, John asks Sonya to sleep with him ("You know, free love!"). She slaps him.

2. Tschaikowskoe at peace: John comes to Sonya's village, pursuing her romantically. They fall in love.
3. Separated by war: John is back in Moscow, while Sonya is at home. Germany attacks the Soviet Union. John and Sonya cannot stand being apart, so John returns to Tschaikowskoe, where they can face the war together.
4. Victory requires sacrifice: Jarrico and Collins describe the first two parts as a romantic comedy. By the end of the third part, the tone has clearly changed: "The farce has become tragedy, the superficiality has become profundity." The tragedy is heightened in part four.

The war comes to Tschaikowskoe. There is a clash between guerrillas and the Nazis. The climax comes when either the hero or the heroine must sacrifice the other for the cause. In this outline, the theme is stated explicitly: "the great theme of our times: no sacrifice is too great to destroy fascism."

Who is to make the sacrifice, and who is to go on fighting, is not given in this sketch of the structure. But a few pages later, in a fuller outline (included in this same file and dated September 2, 1942), more details about the ending of the story are provided. John and Sonya are captured, and they are married in jail. Unbeknownst to the Germans, John has important information, which he needs to get to the guerrillas. An opportunity arises to pass this information on, but it requires the death of Sonya, who urges John to sacrifice her. He accepts; she is tortured. He falters, but Peter urges him on. John escapes, delivers the information, and the story ends with John and the guerrillas avenging Sonya's death.

Following this sketch by Jarrico and Collins are a screenplay and a number of revisions, notes, outlines, etc. The basic structure is the same. The key differences concern (1) the amount of explicit propaganda that does not make it into the final version (this is covered later) and (2) the story's ending.

Screenplay sections (SCORCHED EARTH) by Paul Jarrico and Richard Collins; 9/11/42, through 9/26/42 (f.2925–26)[53]

At the airport in Moscow, the band plays "Stars and Stripes Forever," not the "Star Spangled Banner," as in the final version. The heroine is at last called Nadya—she plays the *cello*—though she is not yet the daughter of Stepanov. In her village, there is still a Tschaikowsky Museum; otherwise, it is much the same as in the film. The romance begins in Tschaikowskoe, culminating in a double wedding ceremony (Nadya's sister gets married as well, to a Red Army officer).

The main conflict is whether Nadya will stay in Russia and fight or go to America with John. Initially she wants to go, but as the Germans get closer to her village, she changes her mind:

Nadya (almost whispering): I'm not going with you, John.
John (simply): I know.
Nadya (jaw tight): There can't be any love in the world until the last Nazi is dead.

They both stay and fight. Boris's son, Peter, tries to destroy a power station (as part of the scorched earth policy) when a Nazi sniper shoots him. Nadya continues his mission; she is shot and killed while successfully blowing up the power station. Shortly thereafter, John conducts a student orchestra—they play Tschaikowsky's *1812 Overture*—in the middle of the burnt out village. The story ends as follows:

John: I'm not going. . . . I know, I know—I can serve better with my music. Well, maybe I can. But I'm going to stay here with you and kill some Nazis.
Stepanov: We'll kill them for you.
John: No. My country's going to have to fight this thing too—that's obvious. Every decent person in the world will fight it. I'm just lucky enough to be where I can start right now.

He marches off with the guerrillas.

Temporary complete screenplay (SCORCHED EARTH) by Paul Jarrico and Richard Collins; 10/30/42, through 12/14/42 (f.2928–29)[54]
This version is the last to be called "Scorched Earth."[55] It has much in common with the previous one, though there are some noteworthy differences. For example, a change to the "Russia" screenplay, as it is called, dated December 1, 1942, has for the first time the story beginning in New York City, at Carnegie Hall. The song that makes its way to Russia is now the "Star Spangled Banner." Nadya is still a cellist, but her romance with John begins in Moscow, where he takes her dancing. As in the film, there is a montage of Moscow. Part of the description reads: "The Park is colorful and gay, with carnival attractions and kids playing games." This fits what we see in the film.

As in the previous version, Nadya dies at the end. But in this version, we cut to John, who is back in the United States, conducting a concert to benefit the war effort. When he's finished, there is a request for a speech. He replies: "There's no need for a speech. America and the Soviet Union ["Soviet Union" is crossed out and changed to "Russia"] are allies and friends. Together we shall win the war—and the peace."[56]

Complete OK screenplay (RUSSIA) by Paul Jarrico and Richard Collins; 1/15/43, through 7/1/43 (f.2931–34)[57]

Of the multiple layers of revisions contained herein, the most interesting that make it into the film are: Carnegie Hall is now Manhattan Hall; Nadya is now a Stepanova and a pianist; Peter picks up John Meredith at the train station in "an open, Ford-type touring sedan"; John is invited to stay at the Stepanovs' house; Stepanov describes their dinner as "a simple peasant farm table"; and Peter is killed by a Nazi *plane.* A number of scenes that make it into the film are added here, for example: Nadya teaching the children about Molotov cocktails, John getting a ride from the woman truck driver, and John and the wounded soldier.

In a revision dated April 5, 1943, Nadya asks John to tell her about America, and he answers: "It's big." But he gives his final answer ("It's wonderful," etc.) on May 3, 1943. In a revision dated April 16, 1943, Nadya still dies at the end, but after she dies, John quotes words Benjamin Franklin uttered at the signing of the Declaration of Independence: "We must all hang together or, assuredly, we shall all hang separately," to which he adds: "The United Nations must hang together." But by June 14, 1943, John and Nadya are both going to America, at Boris's request. By July 1943, the screenplay is very close to what we find in the film.

Notes and speeches (RUSSIA) by Laslo Benedek and John Wexley; 4/7/43, through 10/20/43; 24 pages total [four items, six copies, two sets of originals and retyped versions; also four-page dialogue by John Wexley, July 8, 1943] (f.2936)

By fall 1943, with shooting in progress, the script pretty much presents what we find in the film. Of these late additions, two from Laslo Benedek (retakes and added scenes, October 20, 1943) are noteworthy: (1) the scene in which Hank Higgins (John's manager) compares Nadya and her countrymen and what they are doing to those who fought at Lexington in the American Revolutionary War; and (2) at the very end, the close-up of Nadya playing Tschaikowsky's Piano Concerto No. 1.

Unwanted Collaborators, Part 1:
The Office of War Information

According to the surviving files, the OWI made four sets of comments on *Song of Russia*, which they presumably sent to MGM, in each case recommending (sometimes very specific) revisions. What follows is a presentation of their suggestions, with an indication of whether they were accepted.

Film analysis of the Jarrico–Collins' script (MHL f.2928–29). Reviewed by Marjorie Thorsen. December 18, 1942

This review contains a two-page synopsis of the story, with a brief comment indicating the reviewer's general evaluation, and a three-page review that makes seven points. The slanted, propagandistic nature of this and other OWI reviews is simply amazing.

The OWI reviewer, Marjorie Thorsen, was a loyal New Dealer and biased reviewer. For example, King Vidor, in his story "America," planned on presenting on film a glorification of the steel industry—of the industrialists, not labor. This did not go over well with Thorsen in her OWI review (November 5, 1942): "This story is a deluxe automobile edition of Horatio Alger, and if Henry Ford had written it, it could scarcely express the Ford philosophy more clearly. . . . Implicit in the story are many leaves from the classic but discredited American myth"—i.e., about any hard working person's ability to rise under capitalism.[58] It is shamefully obvious that the OWI was not seeking simply to support the war effort but also to push a particular political philosophy—and to push out any others. As with Poynter, freedom of speech here means everybody's right to advocate the views of FDR.

Given her denunciation of capitalism, it is interesting to see what she would say, one month later, about a film glorifying not the American steel industry, but the Soviet Union. First, her brief comment on "Russia," which I quote in its entirety:

> This is a very excellent story about Russia—within the simple framework of the story, it tells a great deal about what is happening in that remarkable country, and will help to allay many fears that Americans may have about the Soviets. However, in some places it is perhaps just a little too good a picture of Russia: in its uncritical and unqualified admiration for all things Russian, it commits the serious boner, as far as audience reaction is concerned, of implying that Russia is not only as good as the United States, but better. This implicit assumption becomes explicit in at least one scene, which should be remedied. [See point 7 below.] On the whole, however, this is one of the first scripts which promises to present a truthful and heartening picture of the life of ordinary people in Russia, and it should play a very useful part in the war information program.

In the fuller review, she makes seven points. The first five praise certain aspects of the film; the other two are critical comments. (The headings are Thorsen's; what follows are, if not in quotes, my paraphrase of her remarks.)

1. *The framework of the story allows for the use of varied Russian backgrounds.* By showing a variety of sides to Russia—all successful—the story, as she puts it, "dispels the impression of many Americans that Russia is composed solely of bleak, snow-covered plains and grubby, primitive villages." If we see the Russians as grubby, we won't have much confidence in them as our allies. (The presentation of Russia that she here praises is retained in the film.)

2. *The Russians are characterized as a peaceful and constructive people.* The Russians are peaceful, but in fighting the Germans, they fully support the war effort. Further, they are motivated not simply by a desire to defeat the Nazis; they are fighting "for [their] way of life," and "for the right to continue to build peacefully, constructively." (This characterization of Russians is retained in the film.)

3. *The community of aims and interests of Americans and Russians is established.* Like Americans, Russians are pro-achievement, pro-education, and pro-democracy. (This presentation of Russia is retained in the film.)

4. *The enemy is well characterized.* A Nazi is bad because of what he destroys (e.g., "children and old people"), and "what he destroys will be understandable to Americans." But the script does not imply that all Germans are bad. (In the film, no characterization of Germans is stressed, only that they are the invaders of Russia.)

5. *The familiar bugaboo of Russia's anti-clericalism is dispelled.* Thorsen praises the fact that the wedding ceremony is Russian Orthodox, and that the decision whether or not to marry in a church is up to the individual, "just as in America." She goes on to give the Party line (there's no other way to describe it) on the Soviet treatment of religion: "This [approach to religion] is well-taken, for while it is true that Russia has broken the political power of the church (and this was a sore point with Americans also for many generations) the Russians have no objection to the church functioning in its spiritual sphere." (This characterization of religion in Russia—though not stressed—is retained in the film.)[59]

The next two points are criticisms. Thorsen provided no headings, so I've devised my own:

6. *The Nazi–Soviet Pact.* In the version of the script under review, John tells Nadya that there is one thing he doesn't like about Russians—their friends (referring to their pact with the Nazis). Nadya laughs, and says:

"It is because we have such good friends that we spent sixty billion rubles for defense this year." Revealing that she knows the Party line better than Jarrico and Collins—for the same criticism of this scene was (by implication) leveled by Stalin in his famous "Scorched Earth" speech and, as we shall see, by a Soviet ambassador—Thorsen complains:

> The fact is that Russia did affix her signature to the "Nazi-Soviet Friendship Pact." Nadya's speech indicates that this was as cynical a gesture as any of Hitler's, that Russia had no more intention of honoring her treaty obligation than Germany did. . . . The dangerous conclusion that such audiences may reach is that no treaty with Russia is worth more than the paper on which it is written.

Thorsen recommends revising the scene, not removing it: "If this reference is to be retained in the picture—and it is my opinion that it should— a much more careful explanation is demanded. To a very substantial group of Americans, the Nazi–Soviet Treaty is something which cannot be passed off with a tinkling laugh." (The scene is revised [January 16, 1943] but does not make it into the film, which is silent about the pact.)

7. *Soviet versus American competition.* In one scene, John tells Nadya of his surprise to find the Russians so competitive, for he thought there was no competition in Russia. She disabuses him of this notion: "Russians are always competing—one worker against another, one brigade against another brigade, one collective farm against the next." John rises to the occasion with his own (i.e., American) brand of competition: During a contest between Nadya's brigade and another, John joins the other brigade and purposely slows it down, to ensure Nadya's brigade a victory. This shows, Thorsen says, "that Americans compete merely to win," and that "an American will resort to sabotaging his opponent" to do so. Thorsen must be objecting in the name of national unity, for surely the conception of American competition she is here criticizing is the same one she maintains in her extremely negative position on "the [Henry] Ford philosophy." (This entire scene is removed from the story. Competition is not an issue in the film.)

In her summary, Thorsen suggests that "trying to tell Americans that the Russians are not only as good as they are, but better, is not apt to sit so well with audiences, who may dismiss the whole picture as propaganda." It is unclear whether she believes the Russians are in fact better than Americans, or whether such an opinion simply won't "sit well with audiences."

Film analysis of Jarrico–Collins' script (MHL f.2928–29). Reviewer's name not given. December 28, 1942

The first part of this review is based on Marjorie Thorsen's. It has two parts: four positive points about the script and five questions raised about it. The first four points are the same as points 1 through 4 above (though in some cases they are briefer), and so are not covered here. Of the five questions, the first is based on point 6 above—though it has been revised—and the others are new.[60]

Here are the five "questions which we would like to raise for consideration":

1. *The Nazi–Soviet Pact.* The reviewer repeats Thorsen's point that the treatment of this issue in the screenplay may lead American audiences to conclude that Russia cannot be trusted to uphold a treaty. He or she then continues:

> A study of Russia's diplomatic history since the last war shows that she perhaps more than any other nation has stood by her diplomatic agreements. She has long recognized that German imperialist ambitions menaced her own peace and that of the world, her efforts toward collective security showed great foresight. Russia's military and diplomatic planning for many years has showed that she knew Germany and Japan were our basic enemies. If Nadya can clear this up in John Meredith's mind, she will clear it up in the minds of millions of other peoples in the world.
>
> There may be an opportunity here to point up the fact that Russia and the United States both desired peace—still desire peace—on the right basis, but the peoples of the world were not prepared for a United Peace. Russia embraced the Nazi-Soviet pact only after all her previous efforts at world collective peace had failed.

This goes far beyond Thorsen's review. Recall that she had recommended revising the scene, not removing it: "a much more careful explanation [of the pact] is demanded." Here we get a "more careful explanation"—from the FDR/OWI point of view—whether she or Poynter or someone else penned it. Note that this explanation is pure Soviet and Communist Party line. (As mentioned earlier, this scene is ultimately removed entirely.)

2. *Russian preparedness for war.* The review complains that the screenplay, as it reads, "indicates that [war] came as a complete surprise" to the Russians.

> Here again is an opportunity to show that Russia had felt that it was almost inevitable that some day she would be attacked by Germany. This fixation on the

part of Russia explains so many things about Russia that are not well understood, such as her war against Finland and extending her frontiers soon after
Germany's invasion of Poland in 1939.

This is pure Soviet propaganda and is really quiet amazing coming from an
American government office. This reviewer is, whether intentionally or not,
acting as a mouthpiece for Stalin: He or she *defends* Russia's attacks on Finland and Poland—calling its treatment of Poland "extending her frontiers"!
(Russian preparedness for war is a major issue in the film, though there are
no references in it to Poland or Finland.)

3. *American luxury.* The reviewer complains that in the opening scene in
New York City, there is too much American luxury: "white ties and silk hats
and limousines and glittering surroundings." Such luxury, the reviewer pre-
dicts, may well be more rare by the time the film is released. Further, its presentation could create problems: "Too many of our allies feel that American
life goes on luxuriously as usual, and may misinterpret this scene." (There is
a sense of luxury in the opening scene of the film: well-dressed men and
women enter the theater, as shiny automobiles drive by.)

4. *Fighting clergy.* "Is it desirable to show the priest as a fighter in the end
of the picture? The enemy, the Japanese especially, afford no immunity to
men of the clergy because they claim they are fighters, too." (In the film, a
priest is present during combat practice, and he is seen at the end with a
group of villagers planning to engage in guerrilla warfare, but he is never
shown actually fighting.)

5. *An American reporter and German victory.* "An American reporter is reported as saying that Germany will win the war over Russia within six weeks.
Russians resent some of the American forecasts regarding the length of the
war. Instead of blaming this on to the American reporter, could he perhaps
have gotten this from the German radio?" The reviewer adds: "it was the
Russian army that first destroyed a ten year myth of Nazi invincibility. . . .
This fact cannot be reiterated too often for the benefit of neutrals." (This
scene remains essentially unchanged in the film, though a reporter is no
longer responsible: Hank, Meredith's manager, says: "Down at the consulate,
they say the Nazis will win this war in 6 weeks.")

The review concludes: "RUSSIA can be of enormous value to the war
program. It should be checked with the Russian Embassy. The OWI is prepared to do this with the proper sanctions from the studio." In a brief memo
to Mellett (December 31, 1942), Poynter writes: "It is well to clear this with
the Russians? If so, it should be done quickly since they [MGM] are almost
ready to shoot. (The review and comments have already been sent to you.)"

Letter from Lowell Mellett to Maurice Revnes (MGM). December 31, 1942
Mellett offers three small suggestions about the screenplay. He has seen the
other reviews, and two of the three points he makes differ from anything
mentioned therein:

1. *American luxury.* Mellett notes that the limousines (with "shiny roofs")
   described in the opening scene "may be rare rather than a common
   sight in this country by the time the picture is in general circulation."
   (As indicated earlier, some luxury is retained in the opening scene.)
2. *Titles rather than names.* In the opening scene, when the announcer introduces "important personages," Mellett suggests that it would be better if they were introduced by title alone, because (1) "there is always
   the possibility of a change of names in high offices," and (2) using real
   names would entail "all the bother of obtaining the permission of the
   people named." (There is no mention of names or titles in the opening
   scene.)
3. *Hall of Koktails.* In this and some earlier drafts, in presenting the prosperity of Moscow, the story includes a description of (and in some cases
   a visit to) "the Hall of Koktails." Mellett, apparently concerned with
   accuracy on some issues, writes: "Is there such a thing in Moscow? I
   don't recall anything of that description as late as 1937, when I visited
   Moscow." (There is no Hall of Koktails in the final version, though
   John and Nadya do go to a fancy nightclub.)

Point 3 gives rise to a larger issue, namely, "the whole question of the
treatment of the Russian scene." Mellett offers to "present the script to the
Embassy here [in Washington D.C.]."

*Letter from Lowell Mellett to Warren Pierce (OWI, deputy to Nelson Poynter).
January 9, 1943*
Mellett informs Pierce that the "script on RUSSIA was submitted to
Vladimir I. Bazykin, First Secretary of the Embassy, and he has brought me
the following notes concerning it." He lists eight points:

1. *Names.* Bazykin reports that some of the names used (e.g., Frumkin)
   are not typically Russian, and suggests some others (e.g., Petrov and
   Ivanov). (Some names were changed; for example, "Frumkin" became
   "Petrov."[61])
2. *Nazi–Soviet Pact.* He suggests that in answer to John's question about
   the pact, Nadya should, in some form, say:

[O]f course, Russia signed a non-aggression pact with Germany, that Russia would sign a non-aggression pact with any country, that Russia is opposed to aggression by any other country and is willing to give guarantee not to be the aggressor against another country. This rather than the explanation given in the present script.

(Again, there is no mention of the pact in the film.)

3. *Trains.* John's train to Tchaikowskoe consists of merely a couple of coaches, but "trains in the Soviet Union are generally of 8–10 coaches." (This scene seems to have been revised accordingly.)

4. *Rachmaninoff.* In one scene, a character called Frumkin (later Petrov) greets John in the name of a long list of Russian composers. Bazykin here suggests adding Rachmaninoff to the list. (Rachmaninoff was added to the list in a later version of the script, but the whole line was eventually cut.)

5. *Intelligentzia.* In what is described as a typical Russian audience—"filled with workers, soldiers, pretty girls"—Bazykin asks that "intelligentzia" be added to the list. (This is especially interesting [and offensive] given what had happened, and continued to happen, to the "intelligentzia" under Stalin.) Bazykin then adds that aside from soldiers in uniform, "it is not possible to tell workers from other citizens by their dress." (Of course, in the film we cannot tell who is who—and certainly not who is an intellectual.)

6. *Car, not wagon.* The script has John going from the train station to the village by wagon. Bazykin comments: "As far as John Meredith is a famous foreign conductor, we feel sure that the village authorities, even if they do not have a car, could get it for such an occasion from the district center." (In the film, Meredith is picked up by Peter, who is driving a car.)

7. *ID tags.* "When Soviet children are evacuated from war zones, *no* identification tags are given to them." (They wear no such tags in the film.)

8. *Air-raid siren.* In this version of the screenplay, at the end of a concert, an air-raid siren is heard, and the "audience sits quietly." But Bazykin points out that this "is not correct, for after an air-raid people must leave immediately." (In the film, the audience is more attentive; they file out immediately, in an orderly fashion.)

At the end of the letter, Mellett tells Pierce: "[I] related to Mr. Bazykin the suggestions made by our office and he said he was completely in accord with them."

If these suggestions were all eventually sent to MGM, then judging by the changes made between the version of the screenplay reviewed by the OWI, and the film as it was released, MGM did not slavishly follow *every* recommendation, though it was willing to listen and did not object on political grounds to the OWI's advice.

The OWI's role in the film industry must be regarded as coercion and an affront to free speech—especially Mellett's clearing a screenplay with the Soviet Embassy! The existence and nature of the OWI is part of the cultural context necessary for understanding and judging the Hollywood Left and its conception of free speech in the 1940s.

Unwanted Collaborators, Part 2: The Hays Office

William (Will) Hays, former Republican National Committee chairman, was by the 1920s head of the Motion Picture Producers and Distributors of America—that is, the Hays Office. By the early 1940s—when MGM was making *Song of Russia*—the Hays Office was reviewing all films, to ensure that they were morally and socially "proper." Unlike the OWI, which was a government organization, the Hays Office wielded no actual political power. It relied on economic power—that is, the threat of boycott—though the studios often caved in to its demands as if they were issued from Congress or the White House. Koppes and Black, in *Hollywood Goes to War*, describe the rise to power of the Hays Office:

> In 1930 Hollywood had agreed to abide by a production code written by Daniel Lord, S.J., in consultation with Martin Quigley, a prominent Catholic layman who ran the trade paper *Motion Picture Herald*. But the studios had ignored the code. In mid-1934 the Catholic bishops made Hollywood a simple proposition: live up to the code and we will call off the boycott [by Catholics, which the American bishops had threatened earlier that year]. Hays agreed and sold the idea to the industry executives. He upgraded the enforcement mechanism, the Production Code Administration (PCA), and at its head placed a conservative Catholic journalist, Joseph Ignatius Breen. Films had to conform to his interpretation of the code to receive a PCA seal. Without that seal none of the Big Eight companies would handle a picture, effectively killing its market. From mid-1934 into the 1950s Breen's tough, narrow administration of the code sharply limited the subject matter Hollywood might undertake.[62]

Whether because Breen himself was sympathetic to Fascism and anti-Semitism, or because he simply loathed all political films—to the Hays Office, movies should be "pure entertainment"—he had the same attitude to-ward anti-Fascism as he did toward sensuous kissing: It simply should not be allowed on screen. As Koppes and Black report:

> The Hays Office would not let the industry make a movie criticizing Mussolini—this in the late 1930s, after Il Duce's aggression against helpless Ethiopia, crucial support for Franco, and adoption of anti-Semitic laws based on those of Nazi Germany. Instead Joseph Breen went to extraordinary lengths to pacify the Italian government.[63]

Just as Mellett would later send a script, with OWI reviews, to the Soviet Embassy, "Breen actually carried the script [for *Idiot's Delight* (MGM, 1939)] with him to Italy in the summer of 1938 for inspection by Mussolini's government."[64]

The *Song of Russia* files at the Margaret Herrick Library show that Joseph Breen and Louis B. Mayer corresponded about *Song of Russia* from December 1942 to December 1943. Naturally, Breen made a number of suggestions. It is worth noting what criticisms a religious conservative chose to level against *Song of Russia*—and which ones he did not—and whether or to what extent Breen's suggestions changed the nature of the story and ultimately the film. Judging by the dates of their letters, the Hays Office was sent the second version of the screenplay by Jarrico and Collins (MHL f.2928–29)—the same one sent to the OWI—and was thereafter regularly fed revisions. What follows are the main points made by Breen.

Letter from Breen to Mayer (December 9, 1942)

Breen is "happy to report" that *Song of Russia* "meets the basic requirements of the Production Code." However, eight points must be brought to Mayer's attention. Four concern sexually suggestive scenes, e.g., "suggestively sensuous movements in this dance with Nadya." Further, at one point, the two are locked in an embrace, kissing sensuously. Also, while at home playing chess, John reaches over, pulls Nadya to him, and—the treatment reads—"as she slides over the board she knocks the chess pieces over." (There is an embrace and kiss in the film, though the chess match was removed; Nadya dances in a ballroom in Moscow, and at her wedding, but there is nothing sensuous about either dance.)

Another problem Breen saw concerned the wedding: The comic lines between Higgins and Meshkov must not interrupt the wedding ceremony, but should come before or after. (This suggestion was accepted; they come after.)

Letter from Breen to Mayer (December 16, 1942)

There are five points that MGM must attend to before final approval can be granted. Three concern drinking; two concern sexually suggestive scenes. (Again, there seems nothing very "suggestive" in the film, though Breen may have sniffed at the amount of drinking done by Higgins at the wedding.)

Letter from Breen to Mayer (March 16, 1943)

On the one hand, the latest script[65] "meets the basic requirements of the Production Code." On the other hand, Jarrico, Collins, and their colleagues in some respects do not seem to be catching on,[66] because this time Breen has twelve criticisms. Three concern drinking; three concern sexually suggestive scenes; two concern a priest "crouching at the machine gun, since this action is not in line with the character of a priest"; one is a general warning against "any undue gruesomeness"; one concerns the possibility of undue cruelty to horses in a cavalry scene (not retained in the film); and one concerns possibly objectionable curses. (Again, it is difficult to determine whether MGM listened to Breen on many of these points, because I have no idea what Breen would consider inappropriate drinking or sexually suggestive. The priest who appears during combat practice is standing in the background, not actually crouching behind a machine gun.)

In all of his letters to Mayer about this film, Breen made only one comment on what he found to be an anti-American feature of the story: "We request that the following line be deleted, as unduly derogatory to the American way, 'I don't know. . . . I hear that in America there's no real family life at all. You want a divorce—You're divorced. They don't even care about the children.'" This line, spoken by an old woman in the village, was added on February 11, 1943, but did not make it into the film. It is highly revealing that this was the one line or scene or aspect of the story that the conservative Breen chose to chastise as unAmerican.

Letter from Breen to Mayer (May 16, 1943)

Here Breen comments on a revision to the story dated May 8, 1943: "We cannot approve this detailed verbal and experimental description of the 'Molotov cocktail' by Nadya, since this is an easily imitated method of making dangerous bombs. It is essential to establish some other business, if this scene is to be approved." (There is a fairly detailed explanation of the Molotov cocktail in the film.)

On December 14, 1943, the Hays Office sent MGM the final approval certificate for *Song of Russia.*

In the case of *Song of Russia*, MGM seemed more likely to listen to the OWI than to the Hays Office. Whereas the former may have had a noticeable effect on the film, and especially on *some* of its political implications, this is not so in the case of the Hays Office contribution. Again, what is most significant about the Mayer–Breen correspondence on *Song of Russia* is what the conservative Breen did *not* complain about or find politically objectionable, namely, much of what Ayn Rand (and others) criticized in the HUAC hearings: its positive (and false) portrayal of Soviet life.

Casting the Hero and Heroine

Our first indication of who Louis B. Mayer originally wanted for the two lead roles comes from Jarrico and Collins's first written contribution to the project (see MHL f.2923), which includes a "possible outline" (dated September 2, 1942), listing Walter Pidgeon and Ingrid Bergman in the star roles. But neither Pidgeon nor Bergman starred in *Song of Russia*. What happened?

In his HUAC testimony, Richard Collins reports:

> We got the assignment on Song of Russia, wrote a first draft of it, corrected the first draft on the basis of—as any first draft is corrected, on what could be helped in it from a writing standpoint. And then the script with which apparently the studio was pleased was sent to David Selznick so he could borrow— so Metro could borrow Ingrid Bergman. Selznick objected to the script on the basis it was too favorable to Soviet Russia.[67]

The first draft referred to is no doubt MHL f.2925 (September 11 to October 29, 1942). The second, approved draft is either MHL f.2928–29 (October 30 to December 14, 1942) or f.2931–34 (January 15, 1943). So Selznick probably read a draft some time between November 1942 and February 1943, at which time Bergman was out of the running for the female lead.

Greta Garbo *may* have been considered for the female lead at one point. Salka Viertel, in her memoirs *The Kindness of Strangers*, mentions Garbo in connection with the casting of *Song of Russia*, but there are problems with her account, and it is difficult to isolate which parts might be based in fact:

> This story [*Song of Russia*] had been concocted by director Gregory Ratoff, a gregarious White Russian with a hilarious accent, and two leftish screenwriters. Anna Louise Strong, for many years a Moscow correspondent to American papers, was called in as "technical adviser." I saw her often in the corridors of the Thalberg building: a large, white-haired woman leaning heavily on a cane,

flanked by her collaborators [Jarrico and Collins] . . . . The story was not merely a tribute to the sacrifice of the Russian people; it was also intended to exploit the then publicized Garbo/Stokowski romance. Ratoff told it in a nutshell: "Russian girl falls in love with famous American conductor, who arrives in Russia to give concerts but gets involved in the scorched earth policy." Mr. Ratoff wanted me to convince Garbo to play the girl, "a magnificent role and written especially for her." He described the scenes in which she sets the torch to the harvest, while her lover conducts Tchaikowsky's 1812 Overture. "Garbo is making the scorrrched earrrth," cried Gregory, carried away and rolling his rrr's. "All alone she scorrrches the Rrrussian earrrth, while Stokowski—I mean, Rrrobert Taylor—conducts."[68]

Ratoff may have discussed the possibility of Garbo with Viertel, but there is no independent evidence that he did so. If Garbo was considered, it was probably before Bergman. In an early script—screenplay sections by Paul Jarrico and Richard Collins (September 1942, MHL f.2925–26)—the conductor plays the 1812 Overture in the (late) heroine's burned out village; this might support an early consideration of Garbo. Further, there is no evidence that the original story, "Scorched Earth," was "concocted" by Ratoff or written especially for Garbo, or that MGM was out to milk the Garbo–Stokowski romance. And there is a problem with the timing: Robert Taylor seems to have been considered fairly late in the casting—after Pidgeon and Heflin— unless his name was being thrown around as a plan B or C much earlier. Finally, referring to Jarrico and Collins—both members of the Communist Party at the time—as merely "leftish" does nothing to bolster Viertel's objectivity or reliability.

Whether or not Garbo was ever in the running for the female lead in *Song of Russia*, by mid-March, Mayer had made his choice. A clipping in the MHL *Song of Russia* files (dated March 12, 1943, provenance unknown) announced in its headline: "Susan Peters given Lead Role in 'Russia'," which the piece describes as "the plum feminine role of the entire year." Susan Peters had been nominated for an Academy Award a year earlier, for her role in *Random Harvest* (MGM, 1942). I asked Collins whether Peters was political, and if so, whether it colored her attitude toward the film. He replied: "I think that if you asked her, 'Where's Russia?' she'd say, 'Well, it's a long ways away.' I don't think she had any interest in what [the film] was about."[69] (Tragically, Peters was paralyzed in a hunting accident on New Year's Day, 1945; she continued acting for a few years, in a wheelchair, playing forgettable roles. She retired, and died of pneumonia in 1952.)

As for the male lead, Collins reports:

When the time came to cast it, we had a meeting in Mayer's office. . . . Now in this meeting, the discussion was about who can play the lead roles. Mayer said this was very important—and who was going to be in some film always was important to him. The whole theory behind MGM, Mayer's theory, was that you made stars—that was the important thing—and then you kept them. "More stars than there are in heaven." So they discussed Walter Pidgeon. But Mayer said, "I don't want to change the relationship between Walter Pidgeon and Greer Garson. That's a great team. I don't want to break that up." Obviously, she couldn't play a Russian girl.[70]

So Pidgeon could no longer be considered for the male lead.

According to Collins, Gregory Ratoff initially believed that not having Pidgeon was a major problem:

Ratoff said, "I think that if we can't get Pidgeon, we really have very little reason to make the film. I'm not sure we should make it." And Mayer said—not talking to him, but sort of to the table—"At MGM, no one is indispensable, particularly directors." Of course, that shut Ratoff up forever. He didn't say another word.[71]

Mayer continued his search.

In an above-mentioned letter to Lowell Mellett (December 24, 1942), Maurice Revnes (MGM) requested that an effort "be made to secure the temporary release of Lieut. Emmett (Van) Haflin [sic, Heflin] who would, if released, play the star role" in *Song of Russia*. MGM got an answer from Mellett a week later (December 31): "I checked with the War Department concerning your desire to obtain a temporary release for Lieutenant Emmett (Van) Heflin, and was advised that there has been no change in their rule against such releases."

Obtaining a release for an actor who was already in the military was apparently impossible; obtaining a *deferment* for an actor about to enter was not. This brings us to Robert Taylor, who ultimately landed the role of John Meredith.

Louis B. Mayer said in his 1947 HUAC testimony:

I thought Robert Taylor ideal for the leading male role in Song of Russia, but he did not like the story.[72] This was not unusual as actors and actresses many times do not care for stories suggested to them. At the time, Taylor mentioned his pending commission in the Navy, so I telephoned the Secretary of the Navy, Frank Knox, and told him of the situation, recalling the good that had been accomplished with Mrs. Miniver and other pictures released during the war period. The secretary called back and said he thought Taylor could be given time to make the film before being called to the service. Accordingly, Taylor made the picture.

Taylor did make the film, but only after complaining to Mayer. Later, on May 14, 1947, at an HUAC executive session in California, he said:

[I]n 1943 we did a picture in the studio, from which I tried desperately to get out, called Song of Russia. They wanted me to do it. I didn't want to do it because I thought it was definitely Communist propaganda. In other words, it happened to paint Russia in a light in which I personally never had conceived Russia.[73]

This was big news in 1947. A front-page story of the New York Times said that Taylor told the HUAC "that he had been prevented by Government officials from entering the Navy in 1943 until he had starred in a pro-Russian film." The piece quotes Chairman Parnell Thomas: "Mr. Taylor protested to the management of MGM." According to the article, Thomas claimed Taylor's "protest was overruled by a Washington 'agent' [that is, Lowell Mellett] who came to Hollywood particularly for the purpose."[74]

FBI files made available under the Freedom of Information Act reveal how unhappy Louis B. Mayer was with Taylor's testimony. The FBI report states:

On July 23, 1947, SAC [Special Agent in Charge] Hood had a lengthy interview with L.B. Mayer of MGM Studios concerning the hearings conducted last spring by the Un-American Activities Committee. According to Mayer, the Committee did itself a great deal of harm by publishing the testimony of Robert Taylor, inasmuch as it was understood by Taylor and other witnesses that their testimony was to be "off the record." Mayer stated that Robert Taylor was mistaken about the actual facts to which he referred, and Mayer attributed this to Taylor's antagonism toward Communism and related that if necessary he, Mayer, would have to state that Taylor was mistaken. . . . Mayer stated positively . . . that Taylor was not ordered by anyone to make the film and he feels that when the hearings are held in Washington in September, Mellett's testimony and his, Mayer's, if he is called upon, will make the Committee look ridiculous for having jumped at the publicity on Taylor's erroneous statement.[75]

Many years after the hearings, discussing her involvement with the HUAC, Ayn Rand said:

[Robert Taylor] told us at a Board Meeting of the MPA [the Motion Picture Alliance for the Preservation of American Ideals], before we left for Washington, that he had volunteered to join the Navy during the war, and before he left he was called into Louis B. Mayer's office, and there was a man from Washington there who point blank told him that if he did not appear in this movie he would not get his commission in the Navy. He told us this, and said he would testify about it. He testified after me, several days later, and when they asked him had there been any pressure to force him to accept the part, he said no. I was shocked to pieces. . . . Now I know that something had happened between the Board meeting in Hollywood and the testimony in Washington. I was disgusted.[76]

A few years later, discussing the same event, she said: "I can't blame [Taylor] too much, though I wouldn't have done it. But I wondered under what kind of psychological torture he did do it."[77]

I assume the story he told at the MPA is similar to the one he told the HUAC subcommittee in California. Here is the beginning of Taylor's "revised" version, from his actual HUAC testimony a few months later:

I must confess that I objected strenuously to doing Song of Russia at the time it was made. I felt that it, to my way of thinking at least, did contain Communist propaganda. However, that was my personal opinion. A lot of my friends and people whose opinions I respect did not agree with me.[78]

As Rand and the FBI report suggest, pressure from Louis B. Mayer—aided by the OWI—helped to sway him. Earlier, he said he was pressured into making the film. Here he moves away from that position:

Taylor: [May] I clarify something?
Stripling: Yes; go right ahead.
Taylor: If I ever gave the impression in anything that appeared previously that I was forced into making Song of Russia, I would like to say in my own defense, lest I look silly by saying I was ever forced to do the picture, I was not forced because nobody can force you to make any picture. I objected to it but in deference to the situation as it then existed I did the picture.[79]

There are two possible reasons for this backpedaling. (1) His original statement was exaggerated. He said he was *forced* to star in the film—make it, or lose your commission in the Navy—when perhaps what Lowell Mellett in fact said was something like "this film will help the war effort, and I can ensure you that making it won't endanger your commission." (2) Whether or not Taylor's statement was accurate (and we cannot rule out the "make it or else" version), the studio's relationship with the government on the making of *Song of Russia* was—by 1947—an embarrassment, so he was pressured by MGM (and perhaps by some members of the HUAC) into revising his story.

Taylor said that one reason he did not want to make the movie was because of his impending entry into the navy, about which he was enthusiastic. Mayer biographer Charles Higham mentions without elaboration *two* deferments,[80] and he is probably right: one arranged by Mayer and the secretary of the navy; the other by the OWI and the navy's director of public relations. The following letter (date unknown)—from Mellett to Captain Leland P. Lovette, director of public relations, Navy Department— was read into the record by HUAC Counsel Stripling during Mayer's HUAC testimony:

> Metro-Goldwyn-Mayer have asked for a delay in the induction of Robert Taylor as a naval aviation cadet to permit the completion of a picture now under production, with Taylor as the star. Much of the picture already has been shot, but there remains several weeks' further shooting. This picture has Russia for its scene and the Office of War Information believes that, based on the script which we have read, it will serve a useful purpose in the war effort. It has no political implications, being designed primarily to acquaint the American people with the people of one of our Allied Nations.[81]

The first deferment must have come in early 1943, not long after MGM discovered that Van Heflin could not play the male lead. But unless Mellett is exaggerating the urgency of the progress of the film ("Much of the picture has already been shot."), this (second) deferment must have been requested later in the year—during the mid-summer of 1943 at the earliest—long after shooting had begun.

In any case, *Song of Russia* had a leading man. MGM's allegiance to the OWI had paid off.

Removing Propaganda

Robert Taylor and Louis B. Mayer both claimed before the HUAC to have insisted that elements of propaganda be eliminated from the script. First Mayer:

> Smith: Did you read the first script, Mr. Mayer?
> Mayer: Yes, sir.
> Smith: What was your opinion at that time?

Mayer: They had farm collectivism in it and I threw it out and said, "This will not be made until they give me the story they told me originally when I approved the making of it". . . .
Smith: As to the last script then, was the script, in your opinion, satisfactorily cleaned up?
Mayer: I think so; yes, sir.
Smith: Who was responsible, if you know, for taking the collectivism and other things out of the script?
Mayer: I ordered it out, and the producer said it would all be rewritten, and it was. That is why Taylor was delayed getting into the service.[82]

Richard Collins, in his 1951 HUAC testimony, seems to confirm Mayer's account. He says that after learning that Selznick was uninterested in the project, Mayer held a meeting with Jarrico, Collins, and Joseph Mankiewicz:

[I]t was decided that there were certain things such as the collective farms that should be omitted. Now, of course, this is really kind of a ticklish point, because if you show the farmers on collective farms you're in trouble, but, on the other hand, if you show that they own individual farms of this nature then you're in trouble, too. So we decided, for better or worse, not to mention what kind of farms these were. And then we took out words like "community" and did a general job of cleaning it up on this level. We did, in short, what we were instructed to do on the film.[83]

Robert Taylor said:

When the script was given to me I felt it definitely contained Communist propaganda and objected to it upon that basis. I was assured by the studio that if there was Communist propaganda in that script it would be eliminated. I must admit that a great deal of the things to which I objected were eliminated.[84]

If Taylor was brought on in early 1943, then the first script he saw was most likely the one "Okayed by Mr. Pasternak," and dated January 15, 1943 (MHL f.2931–34). In any event, if we can trust the testimony of Mayer and Taylor here, they were both on the lookout for Communist propaganda as the script evolved toward completion during 1943. So along with the comments from the OWI and the Hays Office, the coscreenwriters and the other contributors must have had to deal with input from Mayer and Taylor as well.

John Wexley, who did not begin to work on *Song of Russia* until the summer of 1943, describes working with Robert Taylor:

I was trying to touch up [*Song of Russia*] and was there as a mollifier or paci-
fier—a diplomat—toward Robert Taylor, who was a very strong reactionary.
He hated anything that had to do with the Soviet Union, and they kept trying to tell him it was his contribution to the war effort. For some reason, he respected me and wouldn't talk to the other two writers. I had never met him before. But now I would go to his dressing room or have lunch with him, and he
would say, "I hate this line," and I would say, "How would you like it changed?"
Actually, I changed very little. But the act of changing seemed to satisfy him.
That was part of my job—four weeks on the set keeping him happy. [Laughs.][85]

Given when Taylor came to work on *Song of Russia*, the most blatant
scenes were therefore not removed on his orders. Wexley is probably right in
claiming that he changed very little for Taylor. Mayer was likely responsible
for much of the blatant propaganda being removed, though we can't know
this with certainty.

Following is a representative sample of the Soviet propaganda that did not
make it into the film—at least not in the form that we find it in the film. (Note
that most of this propaganda was removed *before* Taylor ever saw a script.)

The items in the list fall under two main headings: "Scorched Earth" (the
pre-Jarrico–Collins material) and "Russia."[86]

"Scorched Earth"

July 31, 1942 (Trosper and Benedek, MHL f.2921):
"Sonia . . . exposes John's barren concept to the point where she is prob-
ing at this essential unhappiness because of his extreme individualism."
August 15, 1942 (Blankfort and Trosper, MHL f.2921):
"Meschkov tries to explain to John that here they decide things on a col-
lective basis."
August 18, 1942 (Strong, MHL f.2922):

(1) Peter: As soon as the curfew is off in the morning, you must go for the priest.
   John (in utter amazement): The priest?
   Peter (nodding): That little house by the church. . . .
   John (still unconvinced): But why the priest? Faber isn't dying.
   Peter: Faber's an atheist. He would never send for the priest for dying but
   only for guerilla business.
   John (in increasing wonder): Does the priest do guerilla business?
   Peter: Every honest Russian does. (enthusiastically) But this priest is a real
   help to us. He knows every trail, every hill and gully.

(2) John: I hope to act with you.
Priest: It seems strange that you, an American. . . .
John: It seems strange that you, a priest. . . .
Priest: I defend my land and my religion. . . .
John: Together with atheists?
Priest: Our Russian atheists only compete with God. The Nazis make God serve the devil. God can survive with us but not in a Nazi world.
John: Free men can't survive in a Nazi world, either. Americans are free men.
Priest (marveling): To come so far to fight . . . to our little village. (He sees that the guard is drawing near so he crosses himself and devoutly adds) Well, it's the will of God.

"Russia"

August 31, 1942 (Jarrico and Collins, MHL f.2923):
"Limousine. The Commissar is enthusiastically showing the sights as they drive to hotel. Hank thinks they're driving them by a special tourist route, asks where the queues are. Commissar says no more queues. John says what's that—a mirage? Commissar says they're waiting to buy tickets for your concert—if you'll consent to play twice."

September 3, 1942 (Strong, MHL f.2924):
Seeing the large amount of John's luggage, Vassily (a minor character) asks: "Did you fear a famine and bring your own supplies?" John replies: "Well, you know the stories they tell about Russia." Strong adds: "The Russians all chuckle, understanding."

September 11, 1942 (Jarrico and Collins, MHL f.2925):
(1) "Frumkin: 'Look! The new Dynamo apartment houses!' PANNING SHOT—THEIR ANGLE. A huge block of modern apartments. Frumkin (enthusiastic): 'Later I show you the subway! Wonderful subway! Most modern in the world!'"
(2) Stepanov: "When the Revolution came I thought now I'll live like a gentleman, with meat on the table every day and shoes as soft as roses for my feet. But it wasn't so simple. . . . Now that we live like human beings, I have to destroy you [i.e., his tractor—scorched earth]! Why doesn't the world leave us alone?!!"

December 12, 1942 (Jarrico and Collins, MHL f.2928–31):
(1) In a couple of versions of the script, John makes a remark about not liking the Russian's friends—the Germans. Here is a typical response:

Nadya: Is that what you think—that the Nazis are our *friends?*
John: You signed a pact with them.

Nadya: It is because we have such good friends that sixty percent of our national budget goes for defense? ["Sixty percent" is changed to "sixty billion rubles."]

A handwritten addition dated February 10, 1943 reads: "Is it for friendship that millions of us learn to jump from parachutes?"

(2) John: I thought you guys didn't believe in competition.
Nadya: Oh, but we do. We compete all the time. This farm against the next one. . . . If we're winning, we send people over there to help them catch up.

January 21, 1943 (Jarrico and Collins, MHL 2931–34):
Stepanov: Which would you prefer—just the registration or a church wedding as well?
John reacts rather violently, staring at Stepanov in amazement. . . .
John: Are church weddings customary?
Stepanov: It's up to the individual. . . . Why—how is it done in America?
John: It's up to the individual.

In these drafts, there are broadly two kinds of items that were removed: (1) overt "clarifications" of supposed misconceptions Americans may have had about Russia, for example, the living conditions in Soviet Russia (that they are not as bad as they used to be), the right to practice religion, the Nazi–Soviet Pact, etc.; (2) relatively subtle praise of Soviet Russia (and especially collectivism) and condemnation of individualism. Whether these items were removed for political reasons, or simply in the course of normal editing, I cannot say for certain. But given the HUAC testimony of Mayer, and given that some of the pro-Soviet material originally praised by the OWI was later removed, surely some of the more overt propaganda must have been removed at the request of Mayer. (Taylor was likely responsible for some minor adjustments to the screenplay.) But as is made clear in chapter 6, the final product is nevertheless a work of propaganda.

Release

Apparently, enough propaganda had been removed to please Mayer and Taylor. And the Hays Office was satisfied sufficiently to issue a certificate of final approval on December 14, 1943. A few days later, the last work on the film was being completed. (For example, records date the dialogue cutting continuity and the footage and music as December 17, 1943—see MHL f.2942.) The film was "tradeshown" in Los Angeles and New York on December 28, 1943, and the first reviews—in *Hollywood Reporter, Motion Picture Daily*, and *Variety*—appeared the next day. (The reviews are discussed in the next chapter.)

The trailer for *Song of Russia* was ready by mid-January:

> Out of the conflict and drama of our day. . . . comes a *great* love story. . . . inspired by the turbulent beauty of the world's great music! . . .
> A Nation's Songs of Battle!
> A People's Songs of Freedom!
> A Girl's Songs of Love!
> Song of Russia. . . . See it with someone you love![87]

Advertisements in the country's major papers would soon appear, and like the trailer, they make it clear that MGM wanted the film to be seen not as a pat on the back to our Russian allies, and certainly not as propaganda, but—in the words of one advertisement—as "A Glorious Romance Set to Tchaikowsky's Loveliest Melodies."[88]

Song of Russia was released nationally in January 1944.

Notes

1. Charles Higham, *Merchant of Dreams: Louis B. Mayer, M.G.M., and the Secret Hollywood* (New York: Donald I. Fine, 1993), 2–3.

2. Interview with author, January 10, 2001, Los Angeles.

3. Quoted in Clayton R. Koppes and Gregory D. Black, *Hollywood Goes to War: How Politics, Profits and Propaganda Shaped World War II Movies* (Berkeley: University of California Press, 1990), 149.

4. Here and elsewhere, the titles of the material and their file numbers are as found at the Margaret Herrick Library (MHL). See appendix 2 for a complete list.

5. *Hearings Regarding the Communist Infiltration of the Motion Picture Industry* (Hearings Before the Committee on Un-American Activities, House of Representatives, Eightieth Congress, First Session, October 20, 21, 22, 23, 24, 27, 28, 29, and 30, 1947) (Washington, DC: United States Government Printing Office, 1947), 71.

6. Higham, *Merchant of Dreams*, 329–30. When I asked Collins about Pasternak's politics, he said: "I don't think he had any views. . . . He was a man who liked to make musicals." (Interview with author, January 10, 2001, Los Angeles)

7. Interview with author, January 10, 2001, Los Angeles.

8. Interview with author, January 12, 2001, Los Angeles.

9. Federal Bureau of Investigation, Freedom of Information and Privacy Acts File (Communist Infiltration-Motion Picture Industry), File Number: 100-138754, Serial: 4, Part 1 of 15, and File Number: 100-138754, Serial: 157x1, Part 3 of 15.

10. On Mittler, see Bruce Murray, *Film and the German Left in the Weimar Republic* (Austin: University of Texas Press, 1990), 204.

11. Patrick McGilligan and Paul Buhle, eds., *Tender Comrades: A Backstory of the Hollywood Blacklist* (New York: St. Martin's Griffin, 1997), 325–50; Victor Navasky, *Naming Names* (New York: Viking Press, 1980), 225–32.

12. John Wexley was named as a Communist by witnesses at various hearings, though he claimed he never joined the Party because he "didn't care for dues paying." See McGilligan and Buhle, *Tender Comrades*, 699.

Not every writer who worked on this project was a Communist. For example, Laslo Benedek, another Hungarian, and assistant to Pasternak, made additions to the screenplay, though Richard Collins says that he was not in the Party. However, FBI files report that he belonged to a group "under control of the Communist Party," which was at the very least leftist if not Communist (Freedom of Information Act Files Federal Bureau of Investigation, Freedom of Information and Privacy Acts File [Communist Infiltration-Motion Picture Industry], File Number: 100-138754, Serial: 157x1, Part 3 of 15). John Hoffman and Fitzroy Davis also made small contributions to the screenplay, though Collins does not remember them (which he most likely would have had they been Party members).

13. Anna Louise Strong, *I Changed Worlds* (New York: Holt, 1935); *People's Daily World*, March 21, 1946.

14. See Salka Viertel, *The Kindness of Strangers* (New York: Holt, Rinehart & Winston, 1969), 268.

15. Peter Bogdanovich, *Who the Devil Made It* (New York: Alfred A. Knopf, 1997), 592–93.

16. Paul Buhle and Dave Wagner, *Radical Hollywood: The Untold Story Behind America's Favorite Movies* (New York: The New Press, 2002). Their scholarship here is just plain shoddy. Consider these four passages:

1. "pro-Russian wartime films . . . included the stagey musicals *Thousand Cheer*, written by Lester Cole and Paul Jarrico, and *Song of Russia* (by Cole, Jarrico, and Guy Endore)" (141). Richard Collins, not Cole, was Jarrico's collaborator on both films; Guy Endore did not share writing credits with Jarrico and Collins on *Song of Russia*, though he was one of three writers of the original treatment, "Scorched Earth."

2. "Richard Collins . . . coscripted *Song of Russia* with Paul Jarrico" (209). This is correct, but contradicts point 1.

3. "The backstory found Jarrico and Richard Collins working from a story by Leo Mittler, Victor Trival [sic, Viktor Trivas], and Guy Endore" (243). Aside from the misspelling of Trivas's name, this is accurate; but again, it contradicts point 1.

4. "[*Song of Russia*] was rewritten in the last stages by Boris Ingster to tone down the pro-Communism" (243). Ingster did make a small contribution to the rewriting of parts of the *Song of Russia* screenplay (see MHL f.2998–f.2939), but it did not consist of toning down Communist propaganda. His main contribution was to dialogue in the scenes wherein John Meredith is trying to get back to Tschaikowskoe.

17. Interview with author, January 10, 2001, Los Angeles.

18. *Communist Infiltration of Hollywood Motion-Picture Industry-Part 1* (Hearings Before the Committee on Un-American Activities, House of Representatives, Eighty-Second Congress, First Session, March 8 and 21; April 10, 11, 12 and 13, 1951) (Washington, DC: United States Government Printing Office, 1951), 236–37.

19. Interview with author, January 10, 2001, Los Angeles.

20. *Hearings Regarding the Communist Infiltration of the Motion Picture Industry* (1947), 71.

21. Interview with author, January 10, 2001, Los Angeles.

22. McGilligan and Buhle, *Tender Comrades*, 715.

23. *Hearings Regarding the Communist Infiltration of the Motion Picture Industry* (1947), 71.

24. *Hearings Regarding the Communist Infiltration of the Motion Picture Industry* (1947), 75.

25. *Hearings Regarding the Communist Infiltration of the Motion Picture Industry* (1947), 80.

26. *Hearings Regarding the Communist Infiltration of the Motion Picture Industry* (1947), 166–67.

27. McGilligan and Buhle, *Tender Comrades*, 339.

28. Interview with author, January 10, 2001, Los Angeles.

29. I here rely on Koppes and Black, *Hollywood Goes to War.*

30. Koppes and Black, *Hollywood Goes to War*, 34.

31. Koppes and Black, *Hollywood Goes to War*, 36.

32. Koppes and Black, *Hollywood Goes to War*, 51.

33. Koppes and Black, *Hollywood Goes to War*, 58.

34. Quoted in Koppes and Black, *Hollywood Goes to War*, 63.

35. Koppes and Black, *Hollywood Goes to War*, 63–64.

36. Koppes and Black, *Hollywood Goes to War*, 65.

37. Quoted in Koppes and Black, *Hollywood Goes to War*, 66–67.

38. Koppes and Black, *Hollywood Goes to War*, 149. See also pp. 66–69, 136–38, 144–45, and 147–48.

39. Koppes and Black, *Hollywood Goes to War*, 67–68.

40. Ayn Rand, *Atlas Shrugged* (New York: Random House, 1953; paperback ed., Dutton, 1992), 500.

41. Koppes and Black, *Hollywood Goes to War*, 125.

42. Koppes and Black, *Hollywood Goes to War*, 105.

43. Quoted in Koppes and Black, *Hollywood Goes to War*, 82

44. Koppes and Black, *Hollywood Goes to War*, 109–12. On leftist defenses of the need for censorship, see pp. 105 and 110. Note that the government still insisted that the OWI had no powers of censorship (p. 109).

45. The OWI files on *Song of Russia* are found at the National Archives and Records Administration (College Park, MD), Record Group 208, Box 3526.

46. See John Earl Haynes and Harvey Klehr, *Venona: Decoding Soviet Espionage in America* (New Haven, CT: Yale University Press, 2000), 196–201.

47. MHL f.2923.

48. Interview with author, January 12, 2001, Los Angeles.

49. McGilligan and Buhle, *Tender Comrades*, 339. Jarrico tells a similar story in an interview in Griffin Fariello, *Red Scare: Memories of the American Inquisition: An Oral History* (New York: W. W. Norton, 1995), 277.

50. On Lardner, Collins continues:

> Lardner keeps saying that the only way to get off the blacklist was to name names; but of course, the fact is that it didn't matter whether you named names or not, you were on the blacklist. The studios didn't differentiate between those who did and those who didn't. They just figured it was safer if they didn't hire anyone. I was surprised at that from Ring, who was a very bright, nice, gentlemanly fellow. I was surprised that he repeated that over and over again—as do they all.

Interview with author, May 2, 2001, telephone.

51. Interview with author, May 2, 2001, telephone.

52. Actually, they present two similar, overlapping outlines, which I combine here.

53. For a full description, see appendix 2, MHL f.2925–26.

54. For a full description, see appendix 2, MHL f.2928–29.

55. In a letter from Mayer to Joseph Breen of the Hays Office (December 12, 1942), "Scorched Earth" is crossed out and replaced with "Song of Russia." This revision may have been made later. All later screenplays, treatments, etc., refer to "Russia." "Song of Russia" seems to have been chosen rather late. Dialogue cutting continuity and footage of music (December 17, 1943, MHL f.2942) is the first item in the files bearing the title *Song of Russia*.

56. An OWI memo on this story, dated December 31, 1942, indicates that "they are almost ready to shoot." It would be a month or so before MGM had signed actors for the two leading roles, but Pasternak et al. may have been ready to shoot at least some preliminary scenes by January 1943, as the okayed script cited below tends to indicate.

57. For a full description, see appendix 2, MHL f.2931–34.

58. Quoted in Koppes and Black, *Hollywood Goes to War*, 147–48.

59. See Robert Mayhew, "MGM's Potemkin Church: Religion in *Song of Russia*," *American Communist History* 1, no. 1 (2002), 91–103.

60. Thorsen's review indicates that copies were sent to, among others, "LM" (Lowell Mellett) and "NP" (Nelson Poynter). It is possible that Poynter read Thorsen's review, kept the parts he approved of or thought necessary (points 1–4 and 6), made some revisions, raised some questions of his own, and then sent the results to Lowell Mellett, who in turn sent one or both reviews to MGM.

61. Bazykin may have had another or different objection to the name "Frumkin." M. I. Frumkin was an Old Bolshevik who perished in Stalin's Terror in 1939. See Richard Pipes, ed., *The Unknown Lenin: From the Secret Archives* (New Haven, CT: Yale University Press, 1998), 93.

62. Koppes and Black, *Hollywood Goes to War*, 14.

63. Koppes and Black, *Hollywood Goes to War*, 22.

64. Koppes and Black, *Hollywood Goes to War*, 23.

65. Probably the Jarrico–Collins script okayed by Pasternak (MHL f.2931–32).

66. Richard Collins recently stated that he has no memory of Mayer or Pasternak ever expressing any concerns about Breen's comments on the screenplay. Interview with author, May 2, 2001, telephone.

67. *Communist Infiltration of Hollywood Motion-Picture Industry-Part 1* (1951), 236.

68. Viertel, *Kindness of Strangers*, 268.

69. Interview with author, January 10, 2001, Los Angeles.

70. Interview with author, January 10, 2001, Los Angeles.

71. Interview with author, January 10, 2001, Los Angeles.

72. There may not be any dishonesty or misremembering here. After Pidgeon and Heflin, Mayer may have looked into Taylor, discovered that he had musical experience, and concluded he was ideal on that basis. See Taylor's HUAC testimony, *Hearings Regarding the Communist Infiltration of the Motion Picture Industry* (1947), 167.

73. Quoted in Mayer's HUAC testimony, *Hearings Regarding the Communist Infiltration of the Motion Picture Industry* (1947), 80.

74. Gladwin Hill, "Red Film Held Forced on Taylor; 'Agent' Halted His Navy Service," *New York Times*, May 15, 1947.

75. Federal Bureau of Investigation, Freedom of Information and Privacy Acts, Communist Infiltration-Motion Picture Industry, File Number 100-138754, Serial: 4, Part 7 of 15.

76. Biographical interviews (Ayn Rand Archives).

77. From the Q&A period following her Ford Hall Forum talk in Boston, "Wreckage of the Consensus" (1967). (Tapes and transcripts in the Ayn Rand Archives.)

78. *Hearings Regarding the Communist Infiltration of the Motion Picture Industry* (1947), 166.

79. *Hearings Regarding the Communist Infiltration of the Motion Picture Industry* (1947), 166–67.

80. Higham, *Merchant of Dreams*, 329–30.

81. *Hearings Regarding the Communist Infiltration of the Motion Picture Industry* (1947), 81.

82. *Hearings Regarding the Communist Infiltration of the Motion Picture Industry* (1947), 75.

83. *Hearings Regarding the Communist Infiltration of the Motion Picture Industry* (1947), 236. See also Paul Jarrico in McGilligan and Buhle, *Tender Comrades*, 339, and Higham, *Merchant of Dreams*, 330.

84. *Hearings Regarding the Communist Infiltration of the Motion Picture Industry* (1947), 166. Richard Collins, in his HUAC testimony, said: "Now, Bob Taylor as it was, I think, objected to *Song of Russia* and to line[s] in it, and so on, and, as I remember, they had to be in some cases changed." (*Communist Infiltration of Hollywood Motion-Picture Industry-Part 1* [1951], 238).

85. McGilligan and Buhle, *Tender Comrades*, 715.

86. Descriptions are in quotation marks; dialogue is indented. For bibliographical details, see the MHL files listed in appendix 2.

87. Ellipses are in the original. "Trailer dialogue cutting continuity and trailer footage; 1/11/44; 3 pages and 1 page" (MHL f.2943).

88. *New York Times*, February 9, 1944. See, for additional examples, *New York Times*, January 21, 1944 ("A dashing Yankee! A musical maid! A thrilling romance!") and *Washington Post*, February 17, 1944 ("A Dashing American, A Lovely Russian, They Make Love Sing! A singing, soaring story of love—a glorious romance, heightened by wonderful music.").

~

CHAPTER THREE

Reactions to *Song of Russia*

Judging by the publicity material MGM prepared for *Song of Russia*, Louis B. Mayer thought (or hoped) he had a hit on his hands. MGM *Production Facts* asserts: "In 'Song of Russia' we have a new global type love story presenting one of the most dynamic new romantic teams ever paired in Hollywood." Similarly, *Publicity Service: "Song of Russia"* declares that the film "catches the pulse of the Russian people in a story that will hold you spellbound."[1]

The pre-release reviews gave MGM reason to be optimistic. The *Hollywood Reporter* called *Song of Russia* "one of MGM's biggest potential grossers of the season." It is, the reviewer says, "basically an engrossing love story and should be sold as such." Much to Louis B. Mayer's pleasure, the review assures the audience that "the screenplay at no time becomes a political tract." As for the stars of the film, "Robert Taylor . . . contributes one of the top performances of his career," and "Susan Peters is lovely and luminous as the heroine, etching a portrait that should gain her many new admirers."[2] In the same spirit, *Variety* reported: "In competition at the boxoffice with other films of Russia now coming from Hollywood, this Joseph Pasternak production will hold its own." The role of Nadya is "an outstanding performance by Susan Peters," whereas "Taylor . . . competently accounts for the assignment with ability." As for the director, "Gregory Ratoff's Russian background enabled him to paint a picture of an unconquerable people."[3] The *Motion Picture Daily* was pleased as well:

M.G.M.'s contribution to the fostering of a better understanding of the Russians is fundamentally a grand, appealing romantic film. . . . It should score

handsomely with the customers; it is entertainment of the better kind. . . . Under Gregory Ratoff's capable direction the romance is neatly fused with more
somber elements. . . . Taylor and Miss Peters are first-rate.[4]

The post-release reviews were for the most part positive as well, though
some were mixed. I begin with the more positive ones. Note that these either
downplay or ignore the issue of propaganda, or treat any propagandistic aspects of the film as part of a good-natured gesture toward our Russian allies.

The first of these to appear, in the *Independent*, reported: "Here is a dramatic love tale with rich emotional values that will not be lost on the
femmes. . . . The film represents another fine production job by Joseph
Pasternak. . . . Robert Taylor and Miss Peters give their best. . . . *Song of Russia* is a merry boxoffice tune."[5]

Bosley Crowther thought so much of the film that he reviewed it twice in
the *New York Times*. In his first review, he is full of praise for Pasternak and
Ratoff, and Taylor and Peters (and the cast generally). He writes:

Prepare yourself for a surprise folks—an exciting surprise. . . . It is really a
honey of a topical musical film full of rare good humor, rich vitality and a
proper respect for the Russians' fight in this war. Indeed, it comes very close to
being the best film on Russia yet made in the popular Hollywood idiom. And
it is sure to have wide appeal.

After describing the story, he writes: "This may sound on the verge of banal-
ity. And it very well might be, if a truly superb production had not been given
this film."[6] In his second review—entitled "Under Two Flags"—he adds:

"Song of Russia" is full of lively movement, a healthy and hopeful gusto, richly
affectionate humor and fine reserve when it comes to war. . . . Being a musical
picture, it uses music most artfully throughout . . . to motivate and background
the movement of vivid images upon the screen. . . . Robert Taylor and Susan
Peters—especially the latter—play it so pleasantly that one finds it easy to
watch both of them—and the whole film—romantically.[7]

Three positive reviews came out of Los Angeles on February 18, 1944.
The *L.A. Examiner* said, "Robert Taylor gives one of his best performances to
date," and called Susan Peters "Metro-Goldwyn-Mayer's most promising
young star." The film's presentation of the Soviet Union is uncritically described as follows: "Hollywood's usual conception of Russian peasant life
which couldn't be happier, gayer or more carefree."[8] The *L.A. Times* was similarly pleased:

This is a big, M.G.M. glorification of our fighting ally, the Soviet Union, easily bigger than Russia itself and, as such, excellent propaganda. I have no intention of arguing the pros and cons of THAT matter, for I can promise you another good Pasternak show regardless. . . . "Song of Russia" is filled with glorious Tschaikowsky music—conducted and not badly, by Robert Taylor, with Susan Peters (and very convincingly, too) at the piano for the concerto. . . . There is too much gayety before the seriousness sets in, and the story, war or no war, is frankly escapist. It works out a shade too patly for belief throughout.[9]

Escapist and pat or not, the film is praised as good propaganda, that is, it does a good job of glorifying our ally, the Soviet Union. The *Hollywood Citizen-News* said the film has a "refreshing quality and delightful charm." Its music, however, "is the major appeal of this photoplay—that and a simple love story." The actors are good as well: "Taylor, although scarcely the part for the role, registers a really brilliant characterization. . . . As for Miss Peters, her frail beauty is the most appealing touch of the photoplay." Did this reviewer detect any propaganda? "There's a speech by Stalin interposed, which highlights the strong propaganda note."[10]

The review from the *Washington Post* was brief but positive. It praised the cast, especially Peters, and the screenplay, and stated that "the exciting and genuinely moving Metro-Goldwyn-Mayer production of 'Song of Russia,' [is] addressed to the fortitude and devotion of an heroic people, hard pressed by a bitter and ruthless enemy."[11]

In my survey of reviews of *Song of Russia*, positive reviews outnumbered mixed ones (there were no purely negative reviews). Here are two with significant reservations.

The second *Variety* review praises certain aspects of the film. For example: "'Russia' has the benefit of a fine production, faithful to detail. No Pasternak production could be otherwise. And Gregory Ratoff, the director, certainly is keenly aware of his Russian backgrounds." Further, like many other reviews, this one singles out Susan Peters:

But if it achieves nothing else, "Song of Russia" at least establishes the stellar value of a comparative newcomer; this is Susan Peters' most important role to date. It reveals her as one of the finest young dramatic actresses to emerge from Hollywood in some time. The word-of-mouth on her performance, beauty and expressive underplaying should make her a 'must' in any future Metro plans.

Robert Taylor—again, as with other reviews—is not treated as well: "it's a question of whether Taylor could be popularly accepted as a noted symphonic conductor." The problem with *Song of Russia*, as this *Variety* review sees it, is that the film has chosen romance over realism:

> Joseph Pasternak has produced for Metro with a sweep that suggests epochal intentions. That these intentions go awry can be attributed considerably to a script that too frequently sacrifices realism for what is seemingly more a love story than an epic of a gallant people's fight against enslavement. "Song of Russia's" boxoffice returns will be dependent to a considerable degree on Robert Taylor's name.[12]

Note that the criticism is not that the film presents a happy, romantic Russia instead of the more realistic, *totalitarian* one, but that it presents a happy, romantic Russia instead of a more realistic, *heroic* one.

The *Newsweek* review's complaint against the film is in part based on MGM's apparent flip-flopping in its attitude toward the Soviet Union:

> Only a few years ago Metro-Goldwyn-Mayer was kidding the Soviet Union unmercifully with such comedy lampoons as "Ninotchka" and "Comrade X." Now, with the changing times and "Song of Russia," M.G.M. performs the neatest trick of the week by leaning over backward in Russia's favor without once swaying from right to left.

Another problem is—as we've heard before—that the film aims for heroism, but achieves a typical Hollywood romance: "Theoretically, 'Song of Russia' is a somewhat belated attempt to tell Americans about the homely qualities of our Russian allies and their valiant resistance to Nazi aggression. In practice, however, the film resolves into a hifalutin' romance." Finally, according to this review, the film—in its enthusiasm to show the Soviet Union in a positive light—strains belief:

> M.G.M.'s tribute goes overboard on the matter of presenting the Russians as a simple, industrious, religious folk who relax from a day's work in night clubs that would put the Rainbow Room to shame, and who love peace, music, their country, and Americans—in the order named. . . . As an uncomplicated love story cagily set to the music of Tchaikovsky, "Song of Russia" undoubtedly has its popular points; but as a sensible contribution to Russo-American understanding it is neither flesh, fowl, nor good Red herring.[13]

This review criticizes the film for its inaccurate portrayal of Soviet Russia, though it does not seem to have a problem with pro-Soviet propaganda in theory, as long as it is well done.

There were two positive reviews from Communist sources, one American, the other Russian.

Joseph Foster, in "Two Films About Russia," which appeared in *New Masses*, praises the film (despite its Hollywood clichés). This review is unique (among American reviews) in that it does not sidestep or tentatively justify the presentation of an overblown Russia. Instead, Foster praises the film for what he considers its accurate portrayal of Russia. (Keep in mind that *New Masses* defended the Soviet Union against "rumors" of the Great Terror and the purge trials, and defended the Nazi–Soviet pact of 1939–1941, as well as Stalin's rape of Poland, Finland, and the Baltic States.)

"Song of Russia" hits upon the very happy idea of bringing the Soviet Union to America in terms of common understanding. . . . As lovers will, they see Moscow together, and the benefits of Soviet life are introduced, not too obtrusively, but inescapably. . . . The people of the village are . . . brought under the camera's eye and presented with much warmth and sympathy. Many of the scenes that follow, however, are too discernibly theatrical and are based foursquare on dramatic clichés. Sometimes too, the Russian character is distorted for the sake of humor, but the central picture of Soviet life comes through intact and in palatable style. For instance, the father of the household interests the visiting celebrity in the quality of the grain grown by the village collective. During dinner he leads the hero to the storage bins and dwells with pride on the beauty of the grain. . . . And the film brings out pertinent facts about the Soviet Union: music is of prime importance for not only the professional musicians but for all the people; a great conductor can be a national hero; the children are the first regard of the country and are given unlimited opportunity to develop. . . . MGM has definitely shown the way with this one.[14]

In November 1944, *Song of Russia* opened in Moscow, and the famous composer Aram Khachaturyan wrote a review that appeared in a number of American papers. As *Motion Picture Daily* points out in its preface to the review, it "must have cleared through the Soviet Foreign Office before it was filed."[15] Consequently, it follows a purely Stalinist line (and includes a reference to collective farms). Khachaturyan writes:

I must say I liked this film. There was a certain noble and idyllic quality about it that spoke for the warm feeling that is drawing the American and Russian people together. . . . Robert Taylor as John Meredith and Susan Peters as Nadya Stepanova give superb recitals. . . . Speaking of understanding, the impact of the war on Russia is particularly effective, I found, in the picture. One of the partisans, when John Meredith looks fixedly at him, assures Meredith simply that he is one of many. This little bit in the film throws a powerful searchlight on the daily heroism of the Soviet people. . . . Nadya Stepanova, the heroine of the film, is also one of many. There are indeed thousands of Russian girls like her who took up their post in battle as soon as the hour struck. . . . On the whole I think as regards the music and directing the film is an amazingly daring and praiseworthy piece of work.

He assures his readers that the film's portrayal of Russia as a land where children—especially talented children (like the character Peter)—can pursue their dreams is accurate:

In fact, I myself, owe my rise to the Government's support. I never took private lessons. While at college my gift for composing music was marked. I was transferred to the State Conservatory. I'm bringing in all this in order to demonstrate that situations, despite their unusualness, are quite plausible.

His only complaints concern the inaccurate "Hollywood" touches, though none of them implies that Russia is anything less than what the film portrays: "I was unfavorably impressed with the scenes of the tractor ploughing where, I think, both the director and the actress forgot that driving a tractor is hard work. An attractively tied kerchief and soft smile are all very well, but it takes more to sow a Victory harvest." And: "Only certain episodes suffer from misconceptions, as, for example, the portrayal of the wedding on the collective farm done in the manner of a stylized ballet." But these touches don't alter his overall conclusion: "'Song of Russia' is a tribute to the cultural collaboration of the American and Russian people."[16]

It is worth mentioning here that in an unpublished note on *Song of Russia*, Ayn Rand writes:

A news dispatch from Moscow, dated May 25, 1947, states that Sergei Gerasimov, a leading Soviet film director, writing in the Soviet Government paper "Izvestia" and discussing the question of whether "Song of Russia" was pro-Communistic, declared that it was "cordial but very naïve." Which is correct. *How* naïve, Gerasimov could probably tell us better than an American.[17]

Despite receiving good reviews, *Song of Russia* did not do so well at the box office. Further, MGM's hopes for financial rewards from overseas distribution would encounter major problems.

In November 1944, the OWI began considering the film for possible overseas release and for dubbing. (Recall that two years earlier, this office's report on *Song of Russia* was extremely positive and supportive.) Here is a different appraisal of *Song of Russia* from the OWI's Los Angeles Overseas Bureau, Motion Picture Division:

> The completed film, although slightly changed in story content, makes all the points which were made in the script. The minor dialogue objections raised by this office have been eliminated. Unfortunately, however, the manner in which this story has been transferred to the screen greatly lessens its value from the standpoint of overseas distribution. Also to be considered is the fact that this picture is being released almost two years after its conception, and most of the things which it says have already been said many times before on the screen.
>
> SONG OF RUSSIA raises no problems from the standpoint of this office.[18]

This last line constitutes damning with faint praise, and things would get worse. A report from the same office dated January 11, 1945, states that, "The war is made the background for a Hollywoodish romance and success story. Russia and Russians are so artificially presented as to discredit the movie." A memo concerning distribution in the Far East dated January 17, 1945, contained the same comment verbatim, and declared the film unsuitable for distribution. MGM complained, naturally, and letters went back and forth between MGM and the OWI. But on February 5, 1945, Arnold M. Picker of the Motion Picture Branch, Overseas Branch, of the OWI sent a letter to MGM that turned out to be the last word on overseas distribution: "this is to advise you that SONG OF RUSSIA cannot be recommended at the present time for preparation in any language or for shipment to any territory."

The power of the OWI was in its ability to affect not only the content of film but also its financial success.

Seven years after the release of *Song of Russia*, at the 1951 House Un-American Activities Committee (HUAC) hearings, coscreenwriter Richard Collins said: "no one suspected when it came out . . . that 5 years later anyone would ever remember it."[19] This is hard to believe, given the positive nature of the reviews of the film, though it *is* quite believable given the film's quality. And Collins was right: Most would come to regard *Song of Russia* as an utterly forgettable film. In fact, many—Louis B. Mayer, for instance—hoped people *would* forget the film; those who did not kept it in mind not for any cinematic brilliance but because of its portrayal of Soviet Russia and the political implications of that portrayal. This became clear at the October 1947 HUAC hearings on Communist infiltration in the motion picture industry.

Louis B. Mayer was one of the first friendly witnesses to testify. He began with a prepared statement containing—among other things—his "review" of *Song of Russia*:

> The final script of Song of Russia was little more than a pleasant musical romance—the story of a boy and a girl that, except for the music of Tschaikowsky, might just as well have taken place in Switzerland or England or any other country on earth. . . .
> Since 1942 when the picture was planned, our relationship with Russia has changed. But viewed in the light of the war emergency at the time, it is my opinion that it could not be construed as anything other than for the entertainment purpose intended and a pat on the back for our then ally, Russia.

Later, his evaluation of the picture was questioned by Congressmen Smith and HUAC counsel Stripling:

> Smith: Going back to the picture Song of Russia. . . . Don't you feel the picture had scene after scene that grossly misrepresented Russia as it is today, or as it was at that time?
> Mayer: I never was in Russia,[20] but you tell me how you would make a picture laid in Russia that would do any different than what we did there?
> Smith: Don't you feel from what you have read, and from what you have heard from other people, that the scenes just did not depict Russia one iota?
> Mayer: We did not attempt to depict Russia; we attempted to show a Russian girl entreating this American conductor to conduct a concert in her village where they have a musical festival every year and as it inevitably happens this girl fell in love with the conductor, and he with her. . . .
> Smith: What are your feelings about the picture, as to the damage it might cause to the people in the United States, that is, misleading them as to conditions in Russia?
> Mayer: What scenes are you referring to?
> Smith: Do you recall scenes in there at the night club where everybody was drinking?
> Mayer: They do in Moscow. . . .
> Smith: Do you feel it represents Russia in 1943 as conditions were in Russia?
> Mayer: This is what I understood, that they go to night clubs there in Moscow. If only the rest of the Russians had a chance to do the same thing, it would be fine, but they don't. This picture was laid in Moscow. . . .
> Stripling: . . . . I saw it myself. I personally think it was Communist propaganda. I would like to present a qualified reviewer and get their opinion of it. . . . Now, Mr. Mayer, you stated that you recently viewed the picture.
> Mayer: Yes, sir.

Stripling: Is it your opinion that there were no political implications in it whatsoever?

Mayer: I am convinced of that. I am under oath, and if I met my God I would still repeat the same thing.

Mayer defends his position by appealing to a number of positive reviews, many of which are (or are like) those discussed earlier in this chapter:

> I have here reviews of the picture from the New York Times, the New York Post, the London Daily Sketch, the Washington Post, and the New York Herald Tribune. There is only two lines or so in each one. The New York Times said: "It is really a honey of a topical musical film, full of rare good humor, rich vitality, and proper respect for the Russians' fight in the war." The New York Post says: ". . . a pretty little romance with a made-in-America back-drop of Russia . . . cozy, clean, luxuriously musical film. . . ." The London Daily Sketch says: ". . . turned out to be strictly an American anthem." The Washington Post said: "It is one film about Russia which will probably be little assailed as propaganda. . . ." The New York Herald Tribune said: "Russia itself has all too little to do with Song of Russia." Here is that.
> Stripling: Mr. Mayer, I would like for you to stand aside for a moment.[21]

Mayer did not stand aside "for a moment"; he was never called back. Consequently, he was furious about the committee's treatment of him—that these congressmen had asked *him* to step down to be contradicted by their expert witness. "I felt I had been kicked aside at the House Committee and hadn't been allowed to finish. I was disgusted; the whole conduct of the Committee was a disgrace."[22]

He was "kicked aside" to make room for Ayn Rand.

> Chairman: Raise your right hand, please, Miss Rand. Do you solemnly swear to tell the truth, the whole truth, and nothing but the truth, so help you God?
> Rand: I do.[23]

Notes

1. Both of these are dated simply 1943, and can be found in the *Song of Russia* clipping file at the Margaret Herrick Library. No other bibliographical information is available.

2. *Hollywood Reporter*, December 29, 1943.

3. *Variety*, December 29, 1943.

4. *Motion Picture Daily*, December 29, 1943.

5. *Independent*, January 8, 1944.

6. *New York Times*, February 12, 1944.
7. *New York Times*, February 20, 1944.
8. *L.A. Examiner*, February 18, 1944.
9. *L.A. Times*, February 18, 1944.
10. *Hollywood Citizen-News*, February 18, 1944.
11. *Washington Post*, February 25, 1944.
12. *Variety*, January 10, 1944.
13. *Newsweek*, February 21, 1944.
14. *New Masses*, February 29, 1944.
15. "First Soviet Review of U.S. Film Sent to 'Daily'," *Motion Picture Daily*, November 17, 1944.
16. *Motion Picture Daily*, November 17, 1944. This review was published elsewhere. For example, it appeared as "What a Russian Thinks of 'Song of Russia'—a Cable" in *Motion Picture Herald*, November 18, 1944.
17. From "Some Film Reviews," in the Ayn Rand Archives.
18. For the OWI material, see National Archives and Records Administration (College Park, MD), Record Group 208, Box 3526.
19. *Communist Infiltration of Hollywood Motion-Picture Industry-Part 1* (Hearings Before the Committee on Un-American Activities, House of Representatives, Eighty-Second Congress, First Session, March 8 and 21; April 10, 11, 12 and 13, 1951) (Washington, DC: United States Government Printing Office, 1951), 236.
20. Mayer was born in the Ukraine in 1885, but left as a child.
21. *Hearings Regarding the Communist Infiltration of the Motion Picture Industry* (Hearings Before the Committee on Un-American Activities, House of Representatives, Eightieth Congress, First Session, October 20, 21, 22, 23, 24, 27, 28, 29, and 30, 1947) (Washington, DC: United States Government Printing Office, 1947), 71–72, 74–76, 81–82.
22. Quoted in Charles Higham, *Merchant of Dreams: Louis B. Mayer, M.G.M., and the Secret Hollywood* (New York: Donald I. Fine, Inc., 1993), 368. Higham provides no bibliographical information; he merely states that Mayer said this under oath in a court case, *Lester Cole v. Loew's, Inc.* I was unable to find the transcript of this case. I did, however, find its disposition: *Cole v. Loew's Incorporated* (No. 8005, United States District Court for the Southern District of California, Central Division), 8 F.R.D. 508, 1948 U.S. Dist. LEXIS 3340 (December 20, 1948, December 30, 1948). The presiding judge wrote the following in his summary of Mayer's testimony: "Mr. Mayer [speaks] of the 'shabby treatment'—as he called it—that he had received at the hands of the Committee. . . . [H]e resented the cavalier manner in which he was 'brushed aside' by the Committee and was allowed to stand up without being excused, while another person was making a statement." An FBI informant was present at the Motion Picture Producers Association meeting of December 2, 1947, and this is what he reported: "L.B. Mayer stood up and said, 'For the first time in my life I am

forced to disagree with my old friend Cecil [B.] DeMille.' Mayer then went on in the meeting saying, 'If you could have seen how they treated me, Cecil,' speaking of the Un-American Committee" (FBI, Freedom of Information and Privacy Acts [Communist Infiltration-Motion Picture Industry], File Number: 100-138754, Serial: 1003 [part 2], Part 9 of 15).

23. *Hearings Regarding the Communist Infiltration of the Motion Picture Industry* (1947), 82.

PART TWO

NAMING FACTS: AYN RAND'S 1947 HUAC TESTIMONY

~

CHAPTER FOUR

From Russia to Washington, D.C., via Hollywood

Ayn Rand was born Alisa Rosenbaum, on February 2, 1905, in St. Petersburg, Russia.

Her father, Zinovy Zacharovich (usually referred to as Z. Z.) Rosenbaum, was an intelligent and principled self-made man. He and his family (his wife, Anna Borisovna, and their three daughters, Alisa, Nora, and Natasha) lived in middle-class comfort in an apartment adjacent to his pharmacy. Z. Z. and Anna Rosenbaum were Jewish, but for the most part nonreligious.

In 1914, while still a young girl, Alisa decided on a career:

> I decided to be a writer at the age of nine—it was a specific, conscious decision—I remember the day and the hour. . . . I decided to become a writer— not in order to save the world, not to serve my fellow men—but for the sim- ple, personal, selfish, egotistical happiness of creating the kind of men and events I could like, respect and admire. I can bear to look around me levelly. I cannot bear to look down. I wanted to look up.[1]

Looking around her in February 1917, from the balcony of her family's apartment on the Nevsky Prospekt in St. Petersburg (then called Petrograd), she witnessed the beginning of the revolution. She later recalled: "at that time everybody of any political denomination was in favor of [the February or Kerensky] revolution. It was the bloodless revolution because everybody was against the Czar."[2] Alexander Kerensky became head of Russia's provi- sional government. Alisa admired him at the time, though her view of him would subsequently change.[3]

In October 1917, the Bolsheviks took Petrograd. Kerensky managed to escape and go abroad; his ministers—who, along with Kerensky, had been freely elected—were captured and shot. To the end of her life, Rand remembered vividly the funeral of Kerensky's ministers, which she watched from that same balcony.

In 1917, her father's pharmacy was nationalized. Many years later, she still recalled the look on her father's face:

> I felt the way he looked, which was helpless, murderous frustration and indignation about which we knew you could do absolutely nothing. . . . It was a horrible silent spectacle of brutality and injustice. And I remember the feeling: this is monstrous injustice and nothing can be done [about it]. But of course, the way I translated it would be: that's the principle of communism, but all of that will end.[4]

Later describing that same period in her life, she wrote:

> When, at the age of twelve, at the time of the Russian revolution, I first heard the Communist principle that Man must exist for the sake of the State, I perceived that this was the essential issue, that this principle was evil, and that it could lead to nothing but evil, regardless of any methods, details, decrees, policies, promises and pious platitudes. This was the reason for my opposition to Communism then—and it is my reason now.[5]

In 1918, Russia was an unsafe place to live; because of Lenin's use of terror, Petrograd was especially dangerous. In a July 1918 letter to Zinoviev, president of the Petrograd Committee of the Bolshevik Party, Lenin wrote: "This is the hour of truth: It is of supreme importance that we encourage and make use of the energy of mass terror directed against the counter-revolutionaries, especially those of Petrograd, whose example is decisive."[6] That year, Z. Z. Rosenbaum took his family to Yevpatoria, in the Crimea, to wait out what he hoped would be the eventual defeat of the Bolsheviks.

When Alisa Rosenbaum entered high school, the Crimea was still White, and so the curriculum was not yet Communist. She was therefore able to take courses in American history and eventually learn about American government:

> It was almost incredible. Before that, America was mentioned in geography books, but not as history. I didn't really know about the Declaration of Independence or what the American system was until that last year [of high school]. I'm not sure that I even would have grasped it all correctly. I would not have

had a clear idea of capitalism or collectivism. All I knew is that that's the country of individualism (in whichever primitive terms I would have had). . . .
I thought: now this is the kind of government I would approve of.[7]

There was little she could approve of in Russia—on either side of the civil
war raging at that time. More than fifty years after her family moved to Yevpatoria, Rand described her life in the Crimea during the 1918–1921 Russian
civil war as follows:

> I was in my early teens during the Russian civil war. I lived in a small town that
> changed hands many times. . . . When it was occupied by the White Army, I
> almost longed for the return of the Red Army, and vice versa. There was not
> much difference between them in practice, but there was in theory. The Red
> Army stood for totalitarian dictatorship and rule by terror. The White Army
> stood for nothing; repeat: *nothing*. In answer to the monstrous evil they were
> fighting, the Whites found nothing better to proclaim than the dustiest,
> smelliest bromides of the time: we must fight, they said, for Holy Mother Rus-
> sia, for faith and tradition. . . .
>
> In a passive, indifferent way, the majority of the Russian people were behind
> the White Army: they were not *for* the Whites, but merely *against* the Reds;
> they feared the Reds' atrocities. I knew that the Reds' deepest atrocity was in-
> tellectual, that the thing which had to be fought—and *defeated*—was their
> *ideas*. But no one answered them. The country's passivity turned into hopeless
> lethargy as people gave up. The Reds had an incentive, the promise of nation-
> wide looting; they had the leadership and the semi-discipline of a criminal
> gang; they had an allegedly intellectual program and an allegedly moral justi-
> fication. The Whites had icons. The Reds won.[8]

By 1921, the Crimea was Red. With few options, and with the faint hope
that he might reclaim his business and property, Z. Z. Rosenbaum decided his
family should return to Petrograd. These next few years would be some of
Alisa's—and the country's—worst. According to the *Black Book of Communism:*

> When the famine was at its worst in the summer of 1922 and nearly 30 million
> people were starving, the Central Commission was assuring an irregular supply
> to about 3 million people. . . . Despite the massive international relief effort,
> at least 5 million of the 29 million Russians affected died of hunger in 1921
> and 1922.[9]

Alisa Rosenbaum entered the University of Petrograd in fall 1921, major-
ing in history and minoring in philosophy. The curriculum was not yet fully
controlled by the Communists, though she did have to take several Soviet

courses (e.g., "Historical Materialism" and "The History of Socialism"). When she entered university, anti-Communist students outnumbered Communists. This would not last long. The Student Purges began in 1921, thus exposing Alisa to her first experience with a Communist blacklist. The slogan behind the purges was: "We will not educate our class enemies." The most outspoken anti-Communists were sent to Siberia or worse.[10]

Alisa did not escape the purges. She was expelled on December 12, 1923. Fortunately, a convention of foreign scientists visiting Petrograd heard about them and were outraged. As a result, the purges were temporarily postponed, and students close to finishing were allowed to graduate. Alisa was readmitted, and graduated in spring 1924 from what was by then called the University of Leningrad.

In the late 1960s, Ayn Rand wrote:

The meaning of that word ["abroad"] for a Soviet citizen is incommunicable to anyone who has not lived in that country: if you project what you would feel for a combination of Atlantis, the Promised Land and the most glorious civilization on another planet, as imagined by a most benevolent kind of science fiction, you will have a pale approximation. "Abroad," to a Soviet Russian, is as distant, shining and unattainable as these; yet to any Russian who lifts his head for a moment from the Soviet muck, the concept "abroad" is a psychological necessity, a lifeline and soul preserver.[11]

By her last year at the University of Leningrad, if not well before, Alisa Rosenbaum—straining to keep her head above the Soviet muck—had decided that to survive, she must go abroad. She took a chance and applied for a passport, ostensibly to *visit* relatives in Chicago.

News about the passport would take some time, and there was no guarantee that she would receive one. So on October 15, 1924, she enrolled in a program at the State Institute for Cinematography, Leningrad. (She had been in love with film for years.) As Michael Berliner explains, she entered the Institute "in order to learn screenwriting, which she thought could be a stepping stone to a career as a novelist. Her studies would also provide a politically acceptable reason for the Soviet authorities to give her permission to visit America."[12] During her year at the Institute of Cinematography, she wrote two booklets: "Pola Negri" (published in 1925) and "Hollywood: American City of Movies" (published without her permission in 1926, after she left Russia).[13]

She did not finish the two-year program at the Institute. On October 29, 1925, she received her passport and permission to go to the United States.

Ayn Rand[14] left Petrograd by train on January 17, 1926. She stopped in Moscow, Riga, Berlin (where she celebrated her twenty-first birthday), Paris, and Le Havre, whence her ship left for the United States. She arrived in New York on February 18. She spent a week in New York City before going to Chicago. After six months there, she left for Hollywood in late August, hoping to fulfill a lifelong dream to work with Cecil B. DeMille.

The day after she arrived, she had a chance meeting with DeMille, who drove her to the set of *The King of Kings*. He later hired her as an extra at $7.50 per day, and then as a junior writer at $25 per week. On the set of *The King of Kings* she met Frank O'Connor, whom she would later marry (on April 15, 1929) and remain married to for over fifty years, until his death.

DeMille closed his studio in 1928. Rand then worked at odd jobs (e.g., as a waitress) until spring 1929, when she began working in the RKO Studios wardrobe department at $20 per week. She would work there for three years, eventually becoming a division manager.

Upon her arrival in America, she had begun working assiduously writing fiction. During her six months in Chicago, she wrote a number of story ideas for silent film. Over the next few years, while in Hollywood, she completed in her spare time several short stories (e.g., "The Husband I Bought" and "Good Copy").[15] Around early 1930, she began work on her first novel.

Ayn Rand became an American citizen on March 13, 1931. In the 1932 presidential election—the first for which she was eligible to vote—she voted for Franklin Delano Roosevelt, since he promised to repeal Prohibition. She considered Prohibition "a complete breach of individual rights" which served "the interests of the worst kind of pressure groups, the religious . . . censorship groups" supported by "a small religious and Bible Belt minority."[16] However, she later realized that she had been mistaken about FDR. He was much more collectivist than she had thought at the time.

This kind of mistake was not limited to her evaluation of FDR in 1932:

> I did not know the degree of "Pink" penetration in America. . . . I did not know very many people in Hollywood, but those I knew were certainly not [on the] left. At that time, Russia was not yet recognized. My impression was that people were not sufficiently aware of the menace and the evil of communism, but that they would be in sympathy with it I did not expect. . . . My conviction was that most people, consciously or not, explicitly or not, lived by my kind of code. . . . I did not at that time [realize] the enormity of what had to be fought.[17]

During the early 1930s, she worked on her first novel, *We the Living*. Set in Soviet Russia, its theme is the evil of statism. In 1932, she also wrote "Red

Pawn," another story set in Soviet Russia. Universal Pictures bought "Red Pawn" on September 2, 1932, enabling her to quit her job at RKO and write full-time.[18]

She completed *We the Living* in 1933 but had difficulties finding a publisher. Earlier, when she had told a Russian woman that she was writing a book set in Soviet Russia, the woman replied: "You will have a very hard time with it and a lot of opposition. . . . The communists have a tremendous influence on American intellectual . . . opinion and you will find a lot of people opposing you." Ayn Rand didn't believe this, dismissing the woman as "a malevolent universe type of Russian" and her claims as "panic-mongering." The woman, however, "turned out to be right."[19]

While working on *We the Living*, Rand also wrote the play *Penthouse Legend* (1932). She sold the film rights to MGM in 1933;[20] the play opened in Hollywood in 1934 (with the title *Woman on Trial*) and on Broadway in 1935 (with the title *Night of January 16th*), where it had a seven-month run.

On November 24, 1934, she followed her play to New York City and became a freelance script analyst for RKO and MGM. In 1935, she signed a contract with Macmillan to publish *We the Living*. One reader at Macmillan, Granville Hicks—a member of the Communist Party and literary editor at the communist journal, *New Masses*—fought against publication of the book because of its anti-Soviet nature. But George P. Brett Sr., former president of Macmillan, said he did "not know whether they will make money on [*We the Living*] or not, but it's a novel that should be published."[21] *We the Living* was published, in March 1936. Unfortunately, Macmillan did not give the book much support, and although it gradually built an audience, the type was destroyed after the first printing (3,000 copies).[22]

Rand was approached about writing a play based on *We the Living*. Bette Davis was interested in playing Kira Argounova, the heroine; unfortunately— and as an ominous sign of the times—Davis backed out, on the advice of her agent, who told her that appearing in an anti-Soviet play would kill her career.[23] In a letter of June 18, 1936, Ayn Rand wrote:

> For the last month I have not been able to do any work at all. I have had to give lectures and speeches about Soviet Russia—and of course, I couldn't refuse the opportunity, feeling as strongly as I do on the subject. I have even been interviewed over the radio. It is all a rather nerve-wrecking experience, but quite enjoyable.[24]

However enthusiastic she was about denouncing Soviet Russia, she was ready to get back to writing. Since her credentials included a novel and a successful Broadway play, she decided to get a job as a screenwriter. This would enable her to make money *and* have some time to work on her next novel. But she was unable to get such a job, because, a Hollywood agent told her, "she talks too much about Soviet Russia." As she put it later: "I was . . . blacklisted; this lasted until *The Fountainhead*."[25]

For Ayn Rand to be told, especially at this time, that she "talks too much about Russia" was cruelly ironic. Since 1926, she had been trying to get her family out of Russia. After she became a fully employed U.S. citizen, she filed all the necessary paperwork and wrote to the proper authorities. But Russia was shut airtight—as Kira says in *We the Living*—and they could not get out. On May 31, 1937, she received a telegram from her parents stating, simply, "Cannot get permission." (She would never see her parents again.)

In 1937, Ayn Rand wrote *Anthem*, a novella written in the same spirit as *We the Living* and "Red Pawn." Its theme is the importance of man's ego, and it describes the consequences of taking collectivism seriously. As Leonard Peikoff points out, this was America's Red Decade, so she had trouble getting it published here. (It was published in England in 1938 but wasn't published in the United States until 1946, after the appearance of *The Fountainhead*.[26])

In 1940, she took time off from writing her next book to support the Wendell Willkie campaign. Throughout the 1930s, she was stunned by the out-and-out Communism and pro-Stalinism of Roosevelt's supporters, and especially of the intellectuals.[27] During the campaign she became increasingly disappointed with the conservatives, including Willkie. Like the Whites in Russia twenty years earlier, they lacked a principled, philosophical base. Roosevelt won in a landslide.

Back in 1935, Rand had begun preliminary work on her next novel, *The Fountainhead*, the theme of which, she said, is "individualism and collectivism, not in politics but in man's soul."[28] When a number of chapters were finished, she began looking for a publisher. "It was rejected by twelve publishers who declared that it had no commercial possibilities, it would not sell, it was 'too intellectual,' it was 'too unconventional,' it went against every popular trend."[29] It was finally accepted by Bobbs-Merrill in 1941 and published in spring 1943. The intellectuals hated it; the American people did not. It became a best seller, and has remained in print ever since. *The Fountainhead*'s success helped to confirm Rand's belief that a huge gulf existed between the predominantly collectivist ideas of the intellectuals and the spirit of the American people.

The same year the novel was published, Rand sold the film rights to Warner Bros. for $50,000. She returned to Hollywood in 1943 to write the screenplay.[30] "During the next four years, she worked primarily for producer

Hal Wallis, for whom she wrote *Love Letters* [released 1945], *You Came Along* [1945] and some never produced screenplays, including one about the development of the atomic bomb."[31] During this period, she also began work on her magnum opus, *Atlas Shrugged* (which would take thirteen years to complete and would be published in 1957).

About a year after *The Fountainhead* was published, during the summer of 1944, Ayn Rand joined the Motion Picture Alliance for the Preservation of American Ideals (henceforth, the MPA), and became a member of its executive committee. The MPA had been organized on February 4, 1944. Rand later said the following of its creation:

> The MPA was formed by some producers and directors at MGM, and the story was—which I strongly suspect is true—that Louis B. Mayer was behind it (he was allegedly conservative) and that the real purpose was not to fight communism in Hollywood, but to have a front so that the Press of the country would not accuse Hollywood of being Red. At that time, the Red penetration in Hollywood was tremendous and a lot of articles had appeared about Red propaganda in movies. I think the organization was formed simply to counteract it— to say that there is an organization which is conservative, but to do nothing. . . . They didn't want to have any real trouble in Hollywood.[32]

She describes two groups within that organization: those who wanted to fight Communists, not Communism—"that is, gather and expose the facts and records of the activities of communists, without engaging in debate on ideas"; and those—like Rand—who wanted to fight Communism in "a battle of ideas."[33] She joined "on the condition and understanding that the M.P.A. would conduct an educational campaign advocating the basic principles of Americanism, Individualism and Free Enterprise—and opposing the principles of Collectivism, Communism, Fascism and all forms of Statism."[34]

Here are the first two paragraphs in the MPA's statement of principles:

> We believe in, and like, the American way of life; the liberty and the freedom which generations before have fought to create and preserve; THE FREEDOM TO SPEAK, TO THINK, TO LIVE, TO WORSHIP, TO WORK AND TO GOVERN OURSELVES, AS INDIVIDUALS, AS FREE MEN; the right to succeed or fail as free men, according to the measure of our ability and our strength.
>
> Believing in these things, WE FIND OURSELVES IN SHARP REVOLT AGAINST A RISING TIDE OF COMMUNISM, FASCISM AND KINDRED BELIEFS, THAT SEEK BY SUBVERSIVE MEANS TO UNDERMINE AND CHANGE THIS WAY OF LIFE; groups that have forfeited their

rights to exist in this country of ours, because they seek to achieve their change by means other than the vested procedure of the ballot and to deny the right of the majority opinion of the people to rule.[35]

Ayn Rand summed up the purpose of the MPA as follows: "to protect our country and our industry from the doctrine of Collectivism (Communism, Fascism, and any other form of dictatorship)—which means, to protect our country and our industry from destruction."[36]

Rand said that the MPA did very little, "except hold meetings or make speeches. It was all very loose in that kind of way." She suspected that "behind the scenes there was some element constantly advocating caution." They published a bulletin, *The Vigil*, and she was "the only one who wrote signed articles. . . . None of them really wanted to take an editorial or journalistic stand."[37]

However little the MPA did at first, judging by Ayn Rand's desk calendars, their activity began to increase in 1946 and especially in 1947. Her 1947 calendar mentions numerous MPA meetings, and meetings with or calls to MPA members. For example, there are six in April, five in May, five in the last week of August, and nine in September. (There is no doubt some connection between this increased activity and the HUAC hearings in Hollywood in May and in Washington in October.)

In the spring of 1947, she was working on a pamphlet for the MPA called the "Screen Guide for Americans," which gave advice to filmmakers on how to avoid certain political errors. But on May 10, 1947, she resigned from the MPA, because a letter to which she objected had been written in the name of the executive committee, without her knowledge or consent. She did, however, agree to finish the pamphlet.[38]

Around the time she resigned from the MPA, the HUAC was in Hollywood investigating Communism, and eventually became interested in her. She explains:

The FBI was helping [the HUAC] investigation, and they attended some of our meetings. . . , and heard about the "Screen Guide for Americans." It was interesting to me that they had heard about it before it was out, and asked us for galleys of it, just for their own interest, which we supplied. . . .[39] About a week later, I got a call from those investigators [asking] me to come to Washington to testify on the ideology of [certain] films.[40]

On October 11, Ayn Rand bought her train tickets and picked up her coat from the cleaners; on October 13, she went to MGM to view *Song of*

Russia; on October 16 she and her husband, Frank O'Connor, were on the 12:01 train bound for Washington, D.C.

She arrived in D.C. a few days later, and on October 20, in the afternoon, she was before the HUAC, swearing to tell the truth, the whole truth, and nothing but the truth.[41]

Notes

1. Michael S. Berliner, ed., *Letters of Ayn Rand* (New York: Dutton, 1995), 669.

2. Biographical interviews (Ayn Rand Archives).

3. See Berliner, *Letters of Ayn Rand*, 42. By 1945, she had met Kerensky and was quite disappointed: "By that time I had no illusions about him, and he was worse than I would have expected. . . . I can't claim that it was any kind of sad loss of an illusion, because I didn't expect him to be much; only what I was surprised by is that he was a real mediocrity" (biographical interviews).

4. Biographical interviews. Howard Koch, in *As Time Goes By: Memoir of a Writer* (New York: Harcourt Brace Jovanovich, 1979), 89, writes: "As I learned later, [Rand's] family had been prosperous in Czarist Russia and had lost their fortune in the revolution. Whether or not this was the reason, Miss Rand had become fanatical on the subject of communism, socialism, or any 'ism' except capitalism." Koch's suggestion that Rand's views on Communism might lack objectivity because the Communists destroyed her family financially (and later, actually) is absurd. One does not doubt the objectivity of a Jewish merchant who hated Nazism because, among other reasons, the Nazis destroyed his business (and later, his family).

5. Foreword to the 1959 edition of Ayn Rand, *We the Living* (New York: Macmillan, 1936; rev. ed., Random House, 1959; Signet paperback ed., 1996), xv.

6. Stéphen Courtois et al., *The Black Book of Communism: Crimes, Terror, Repression*, trans. Jonathan Murphy and Mark Kramer (Cambridge: Harvard University Press, 1999), 70. See also pp. 60–83.

7. Biographical interviews.

8. "The Lessons of Vietnam" (1975), in Ayn Rand, *The Voice of Reason: Essays in Objectivist Thought*, ed. Leonard Peikoff (New York: New American Library, 1988), 138–39.

9. Courtois et al., *Black Book of Communism*, 123. In general, see ch. 5.

10. For a portrayal of the student purges, see Rand, *We the Living*, 209–13; see also Berliner, *Letters of Ayn Rand*, 636–37.

11. "The 'Inexplicable Personal Alchemy'" (1968), in Ayn Rand, *Return of the Primitive: the Anti-Industrial Revolution*, ed. Peter Schwartz (New York: Meridian, 1999), 125.

12. "Introduction," in *Ayn Rand: Russian Writings on Hollywood*, ed. Michael S. Berliner (Marina del Rey, CA: Ayn Rand Institute Press, 1999).

13. See Berliner, *Rand: Russian Writings*, 15–40, 43–106.

14. She chose the name Ayn Rand before leaving the Soviet Union, and began calling herself that upon arriving in the United States.

15. See Leonard Peikoff, ed. *The Early Ayn Rand: A Selection from Her Unpublished Fiction* (New York: Signet, 1986).

16. Biographical interviews.

17. Biographical interviews.

18. "Red Pawn" was never made into a movie; it was later published in Peikoff, *Early Ayn Rand.*

19. Biographical interviews. See Richard Ralston, "Publishing *We the Living,*" in *Essays on Ayn Rand's* We the Living, ed. Robert Mayhew (Lanham, MD: Lexington Books, 2004).

20. A film was made in 1941, but it retained nothing of the play. See Ayn Rand's introduction to the 1968 revision of *Night of January 16th* (New York: Plume, 1987), 14.

21. Biographical interviews.

22. A revised version was published in 1959; it has remained in print ever since.

23. Later, Alida Valli, who starred in the Italian film version of *We the Living* (made without Rand's consent), approached David Selznik about remaking the film; he had no interest in making an anti-Soviet film. See the documentary film *Ayn Rand: A Sense of Life* (Michael Paxton, Strand, 1998). As was seen in chapter 2, Selznik had no interest in making a *pro*-Soviet film, either. On the play and film versions of *We the Living,* see Jeff Britting, "Adapting *We the Living,*" in *Essays on Ayn Rand's* We the Living.

24. Berliner, *Letters of Ayn Rand,* 31.

25. Biographical interviews.

26. Leonard Peikoff, introduction to the 50th anniversary edition of Ayn Rand's *Anthem* (New York: Signet, 1996), ix–x.

27. On the vast number of Communist spies working in government during FDR's administration, see: Allen Weinstein and Alexander Vassiliev, *The Haunted Wood: Soviet Espionage in America—The Stalin Era* (New York: Random House, 1999); Harvey Klehr, John Earl Haynes, and Fridrikh Igorevich Firsov, eds., *The Secret World of American Communism* (New Haven, CT: Yale University Press, 1995); and, Harvey Klehr, John Earl Haynes, and Kyrill M. Anderson, eds., *The Soviet World of American Communism* (New Haven, CT: Yale University Press, 1998).

28. Ayn Rand, *The Art of Fiction: A Guide to Writers and Readers,* ed. Tore Boeckmann (New York: Plume, 2000), 17.

29. Berliner, *Letters of Ayn Rand,* 672.

30. After a delay owing to the war, the film was released in 1949, starring Gary Cooper and Patricia Neal.

31. Berliner, "Introduction," in *Rand: Russian Writings,* 11.

32. Biographical interviews.

33. Biographical interviews.

34. From "Inserts for Memorandum," unpublished, in the Ayn Rand Archives.

35. This statement of principle was included in MPA information pamphlets and in advertisements—for example, in *The Hollywood Reporter*, June 9, 1947.

36. From "The Double-Standard," unpublished, in the Ayn Rand Archives.

37. Biographical interviews.

38. This statement was widely circulated and published in a number of places (for example, in *Plain Talk*, November 1947). It was reprinted in David Harriman, ed., *Journals of Ayn Rand* (New York: Plume, 1997), 356–66. Here are its main headings (each of which is followed, in the article, by Rand's explanation): 1. Don't Take Politics Lightly; 2. Don't Smear the Free Enterprise System; 3. Don't Smear Industrialists; 4. Don't Smear Wealth; 5. Don't Smear the Profit Motive; 6. Don't Smear Success; 7. Don't Glorify Failure; 8. Don't Glorify Depravity; 9. Don't Deify "The Common Man"; 10. Don't Glorify the Collective; 11. Don't Smear an Independent Man; 12. Don't Use Current Events Carelessly; 13. Don't Smear American Political Institutions.

39. There is no longer any mystery over how "they had heard about it before it was out." There was an informant at MPA meetings who reported to the FBI. Here are some sample passages from FBI reports in the FBI Freedom of Information Act files: "On October 14, 1944, a confidential informant of the Los Angeles Field Division saw in the offices of the Alliance a document containing the names of Communists." "During the month of November, 1944, this anti-Communist group [the MPA], according to the informant, continued its inactiveness." "Confidential informant [name crossed out] advised that after inactivity for six months, this organization came forward during the first part of May, 1945." "Confidential Informant [name crossed out] of the Los Angeles Office related that this anti-Communist organization [the MPA] held a meeting on April 29, 1947." (The informant goes on to describe events at this meeting that contributed to Ayn Rand's decision to resign from the MPA. She is not mentioned.) See Federal Bureau of Investigation, Freedom of Information and Privacy Acts File (Communist Infiltration-Motion Picture Industry), File Number: 100-138754, Serial: 157x1, Part 3 of 15.

40. Biographical interviews.

41. The information in these last two paragraphs comes mainly from Rand's 1947 desk calendar (in the Ayn Rand Archives). For October 13, her calendar has "MGM"; and in her HUAC testimony, she says she viewed *Song of Russia* on October 13.

~

CHAPTER FIVE

Ayn Rand on the House Un-American Activities Committee

That Ayn Rand agreed to cooperate with the HUAC might suggest that she gave it her wholehearted support. She did not. What then did she think of the HUAC? And what did she expect to achieve by testifying?

Rand was not impressed by the HUAC. She thought they were a "bunch of fools, way out of their depth."[1] Basically, she found the committee inefficient and unnecessary, and its members publicity seekers:

> What I considered wrong is simply the futility of it, that they go through a great many motions and publicity and very little action comes out of it or can come out of it because, if they needed information, they certainly have all the information they need without public witnesses reciting pieces.[2]

I assume she means that because this was a proper criminal investigation, it should have been handled as such, by the police, FBI, secret service, etc. Having public hearings did not contribute to solving a case or discovering the truth about Communist infiltration into Hollywood.

Then why cooperate with the HUAC? "I wouldn't have any Hollywood hearings," she said, "because that's really only publicity; the only reason it was valuable . . . is that there was no other way to call public attention to the conspiracy that was going on." She had no moral qualms about testifying, because she did not "consider it an evil institution," only "a futile one. I certainly don't think it's any kind of interference with anybody's rights or freedom of speech." By "the conspiracy that was going on," she is referring specifically to the Communist influence on the content of films. She claimed that "there were quite a few articles appearing about Reds in Hollywood, but never about propaganda on the screens; that was the real issue." Making this issue public was, she believed, the only good that came out of the 1947 HUAC hearings.[3]

In rejecting the idea that the HUAC violated "rights or freedom of speech," Rand differs radically from the standard picture of the 1947 HUAC hearings and what happened to the unfriendly witnesses (i.e., the Hollywood Ten). According to this picture, the HUAC went on a witch hunt, trampled on the Constitution, violated the Hollywood Ten's right to free speech—since it condemned them for being Communists and inquired after their political beliefs—as well as their right to earn a living—since, it is claimed, the hearings made possible the blacklisting of Hollywood Communists. It is further claimed that the HUAC encouraged and relied on the immorality of a number of Communists and ex-Communists, because it asked them to *name names* (which, in this view, is a moral "crime"[4]). How would Rand reply?

She addresses most of these issues in a note she wrote not long after testifying in Washington, entitled "Suggestions Regarding the Congressional Investigation of Communism" (published for the first time in *Journals of Ayn Rand*[5]). I begin with the issue of free speech.

The HUAC and Free Speech

When describing what he calls "the paradoxical feelings of that crazy time when HUAC terrorized us in our middle-class Hollywood houses," Arthur Laurents writes, in a statement typical of the inaccuracies that plague his autobiography: "We weren't standing up for Communism, we were standing up for the Bill of Rights."[6] This is a leftist cliché, and Rand rejects it.

I quote Rand's "Suggestions" at length, because it is the best statement in opposition to the standard leftist fare concerning the HUAC and the Hollywood Ten:

> The whole conception of civil rights (of free speech, free assembly, free political organization) applies to and belongs in the realm of ideas—that is, a realm which precludes the use of physical violence. These rights are based on and pertain to the peaceful activity of spreading or preaching ideas, of dealing with men by intellectual persuasion. Therefore, one cannot invoke these rights to protect an organization such as the Communist Party, which not merely preaches, but actually engages in acts of violence, murder, sabotage, and spying in the interests of a foreign government. This takes the Communist Party out of the realm of civil law and puts it into the realm of criminal law. And the fact that Communists are directed and financed by a foreign power puts them into the realm of treason and military law.

The Thomas Committee [i.e., the HUAC] was inquiring, not into a question of opinion, but into a question of fact, the fact being membership in the Communist Party.

The Thomas Committee did not ask anyone whether he believed in Communism, but asked only whether he had joined the Communist Party. Membership in the Communist Party does not consist merely of sharing the ideas of that Party. That Party is a formal, closed, and secret organization. Joining it involves more than a matter of ideas. It involves an agreement to take orders to commit actions—criminal and treasonable actions.

The Communists have been trying to claim that belonging to the Communist Party is the same as belonging to the Republican or Democratic Party. But membership in the Republican or Democratic Party is an open, public matter. It involves no initiation, no acceptance of an applicant by the party, no card-bearing. . . .

Membership in the Communist Party is a formal act of joining a formal organization whose aims, by its own admission, include acts of criminal violence. Congress has no right to inquire into ideas or opinions, but has every right to inquire into criminal activities. Belonging to a secret organization that advocates criminal actions comes into the sphere of the criminal, not the ideological. . . .

In America, no man can be sent to jail for holding any sort of ideas. And no man is allowed to demand a consideration of his ideas as a mitigating circumstance when and if he has committed an act of violence.

The entire conception of American law is based on the principle of inalienable individual rights. This principle precludes the right of one citizen to do violence to others—no matter what ideas or convictions he may hold. Therefore, any man may preach or advocate anything he wishes, but if he undertakes acts of violence in pursuit of his beliefs, then he is treated as a common criminal. American law is not asked to share *his* conviction—his idea that his rights include the right to use force against other men. (As an example: American citizens have freedom of religion; but if some sect attempted to practice human sacrifices, its members would be prosecuted by law—not for their religious beliefs, but for murder; their beliefs would not be considered or recognized as pertinent to the case.)

Therefore, it is totally irrelevant to Congress whether a man enters a criminal conspiracy for criminal reasons or for reasons he considers political or ideological. This is precisely where his ideas do not concern Congress at all and do not enter the question. When Congress investigates the Communist Party, it is investigating a factual matter, a criminal conspiracy, and not a matter of ideas. . . .

If the Communist Party were purely a national American organization, the above points would be sufficient to give Congress the right to inquire into its activities. But when we add to it the fact that the Communist Party is an organization which owes allegiances to a foreign power, then it becomes not only a matter of crime, but also of treason. A party which is the agent of a foreign power cannot claim the same rights as an American party. . . . An investigation into a man's or an organization's allegiances to a foreign power is not an ideological matter, but a military one.[7]

Two additional points are worth making here. First, the availability of previously secret documents from both the United States and the former Soviet Union confirms Rand's claims about the nature of the Communist Party: It was an organization funded by, controlled by, and working in the interest of a foreign government, namely, Soviet Russia. Further, a number of members of the Communist Party were engaged in espionage and worked directly with the Soviet government.[8] And it makes no difference that not every member of the Party was engaged in espionage or sabotage (or even was as devoted to the Party as the Party demanded). The HUAC was investigating possible illegal activities of the Communist Party; no one was on trial for treason. But given the nature of the Party, membership alone *was* enough to justify the government simply asking questions as part of a criminal investigation.[9]

Writer-director Fred Niblo, Jr., was right when he said, at the 1947 HUAC hearings: "it is grotesque that a Russian political party enjoys a legal existence as an American political party in this country. . . . It is a secret organization no less than the Ku Klux Klan." The next witness, actor Robert Montgomery, made the same point: "I consider it [the Communist Party] a subversive group just as I consider the German-American Bund a subversive group."[10]

Second, it is transparently clear that the Communist Party members who opposed the HUAC (the Hollywood Ten, for example) should in no way be considered defenders of free speech and constitutional rights, as they often are. They were the opposite: Any late-in-life revisionist claims to the contrary notwithstanding, the Communists wanted a Soviet America; and as good Marxists, they regarded the rights contained in the Declaration of Independence and the American Constitution as bourgeois rights, and thus not to be respected.

Ring Lardner Jr.—one of the Hollywood Ten—claims: "Neither I nor any of my friends in the party wanted the U.S. remodeled along Soviet lines."[11] Richard Collins has corrected Lardner's memory: "I read Ring Lardner saying that we really didn't expect it to turn into a Soviet America. Of course we always thought just that. That was the whole intention. That's what it was all about. We didn't say so, because that would've been dumb. But we believed it."[12] Consider also this pledge read by Earl Browder (head of the U.S. Communist Party) to 2,000 people initiated into the Party in New York City in 1935:

I pledge myself to rally the masses to defend the Soviet Union, the land of victorious Socialism. I pledge myself to remain at all times a vigilant and firm defender of the Leninist line of the Party, the only line that insures the triumph of Soviet power in the United States.[13]

A few years before the 1947 hearings, there appeared in *New Masses* a series of pieces discussing the liberal versus the Communist conception of free speech. The center of the discussion was an exchange between Alexander Meiklejohn (the liberal) and Earl Browder (the Communist). Meiklejohn held that "liberals, taking their stand on the Bill of Rights, believe that everyone should be free to "'speak' what he thinks," and being consistent, he adds that this would include Fascists, who have the right to say whatever they want (though not the right to act on what they say). As Meiklejohn points out, the Communists, by contrast, wish "to deny to those Americans *whom it calls 'fascists'* the freedom of speech which it claims for its own members." Browder replies: "Of course we demand the suppression of American fascists! We fight for the complete, merciless, and systematic destruction of fascism *in all its aspects, everywhere.*"[14] Browder goes on to mention racism and anti-Semitism, but it is perfectly clear that "Fascism"—as the Communists use the term—refers to the views of virtually anyone not on the Left, that is, anyone who is not a Communist, or a socialist or liberal willing to work with Communists. For instance, the Party considered Fascist anyone who accepted—in the words of Lillian Hellman and Dashiell Hammett—the "fantastic falsehood that the USSR and the totalitarian states are basically alike."[15]

Note that in the same issue of *New Masses*, immediately preceding the article under discussion, there is another article condemning the "Pro-fascist, anti-Soviet Americans of Polish descent who pretend to speak for Poland." Why were they considered pro-Fascist? Because they correctly blamed the Soviet Union for the Katyn massacre, and because they generally feared what Stalin had planned for Poland.[16] It is clear that if the American Communists ever took power, such Polish-Americans, being "Fascists," would be denied free speech.

In the next issue of *New Masses*, the discussion continued under the heading "Free Speech for Fascists?" Here is the contribution of the writer Howard Fast—a man later called "Big Brother's U.S. Pen Pal" by *Time* magazine, and the only American besides Paul Robeson to win the Stalin Peace Prize:[17]

[M]y answer is flatly—no. Take Voltaire's old epigram—and I call it that with reason—"I do not agree with what he says, but I will defend to the death his right to say it." How often has that been quoted, and what arrant nonsense it is!

Are we to defend to the death Adolf Hitler's right to promulgate his vicious race theories? Are we to defend to the death the right of all other fascists, native and foreign, to mouth their lies, their attacks upon democracy? Is it inherent in democracy that it must, for the sake of a vague and mystical ideal, give its enemies a legal opportunity to destroy it? . . . [The constitutional] guarantee [of freedom of speech] is interpreted to operate as a defense of that democracy which is defined by the Constitution. And such was its original conception—free speech as a weapon to forge and uphold the republic.

Fast goes on to argue that "any promulgation of fascism . . . becomes a degree of treason to the United States."[18]

This position is typical of what is found in *New Masses* and can be regarded as the Party line. According to this view, any member of a political group that acts contrary to the Constitution—such as the American Nazi Party—has no right to free speech. Of course, the Communists are willing to make an exception—when it comes to Communists.

The Communist Party did not object to the actions of the HUAC when the HUAC was interested in the activities of the German-American Bund and other American pro-Nazi groups.[19] (It turns out that the U.S. congressman who founded what was to become the HUAC was actually a Soviet agent.[20]) What the Hollywood Communists objected to was any attempt to make *them* speak about their activities as members of the Communist Party, and any attempts—as they saw it—to "violate" *their* desire to keep their political activities to themselves. They had no problem with the violation of the rights of Americans generally, because they recognized no such rights. And they were utterly unconcerned about the violation of human rights in the Soviet Union.

In light of what they were defending and hoping to achieve, and in light of their hypocrisy on the issue of the right to free speech, the standard picture of the Hollywood Communists as champions of the Constitution (and specifically of the First Amendment) is absurd.

Blacklists of Communists, and Communist Blacklists

According to Ayn Rand, the facts that make the HUAC investigation not a violation of anyone's right to free speech or opinion are directly connected to the morality of "the Hollywood blacklist." I again quote from her "Suggestions Regarding the Congressional Investigation of Communism":

Now if the Hollywood Ten claim that a public revelation of their Communist ideas damages them because it will cost them their Hollywood jobs—then this means that they are holding these jobs by fraud, that their employers, their co-workers and their public do not know the nature of their ideas and would not want to deal with them if such knowledge were made available. If so, then the Communists, in effect, are asking that the government protect them in the perpetuation of a fraud. They are demanding protection for their right to practice deceit upon others. They are saying, in effect: I am cheating those with whom I am dealing and if you reveal this, you will cause me to lose my racket—which is interference with my freedom of speech and belief. . . .

If, in the course of an inquiry into criminal and treasonable activities, Congress reveals the nature of the political beliefs of certain men—their freedom of speech or belief has not been infringed in any manner. If, as a consequence, their employers—who had been foolish, ignorant, or negligent before—now decide to fire these men, that is the employers' inalienable right. It is also the inalienable right of the public not to buy the product of these men—in this particular case, not to attend the movies written or directed by the Hollywood Ten. The damage which the Ten claim to have suffered in this case is a private damage, not a legal one, a damage which consists of the refusal of private citizens to deal with a Communist, if they learn that he is a Communist. . . .

They [the Hollywood Ten] are attempting to claim that there is no difference between private action and government action—that a citizen's refusal to deal with a Communist is equivalent to a government order forbidding him to be a Communist. . . .

Under the American system, a man has the right to hold any ideas he wishes, without suffering any government restraint for it, without the danger of physical violence, bodily injury, or police seizure. That is all. Should he have to suffer some form of private penalty for his ideas from private citizens who do not agree with him? He most certainly should. That is the only form of protection the rest of the citizens have against him and against the spread of ideas with which they do not agree. . . .

Should the Hollywood Ten suffer unpopularity or loss of jobs as a result of being Communists? They most certainly should—so long as the rest of us, who give them jobs or box-office support, do not wish to be Communists or accessories to the spread of Communism. If it is claimed that we must not refuse them support—what becomes of our right of free speech and belief?[21]

So long as this blacklist was a private matter—a boycott arranged by private individuals, and not a government action punishing people for their beliefs—there is nothing wrong with it politically (i.e., legally). And since this was a blacklist of members or supporters of the Communist Party, there was nothing morally wrong with it either.

Here as on many other issues, leftists are hypocritical. *Leftist* boycotts (including government-sponsored "boycotts," that is, censorship and political discrimination) are considered progressive and humane, but blacklists—that is, private boycotts—of Communists are oppressive violations of the right to free speech.[22] For example, how did many European leftists react to the HUAC hearings and blacklists? With blacklists. An FBI report states:

> Since the publication in Humanite on October 24, 1947, of a summons addressed to the people of France to fight the 'degrading spirit' of American civilization, the Communist campaign in the sphere of motion pictures has assumed fantastic proportions. An invitation of a general nature to boycott American production, which appeared in the Communist press at the end of October 1947, was soon followed by more definite injunctions, i.e., 'to boycott Robert Taylor,' 'to hiss during the presentation of American films,' etc. . . .
>
> The Washington "Star" newspaper for February 4, 1948, carried a news item regarding the banning of certain films in Hungary. This article stated that on January 16, 1948, films of Adolphe Menjou, Allan Jones, George Murphy, Robert Montgomery, Robert Taylor, and Gary Cooper had been banned by the Hungarian Interior Ministry. Also, effective February 12, 1948, the same governmental agency banned films starring Clark Gable, Ginger Rogers, and Barbara Stanwyck. . . .
>
> The March 8, 1948, issue of the "Washington Post" carried a news item datelined March 7, at Prague, Czechoslovakia, indicating that the Czechoslovakian Government had banned movies starring certain individuals who gave testimony of an anti-Communist nature before the House Committee on Un-American Activities. The article stated that the films of the following stars had all been barred: Adolphe Menjou, Gary Cooper, Robert Montogomery, Robert Taylor, and Ginger Rogers.[23]

The French Communists (and their American cousins) are merely hypocrites, in that they object to boycotts and blacklists with boycotts and blacklists. But the Czechoslovakian and Hungarian Communists give us a clearer picture of Communists in power: In response to an American investigation into criminal, treasonable activities, and a private boycott of those who were exposed or refused to cooperate, these Communist regimes violated the rights of their citizens by banning certain American films. Granted, such violations are not much when compared to the enormous evils committed by Soviet and Eastern European governments, but they do underscore the hypocrisy of Communists.

As we have seen, Ayn Rand believed that—at least in the case of the Hollywood Ten—there was no (or no effective) Hollywood blacklist of Communists. Moreover, leftists—maintaining a double standard—were guilty of *establishing* a blacklist against those who opposed Communism and the Hollywood Ten.

In the 1960s, following a lecture she gave at the Ford Hall Forum in Boston, Ayn Rand was asked: "At the time you testified before the HUAC, did you support the blacklisting of communist actors and writers?" She replied:

I do not know anything about a Red blacklist, but I know a great deal about the blacklist of conservatives by the Reds. I am the last person to whom you should address this question, unless you are interested in the truth.

The investigation I was involved in took place in 1947. It's before the McCarthy Era—McCarthy was not involved. This was the hearing at which ten unfriendly witnesses were asked about their Communist Party affiliation, and they refused to answer. (Their Communist Party cards were produced at the hearings by the Committee's investigators.) Another group of witnesses were the so-called "friendly witnesses"—friendly to the investigation—and they testified about Communist penetration into the motion picture industry. I was one of the friendly witnesses. . . .

I do not know of any Red who had been blacklisted in Hollywood. I do know, if the newspaper stories can be trusted, that many of those "blacklisted" people, including the Hollywood Ten (who went to jail for a year, for contempt of congress), were working in Hollywood thereafter under assumed names. They had enough friends in the industry to be able to sell stories under phony names; and today, most of them are back in business. But have you ever inquired into what happened to the *friendly* witnesses?

Observe that some of the friendly witnesses at those hearings were famous stars, such as Gary Cooper and Robert Taylor, and they remained working, of course, because the leftists are the greediest people in Hollywood. They want most of all anyone who is box office. So the stars involved in that hearing did not particularly feel any pressure or blacklist thereafter. The real tragedy is what happened to the second rank people, i.e., people like Adolph Menjou, for instance, who was a famous character actor, but not a star. He used to work all the time, freelancing in various movies. But he was one of the friendly witnesses, and after that hearing, he could not find work. He made a few more movies, with small, supporting roles, and I heard got into financial trouble, so he descended from a very prominent position. Or take the writer Morrie Ryskind, who was famous. (He wrote the comedy *Of Thee I Sing.*) In Hollywood, he was a top writer, getting $3000 a week, which at the time was top money for writers. He has not worked as a writer one day since appearing as a friendly witness. Writers are dispensable in Hollywood; they were treated quite contemptuously; so the writers who cooperated with the HUAC were the worst victims. Now young, junior writers are the most vulnerable people in Hollywood. I know of two of them who cooperated with the HUAC, one was Fred Niblo, Jr.—the son of the director—and the other was Richard Macaulay. They were rising writers, working very well, both men with families, and making about $350 a week. To my knowledge, neither of them has worked as a screenwriter again. When I left Hollywood, Fred Niblo, Jr., was a laborer at Lockheed in California. This is what happened to the friendly witnesses.

At that time, I was under contract to a movie studio, and my producer [Hal Wallis] was a little more decent than the others. I quit voluntarily some years later, because I didn't want to write for Hollywood anymore. But I don't want to tell you what kind of victim of what kind of smear brigade I have been since—what kind of blacklisting of public opinion is going on. You talk about the blacklisting of Reds. I don't know of one leftist that has suffered for his views. And conversely, I don't know of one pro-capitalist who in one form or another did not have to suffer for his views.[24]

A few years later, following another lecture, she was asked a similar question. She ended her answer with the following:

If someone wanted to do something humanitarian, do a research project on what became of the friendly witnesses. A monstrous silent blacklist was exercised by those same goddamned Communists in Hollywood. Did those talented people who were in demand suddenly lose their talent? . . . The Communists work their way into every position of influence, and so the friendly witnesses suffered for their testimony, in one way or the other. That's never mentioned.[25]

I am not here undertaking this humanitarian project—that would itself require a book. I'll simply point out that compared to the attention given to the blacklisting of Communists, there is virtually no mention of "the other blacklist."

When I asked Richard Collins whether he was out of work because of the blacklist against people who cooperated with the HUAC, he responded:

Probably. I don't know. I know it existed. But the fact is that it didn't matter whether you gave the fifth, which they did later on [at the 1951 HUAC hearings], or whether you testified. No matter which way you went, you didn't work. I think the studios in the main felt they'd be safer not to hire anybody who was involved in it, no matter which way they went. There may have been some people who really did figure that the guy's a stool pigeon, a rat, and so forth. And I know a lot of them didn't work ever again—or at least very little.[26]

Friendly witnesses could be blacklisted as a result of the cowardice of moderate liberal or middle-of-the-road or conservative studio executives. Or they could be blacklisted owing to the influence of Hollywood Communists and their sympathizers, who simultaneously complained about the blacklisting of Communists. (See appendix 4, which provides more information on this other blacklist.)

In summary: Ayn Rand claims that she did not know about an official blacklist of the Hollywood Ten, though she would have approved of such a blacklist, because there is a difference between government action (e.g., censorship) and private action (e.g., a boycott). Further, she would argue that the Hollywood Ten got back to work (at least under assumed names), which is more than can be said about many of the "friendly witnesses," who are the genuine victims of a blacklist.

Naming Names

The major study of "naming names" in the context of Hollywood Communism and the HUAC hearings is, unfortunately, Victor Navasky's *Naming Names*.[27] Though valuable as a collection of interviews of many who cooperated with the HUAC, it is utterly lacking in objectivity. (Eric Breindel accurately describes it as an "error-ridden pseudo-histor[y]."[28]) For Navasky makes it clear that he accepts as fundamental two claims that are, in fact, false, but which color his entire study:[29]

1. Anyone who names names is an informer, which Navasky defines "as someone who betrays a comrade, i.e., a fellow member of a movement, a colleague, or a friend, to the authorities."[30] So, those who named names before the HUAC are, he believes, morally tainted.[31] In fact, his book is a study of what could make these informers commit such an evil act. Navasky, however, is no moral philosopher. Arguments for his outlook are rare; instead we are given a brief cultural survey showing how people have tended to regard informers negatively.[32]
2. Hollywood Communists—however misguided or wrong about Stalin, human rights violations in the Soviet Union, etc.—were basically motivated by social conscience; moreover, their activities were neither criminal nor harmful.

A proper study of the 1947 and 1951 HUAC hearings on Hollywood Communism, including a study and evaluation of the friendly and unfriendly witnesses—who they were, what they said (and who named what names) and why, and what became of them—is desperately needed, but beyond the scope of this book.

Ayn Rand apparently never discussed the propriety of naming names. But since the Left seems to view naming names—in the context of the HUAC investigation of Communism in Hollywood (and only in that context)—as the essence of immorality, it is worth discussing. This section sketches what

I believe is the proper approach to "naming names"—from the standpoint of my understanding of Rand's philosophy and of these issues.

My guess is that Rand would no more disapprove of "naming names" in the context of the HUAC investigation than she would disapprove of anyone cooperating with the authorities in any valid criminal investigation. She *would*, however, condemn a person who "named names" in Stalin's Russia, for instance, by reporting a neighbor's anti-Soviet statements to the authorities. There is no moral commandment: Thou Shalt Not Name Names. Naming names must be discussed in a certain context. The real issue is not whether one has named names, but whether one is supporting what is good or what is evil. Has a person cooperated with authorities in a legitimate investigation of criminal activity, in the context of a free society with objective laws, or has a person turned someone in to the secret police?

According to Rand, integrity is a virtue.[33] It is morally wrong to betray your ideals, your values, your friends. But this assumes we are talking about legitimate ideals, values, and friends.[34] At a certain point, one can go so far outside the boundaries of morality that one's ideas themselves are a betrayal—a lack of integrity. For example, how should we morally evaluate an American Nazi or ex-Nazi providing information to the authorities that saved his skin and enabled them to fight Nazism? We might understand why *Nazis* would hate the Nazi informer; but why should we care about that? Looking at it from the outside—as anti-Nazis—we can be glad he did it. The same is true of (ex-) Communist "informers" in the United States during the HUAC hearings. Either they were like the Nazi informer in my example—in which case, however much we might not admire the person, we can be glad he cut a deal—or they were motivated by a genuine change of heart about the nature of the Soviet Union and the U.S. Communist Party.

We must reject the assumption, conveniently accepted by most leftist commentators, that any ex-Communist who cooperated with the HUAC did so to save his neck and/or advance his career.[35] For example, Edward Dmytryk—the one member of the Hollywood Ten to have a change of heart—had quite a different reason: "I deserted my comrades *because* they were 'comrades'."[36] There is no reason for doubting his sincerity.

It is worth mentioning another leftist double standard here. The Left generally treats the refusal to name names as a moral absolute, which in part explains their insistence that this is not a political issue, but a moral one. Patrick McGilligan and Paul Buhle, in their introduction to *Tender Comrades*, write: "Whether or not to inform was, for those who refused, above all not a question of politics but a matter of ethics and morality."[37] In the same book, Walter Bernstein says: "It comes down to something I've said repeatedly: informing was not a matter of politics but a matter of morality."[38] This has become something of a Party line; it is also nonsense.

When it's convenient, the Left (at least implicitly) recognizes that the refusal to name names is not a moral absolute. For example, leftists tend to have no problem with corporate whistle-blowers, or with John Dean's testimony against Nixon—which was not only "naming names," but arguably a violation of lawyer–client privilege.[39] One may legitimately wonder what these same Hollywood Stalinists who moan about the evil of naming names would have thought about the "heroic" informers of their beloved Soviet Union—for example, Pavlik Morozov, who was made a hero for turning his own father in to the authorities.[40]

In his 1951 HUAC testimony, Paul Jarrico said that "one man's subversion is another man's patriotism."[41] I wouldn't put it that way, because I'm not a relativist. But if I accepted that language, I would say the same is true for naming names (though the Left won't admit it): One man's snitch is another man's patriot. Pavlik Morozov is a hero if you're a Communist, a despicable swine if you're not. John Dean is a hero if you're a Democrat, a villain if you're pro-Nixon. (These do not exhaust the possibilities; one may loathe them both.) To leftists, corporate whistle-blowers are heroes, Communist Party whistle-blowers are not. And to leftists, Elia Kazan and Richard Collins are snitches; to those who applaud their change in evaluation of the Soviet Union and the U.S. Communist Party, they are not.[42]

How you evaluate those who named names before the HUAC depends in part on the motives of the informants; but it depends more on what they were providing information about—and in the case of the 1947 hearings, they were providing information about Americans who supported Stalin and the Soviet Union. It is only in this context that one can evaluate "naming names."

On March 21, 1999, on the day Elia Kazan received the Irving Thalberg Lifetime Achievement award, some protestors stood outside the Dorothy Chandler Pavilion with signs reading "Elia Kazan: Nominated for the Benedict Arnold Award."[43] Now I understand why those sympathetic to Hollywood Communists felt this way; but for those of us who despise Communism, the statement is ludicrous, for the Hollywood Communists supported the Soviet Union during its worst period, and wished to import that Soviet hell to America. From that perspective—and in fact—*they* are the Benedict Arnolds.

Ayn Rand and the HUAC

Ayn Rand had no moral qualms about cooperating with the HUAC. But what did she expect from them? What did she plan to say? She later explained that she agreed to cooperate with them with the understanding that she could "testify without any censorship or compromise":

> They assured me that I could. . . . So, I went there on condition that I would be allowed to present a full case. I was going to start my testimony—establish the foundation—reading from my "Screen Guide" and explaining it; and then I would testify about [*Song of Russia* and *The Best Years of Our Lives*]. That's the way it was planned, and I was to appear on the second day. When we arrived in Washington they told me that the first day they had three big shots scheduled. I don't remember who the other two were [Jack Warner and Sam Woods], but the biggest one was Louis B. Mayer. They were going to ask him whether MGM had ever had any communist propaganda in their movies. They were angling for *Song of Russia*. They told me that if he denies that they ever had, [they would like me to take] the stand the first day, right then, and testify specifically about *Song of Russia*—in effect, to give him the lie. They asked if I'd be afraid of him. I said I certainly would not be; if he does that, I'll go ahead. So that is the way it happened. He denied it; and I really hoped he wouldn't, because I didn't want to start on *Song of Russia*.[44]

There is some evidence that the HUAC (or at least those congressmen who spoke to Rand) lied to her—that they had no intention of using her for any other purpose than to refute Louis B. Mayer. The FBI's Freedom of Information Act files on Communist Infiltration in the Motion Picture Industry reveal that although Ayn Rand was on the list of friendly witnesses, she was not a part of the tentative schedule of witnesses. She is nowhere to be found in what looks like a carefully crafted program that puts a great deal of emphasis on *Song of Russia*, Louis B. Mayer, and Robert Taylor. Nor does the program mention any proposed discussion of the MPA's "Screen Guide for Americans." (See appendix 3.)

A comparison of this tentative schedule with the actual order of appearance at the October 1947 HUAC hearings does show that there was a great deal of reshuffling of witnesses (perhaps owing in part to the witnesses' schedules); but Rand's name appears nowhere on the program. She was probably an ace-up-their sleeve, which they intended to play only if Mayer failed to play the cards they wanted him to, and that's what happened.

It is unfortunate that Ayn Rand never got the chance to say before the HUAC what she wanted to say. But we can be glad that she appeared before the committee in 1947 and said what she *did* say. The content of her testimony is analyzed in the next two chapters.[45]

I conclude this chapter with her thoughts on her HUAC experience:

> [After testifying on *Song of Russia*,] I thought my main testimony would be [the next day]. I see McGuinness go into a huddle with Congressman Thomas, the head of the Committee. And shortly thereafter, Thomas approached me and said that they didn't think that they would put me on tomorrow, would I mind staying a little longer. They would probably put me on the day after tomorrow or the next day. I thought there was something funny [going on], but I certainly didn't refuse. The upshot is that I stayed to the end, through the whole hearings, and they never called on me again. . . . I explained to them why I was upset. If I testify only about *Song of Russia*, which was a bad-plot movie and [three] years old, [and] was of no importance—if this is the worst that Hollywood has done—it amounts to almost a whitewash, precisely the sort of thing I wouldn't do. What was much more important was to show the really serious propaganda going on right now and about America—not some musical about Soviet Russia that wouldn't fool anybody, and that had failed very badly at the box office anyway. So they kept promising that they would put me on. . . .
>
> I had a violent scene with Parnell Thomas, the head of [the HUAC], in his office. . . . He said he was convinced that there should be a whole special hearing devoted to nothing but ideology. . . . [The October 1947] hearing was specifically much more factual—an expose of names and party tickets, and union penetration—rather than ideological. . . . He wanted a full ideological hearing, and that's when he would call on me to bring out all the facts. . . . I told him that if I come next time, it will be on my terms. The funny thing was, he looks at me and he says, "Just what do you mean? What terms?" I said, "ideological of course, philosophical." He says, very relieved, "Oh, I thought you meant money." That gave me an insight into that psychology. You know in Washington, if you talk about terms, it's not philosophy.[46]

On November 7, 1947, she received a letter from H.A. Smith of the HUAC, thanking her "for the very fine cooperation which you extended to us during the investigation and hearings in connection with the Committee on Un-American Activities. You are indeed to be commended on your loyalty, and your courage to testify before the committee."[47] Of course, such sentiments did nothing to alter her view of her HUAC experience, which she later described as "nothing but disappointments."[48]

Notes

1. Biographical interviews (Ayn Rand Archives).
2. Biographical interviews.
3. Biographical interviews.
4. For example, Rod Steiger said of Elia Kazan: "Age and ability in the arts or anything else, in my opinion, does not excuse a crime." Quoted in Jerry Schwartz, "Some Actors Outraged by Kazan Honor," *Associated Press*, March 13, 1999. Of course, for those of us who identify the criminals differently, if we took Steiger's approach, no one who supported Stalinist Russia and did not repent and apologize should ever achieve such an award.
5. David Harriman, ed., *Journals of Ayn Rand* (New York: Dutton, 1997), 381–86.
6. Arthur Laurents, *Original Story By: A Memoir of Broadway and Hollywood* (New York: Alfred A. Knopf, 2000), 304.
7. Harriman, *Journals of Ayn Rand*, 381–84.
8. There are a number of books on these subjects. See, for example, Harvey Klehr, John Earl Haynes, and Fridrikh Igorevich Firsov, eds., *The Secret World of American Communism* (New Haven, CT: Yale University Press, 1995), and Harvey Klehr, John Earl Haynes, and Kyrill M. Anderson, eds., *The Soviet World of American Communism* (New Haven, CT: Yale University Press, 1998).
9. Jonathan Foreman (son of blacklisted writer Carl Foreman) asks, in his (inept and unfair) review of Kenneth Billingsley's *Hollywood Party*:

> While there is absolutely no question that the American Communist Party leadership took its orders directly from the Kremlin, it is far from clear to what extent the Soviet contacts of the Party's deeper echelons affected the hundreds of thousands of Americans who passed through the Party. How did they in fact balance their allegiance to it with their allegiance to their country. . . ?

"Blacklist Whitewash," *National Review*, March 22, 1999, 53. But this is precisely the kind of information the government was (or should have been) attempting to discover in its investigation of Hollywood Communism—whatever one thinks of the HUAC as the means of gathering such information. Foreman, however, seems to think that such an investigation is wrongheaded because not all Communists were (equally) evil.
10. *Hearings Regarding the Communist Infiltration of the Motion Picture Industry* (Hearings Before the Committee on Un-American Activities, House of Representatives, Eightieth Congress, First Session, October 20, 21, 22, 23, 24, 27, 28, 29, and 30, 1947) (Washington, DC: United States Government Printing Office, 1947), 195, 206.
11. Ring Lardner Jr., *I'd Hate Myself in the Morning: A Memoir* (New York: Thunder's Mouth Press, 2000), 6.
12. Interview with author, January 10, 2001, Los Angeles.
13. From the "Manual on Organization of the Communist Party," by J. Peters, quoted in Federal Bureau of Investigation, Freedom of Information and Privacy Acts

File (Communist Infiltration-Motion Picture Industry), File Number: 100-138754, Serial: 251x1, Part 6 of 15.

14. *New Masses*, December 7, 1943, 12 (emphasis added).

15. Joan Mellen, *Hellman and Hammett: The Legendary Passion of Lillian Hellman and Dashiell Hammett* (New York: HarperCollins, 1996), 165–66. Mellen describes a 1940 meeting of the Committee on Free Elections, chaired by Hammett, in which a man in the audience named Hamilton stood up and said: "The Communist Party protests the denial of civil rights against themselves. . . . But at the same time it organizes movements to deny civil liberties and election rights to the Socialist Party." This was true. How did Hammett respond? "Mr. Hamilton has violated the spirit and purpose of this meeting. Only antidemocratic elements could benefit by disrupting this rally" (168).

16. Ed Falkowski, "The Polish Hearsts," *New Masses*, December 7, 1943, 10.

17. Kenneth Lloyd Billingsley, *Hollywood Party: How Communism Seduced the American Film Industry in the 1930s and 1940s* (Rocklin, CA: Prima, 1998), 256.

18. *New Masses*, January 11, 1944, 18.

19. See Billingsley, *Hollywood Party*, 170.

20. U.S. Congressman Samuel Dickstein worked to create the Dies committee, which eventually became the HUAC. See Allen Weinstein and Alexander Vassiliev, *The Haunted Wood: Soviet Espionage in America—The Stalin Era* (New York: Random House, 1999), ch. 7.

21. Harriman, *Journals of Ayn Rand*, 384–86.

22. See Billingsley, *Hollywood Party*, ch. 9.

23. Federal Bureau of Investigation, Freedom of Information and Privacy Acts File (Communist Infiltration-Motion Picture Industry), File Number: 100-138754, Serial: 1003 (part 2), Part 9 of 15.

24. From the Q&A period following her talk in Boston in 1967, Ford Hall Forum lecture, "Wreckage of the Consensus." (Tapes and transcripts in the Ayn Rand Archives.) For additional examples of the silent blacklist of "pro-capitalists," see David Horowitz, *Radical Son: A Generational Odyssey* (New York: Simon & Schuster, 1997), 404–408.

25. From the Q&A period (in which Rand took part) following lecture 6 of Leonard Peikoff's "Philosophy of Objectivism" course (1976). (Tapes and transcripts in the Ayn Rand Archives.) Richard Collins recently reported:

One of the things the Party did was to get people jobs. That, in a strange way, worked. So, if [someone] came in and suggested to a producer that so and so would be a good writer, the secretary [who was in the Party] would say, "Oh, yes, I hear he's wonderful." And it could work the other way. Leo Townsend told me that he was with Phil Yordan, and a communist came in and said: "To whom are you going to give the story?" And the producer [Yordan] said: "I thought I'd give it to Richard Collins," and the man said, "you can't do that, he'll steal your money, he can't write at all." I figured that's the way it is.

Interview with author, January 10, 2001, Los Angeles.

26. Interview with author, January 10, 2001, Los Angeles.

27. Victor Navasky, *Naming Names* (New York: Penguin, 1981).

28. John Podhoretz, ed., *A Passion for Truth: The Selected Writings of Eric Breindel* (New York: HarperCollins, 1999), 35.

29. See especially Navasky, *Naming Names*, x–xix.

30. Navasky, *Naming Names*, xviii.

31. To avoid the hypocrisy involved in condemning anti-Communists who name names while praising whistle-blowers and John Dean, Navasky asserts that naming names is like murder and lying: basically immoral, though there are legitimate exceptions. See Navasky, *Naming Names*, xviii.

32. Navasky does present (weak) objections to the arguments given by those who named names. And, toward the end of his book, he does provide a consequentialist argument of sorts against naming names: "The Blacklist savaged private lives, but the informer's particular contribution was to pollute the pubic well, to poison social life in general, to destroy the very possibility of a community; for the informer operates on the principle of betrayal and a community survives on the principle of trust" (*Naming Names*, 347). There is no evidence for such a conclusion. True, the blacklist and the possibility of ex-Communists naming names may have negatively affected the "community" that was the U.S. Communist Party and its fellow travelers. But why should a non-Communist care? And how generally applicable does Navasky think this argument is? There are villages in Southern Italy and Sicily that would be much better off had they not been crippled by a culture of silence, wherein it was frowned upon to cooperate with the authorities in fighting organized crime. Finally, the existence of Communists in America in the 1930s, 1940s, and 1950s—existing underground, dishonestly, and in allegiance to a foreign tyrant—did enormous harm to a feeling of community in America.

33. For Rand's views on integrity, see Leonard Peikoff, *Objectivism: The Philosophy of Ayn Rand* (New York: Dutton, 1991), 259–67.

34. It is superficial to regard whether one ought to "name names" as simply an issue of loyalty to friends and former political comrades. Unfortunately, it is often treated in just such a way. In addition to Navasky's *Naming Names*, see for example Laurents, *Original Story By*, 242–43, 305. According to Laurents, there are good guys and bad guys, and good guys are people who refuse to inform on their friends. Laurents has no problem including in the ranks of good guys people who blindly accepted Stalin, just so long as they never named names—or, in the case of Lillian Hellman, befriended Hannah Arendt! "I would very willingly have attacked [Hellman] myself, not for her idolatry of Stalin but for her admiration of Hannah Arendt" (243).

35. Patrick McGilligan and Paul Buhle, in their introduction to *Tender Comrades: A Backstory of the Hollywood Blacklist* (New York: St. Martin's Griffin, 1997), write: "Informing, in the context of the blacklist, constituted a personal career move" (xviii). Later in the book, Buhle asks Walter Bernstein the following loaded question: "Do you have a general approach to understanding the motivations of the friendly witnesses, aside from the feeling that they all did it for their careers?" (Bernstein re-

sponds: "I think it's a mistake to try psychologizing"—and then proceeds to psychologize about the motives of Schulberg, Kazan, and others [44–45].)

36. Edward Dmytryk, *Odd Man Out: A Memoir of the Hollywood Ten* (Carbondale: Southern Illinois University Press, 1996), 200.

37. McGilligan and Buhle, *Tender Comrades*, xviii.

38. McGilligan and Buhle, *Tender Comrades*, 45.

39. See note 32 above. It is worth presenting Ayn Rand's view of John Dean (from "The Principals and the Principles," *The Ayn Rand Letter* 2, no. 19 (June 18, 1973): 2–3.

As a general rule, whenever a man refuses to put his words in writing, one may be certain that he has been lying. When Dean was asked by Mr. Nixon to prepare a *written* report on Watergate, he would not comply; he ran to the prosecutor, instead (knowing, apparently, that the jig was up). This alone should be sufficient to impeach Dean's credibility.

But all these are merely details [Rand had made a number of points about Dean], of no importance compared to one overriding fact: John Dean is a lawyer who bargained for his own immunity in exchange for the confidential documents he stole from his former clients. Nothing else need be known—or considered—about him. That this should be accepted and passed over in silence by a Senate committee—a committee whose alleged purpose (and rhetorical theme) was to protect the right of *privacy*, to deplore this country's *moral* deterioration, to seek a rebirth of public *morality*—that Dean should be given a respectful, almost friendly treatment by such a committee, will contribute more to this country's demoralization than any grafters or wiretappers ever could. *This*—more than all the other manifestations of a cynical double standard—can destroy the last of people's confidence in anyone's appeals to decency, morality and justice.

40. See Sheila Fitzpatrick, *Everyday Stalinism: Ordinary Life in Extraordinary Times: Soviet Russia in the 1930s* (New York: Oxford University Press, 1999), 73. Fitzpatrick points out that Morozov was considered a hero by young Communists but loathed by Russian intellectuals. Ayn Rand presents this particular evil in her portrayal of Victor Dunaev, in *We the Living*. Victor turns in his sister and her boyfriend to secure his position in the Party and advance his career.

41. *Communist Infiltration of Hollywood Motion-Picture Industry-Part 1* (Hearings Before the Committee on Un-American Activities, House of Representatives, Eighty-Second Congress, First Session, March 8 and 21; April 10, 11, 12 and 13, 1951) (Washington, DC: United States Government Printing Office, 1951), 278. Shortly thereafter, Jarrico says: "I believe this country was founded on the doctrine of freedom, the right of a man to advocate anything he wishes—advocate it, agitate for it, organize for it, attempt to win a majority for it" (278). I doubt he thought this applied to anti-Communists in Hollywood, for a bit later he says: "I know that today the basis is being laid for an increase of [the blacklist of Hollywood leftists], so that anyone who has advocated anything progressive is going to be suspect. And the Motion Picture Alliance for the Preservation of American Ideals, quaintly named, is going to be the organization in Hollywood that decides who shall work and who shall not, what pictures shall be made and what pictures shall not be made," etc. (279).

(Recall that Jarrico had no problem with the OWI, a *government* propaganda office with strong pro-Soviet leanings.) One may legitimately wonder whether Jarrico thought a member of the MPA (a private organization) had the right to advocate whatever he wanted, agitate for it, organize for it. More leftist hypocrisy.

Jarrico's conception of patriotism is shared by leftist historian Ellen Schrecker, who uses it to defend American Communists who engaged in espionage for the Soviet Union: "it is important to realize that as Communists, these people did not subscribe to traditional forms of patriotism; they were internationalists whose political allegiances transcended national boundaries." *Many Are the Crimes: McCarthyism in America* (Boston: Little, Brown, 1998), 178–79.

42. Kazan and Collins both wrote articulate defenses of their rejection of the U.S. Communist Party, both of which are reprinted in Billingsley, *Hollywood Party*, 223–25, 308–13. Navasky responds to such defenses as follows: "to cite one's defection from the CP as a reason to testify before the Committee is to miss the point. The principle at stake was not the well-being of the Communist Party but rather the rights of all Americans and the well-being of the First Amendment" (*Naming Names*, 306). As I follow Rand in rejecting the view that the hearings and the blacklist represented threats to the First Amendment, I think this objection fails completely.

43. Patrick Goldstein, "Many Refuse to Clap as Kazan Receives Oscar," *Los Angeles Times*, March 22, 1999.

44. Biographical interviews.

45. Her entire testimony is provided in appendix 1.

46. Biographical interviews.

47. In the Ayn Rand Archives.

48. Biographical interviews.

CHAPTER SIX

Big Lies: *Song of Russia* versus Soviet Russia—An Analysis of Ayn Rand's HUAC Testimony, Part 1

Communist Propaganda

At the beginning of her HUAC testimony, when asked about *Song of Russia*, Ayn Rand begins her response by defining "propaganda."

> We have all been talking about it, but nobody . . . has stated just what they mean by propaganda. Now, I use the term to mean that Communist propaganda is anything which gives a good impression of communism as a way of life. Anything that sells people the idea that life in Russia is good and that people are free and happy would be Communist propaganda. Am I not correct? I mean, would that be a fair statement to make—that that would be Communist propaganda?[1]

In the course of her testimony, Rand attempts to demonstrate that *Song of Russia* is clearly a work of Communist propaganda.

As we have seen, many of the reviews of *Song of Russia* saw the film as a piece of propaganda but disagreed about the nature of the propaganda, and whether or not it was proper propaganda. But some have rejected Rand's appraisal completely. At the time of the 1947 hearings, Lillian Hellman wrote that "there has never been a single line or word of communism in any American picture at any time."[2] This became the Communist gospel truth. For example, when presented with the opinion that *Song of Russia, Mission to Moscow*, and *North Star* (the last penned by Hellman herself) were examples of "overt propaganda," Arthur Laurents replied: "Nobody has been able to point to one movie that was propaganda for the Soviet Union."[3] One wishes that Hellman and Laurent had, like Rand, explained what they meant by propaganda, because their claims are nonsense. These films are classic propaganda. What follows should make that clear in the case of *Song of Russia*.

Moving beyond Laurent's knee-jerk, Party-line response, the serious issue is the *nature* of the propaganda in films like *Song of Russia*. Most commentators acknowledge that *Song of Russia* shows the Soviets in a good light and tend to justify such films on the grounds that Russia was an ally at the time. (More on that issue in chapter 7.) But, it is claimed, the film does not portray Communism positively, because it does not portray Communism at all. Thus, *Song of Russia* contains no *Communist* propaganda.

One may attempt to make a distinction between pro-Communist, pro-Soviet, and pro-Russian propaganda; however, I demonstrate in this chapter and the next that there is in fact no difference. Russia was the heart of the Soviet Union: in the 1940s, to be pro-Russia—if we include its people, government, military, and way of life—is to be pro-Soviet Union. But you cannot be pro-Soviet Union without being pro-Soviet. As will be clear in the following analysis of Rand's HUAC testimony, pro-Soviet propaganda *is* a form of Communist propaganda, just as pro-German and pro-Italian propaganda in the 1930s were (forms of) pro-Fascist propaganda.[4]

There are hints of overt Communist propaganda in the film, a couple of which Ayn Rand mentions in her testimony.

[T]he heroine decides that she wants to stay in Russia. Taylor would like to take her out of the country, but she says no, her place is here, she has to fight the war. Here is the line, as nearly exact as I could mark it while watching the picture: "I have a great responsibility to my family, to my village, and to the way I have lived." What way had she lived? This is just a polite way of saying the Communist way of life. She goes on to say that she wants to stay in her country because otherwise "How can I help to build a better and better life for my country?"[5] What is meant by "better and better"? That means she has already helped to build a good way. That is the Soviet Communist way. But now she wants to make it even better.[6]

Ayn Rand is right. The implication is that Communism is good—or at least that it's good for Russia. According to *Song of Russia*, America and Russia—whatever their differences—are both good countries.[7] And in case you've heard about the differences between them (and held, like Nadya at first, that "We have serious differences—socially, culturally"), the film assures its audience that Communism is nothing for America to worry about.

Most of the propaganda dealt with in this chapter, however, is not *overt* Communist propaganda—that is, propaganda that overtly makes a point of defending the Communist way of life—rather, it is overt *Soviet* propaganda, which is by implication Communist propaganda.

Freedom

Song of Russia proclaims that what it presents is the truth. At the beginning, the announcer declares that John Meredith witnessed what was going on in Russia firsthand; then we flash back to what he witnessed. At the end of the film—as Ayn Rand points out in her testimony—Boris "asks Taylor and the girl to go back to America, because they can help them there. How? Here is what [Boris] says, 'You can go back to your country and tell them what you have seen.' Now, that is plainly saying that what you have seen is the truth about Russia."[8]

The bulk of Ayn Rand's testimony is a refutation of the idea that *Song of Russia* presents an accurate picture of the Soviet Union. This chapter examines the details of her testimony. But here, at the outset, I wish to make a general point about the film's inaccuracy—one that is later confirmed by the details—namely, that from *Song of Russia*, one gets *no* sense of the lack of individual freedom that existed in Soviet Russia.

This point is made at least twice during Rand's testimony:

(1) when all this sweetness and light was going on in the first part of the picture, with all these happy, free people, there was not a G.P.U. agent among them. . . , no persecution—complete freedom and happiness.[9]

(2) Taylor's manager, an American, tells [Nadya] that she should leave the country, but when she refuses and wants to stay, here is the line he uses: he tells her in an admiring, friendly way that "You are a fool, but a lot of fools like you died on the village green at Lexington."[10] Now, I submit that this is blasphemy, because the men at Lexington were not fighting just a foreign invader. They were fighting for freedom and what I mean—and I intend to be exact—is they were fighting for political freedom and individual freedom. They were fighting for the rights of man. To compare them to someone fighting for a slave state, I think is dreadful.[11]

I would add three more lines from the film which, in their context, convey the idea that Russia is a free country—like the United States. Greeting John at the beginning of the film, Petrov, of the Central Art Committee of the government, says: "All hail the cultural achievements of our free country." And after the Nazis attack Russia, Stalin, in his famous "Scorched

Earth" speech to rally the nation, proclaims: "the issue is one of life and death for the peoples of the Soviet Union. Whether they shall remain free, or fall into slavery." And finally, at the end, when Boris urges John and Nadya to go to America, he tells them:

> We will feel you fighting side by side with us, all soldiers in the same army. Fighting to bring a new light to our children, for that great day when the whole world will ring with a new song of freedom; for you will bring our great countries closer together, in the fight for all humanity.

Song of Russia presents Russia as a free country. But in fact there is a huge gulf between this presentation and Soviet reality. There is no indication in the film that the U.S.S.R. is a totalitarian dictatorship. The unwary or ignorant could watch it and be oblivious to the fact that there was no freedom of thought and speech, no free elections, no freedom of trade, no freedom of assembly, no freedom of emigration; there is no suggestion of the use of terror, or of a war against—and even the liquidation of—certain classes of people. But the Soviet Union during the period covered in *Song of Russia* was characterized by all these things. As Sheila Fitzpatrick describes it:

> Soviet society may be conceptualized as a prison or a conscript army. This catches the elements of regimentation, strict discipline, and confinement within a closed institution with its own strict codes of behavior, often bewildering to outsiders. The behavior of prisoners and conscripts reflects their fear of punishment, which may be incurred by failing to follow orders or random mischance. A sharp dividing line separates guards and officers in such institutions from inmates and recruits: these are "us" and "them" situations. Bullying by guards/officers produces resentment, though it is also seen as part of the natural order of things. There are informers among the inmates, but "ratting" to authorities on other inmates is nevertheless strongly condemned in the inmate community. Desertion/ attempting to escape is severely punished.[12]

Leaving Russia, the writer John Dos Passos wrote to Hemingway, "was like being let out of jail."[13] *Song of Russia* not only ignores all of this, it paints a picture of the opposite: a free and happy Russia.

During the wedding party of Nadya and John, Hank (John's manager) makes a feeble (and drunken) attempt at an objection to the marriage. He tells Nadya's father that he just doesn't see it: "He's an American. It's unpatriotic." Her father responds: "You'll see it, you'll see it," and pours Hank another shot of vodka. This scene could be a symbol of *Song of Russia*. For Americans who had objections to the marriage of the United States and the

Soviet Union during World War II (and after), this film is a shot of vodka poured down their throats, to make them see it—not the truth, of course, but what the creators of this film wanted them to see. What follows—a close analysis of the part of Ayn Rand's HUAC testimony that focuses on the inaccuracy of its portrayal of Russia—is a confirmation of this.

City Life

Roughly the first half of *Song of Russia* takes place in Moscow. Moreover, much of it—certainly the scene in which John and Nadya see Moscow together—is presented as travelogue: It acquaints its American audience with Moscow. Is the picture it paints of Moscow accurate?

Ayn Rand answers with an emphatic "*no!*"

The picture then goes into a scene of Moscow, supposedly. I don't know where the studio got its shots, but I have never seen anything like it in Russia. First you see Moscow buildings—big, prosperous-looking, clean buildings, with something like swans or sailboats in the foreground. Then you see a Moscow restaurant that just never existed there. In my time, when I was in Russia, there was only one such restaurant, which was nowhere as luxurious as that and no one could enter it except commissars and profiteers. Certainly a girl from a village . . . could not afford to enter it, even if she worked ten years. However, there is a Russian restaurant with a menu such as never existed in Russia at all and which I doubt even existed before the revolution. From this restaurant they go on to this tour of Moscow. The streets are clean and prosperous-looking. There are no food lines anywhere. You see shots of the marble subway—the famous Russian subway out of which they make such propaganda capital. There is a marble statue of Stalin thrown in. There is a park where you see happy little children in white blouses running around. I don't know whose children they are, but they are really happy kiddies. They are not homeless children in rags, such as I have seen in Russia. Then you see an excursion boat, on which the Russian people are smiling, sitting around very cheerfully, dressed in some sort of satin blouses such as they only wear in Russian restaurants here [in the U.S.]. Then they attend a luxurious dance. . . . Of course, it didn't say whose ballroom it is or how they get there. But there they are—free and dancing very happily.

Rand claims that the dishonesty of the movie is clear: *Song of Russia* presents Moscow (and Russian urban life generally, is the implication) as prosperous, clean, and happy, when in fact Moscow and Muscovites—Soviet cities and city-dwellers—were on the whole poor, hungry, filthy, and miserable.

Ayn Rand's critique of the film's portrayal of Soviet urban life is accurate. One cannot in a few pages do justice to just how awful conditions were in Soviet cities in the decade prior to and including the time covered in *Song of Russia*. This section presents a montage, of sorts, of Soviet urban life.[14] For a general account of the conditions, see Sheila Fitzpatrick's *Everyday Stalinism*, which shows that Soviet cities were lacking in housing, clothes, shoes, and all sorts of consumer goods—and especially food; that they were crowded, filthy, and dangerous.

In what follows, keep in mind (1) that Moscow was the Soviet showcase city—however bad conditions were there, they were better than in other Soviet cities; and (2) that Communist Party members were privileged, and thus better off than other citizens—though they nevertheless tended to be miserable, too.[15]

Song of Russia, as Ayn Rand points out, presents city life as prosperous and happy. The reality was quite different. Fitzpatrick writes:

> The most extraordinary aspect of Soviet urban life, from the perspective of those living it, was the sudden disappearance of goods from the stores at the beginning of the 1930s and the beginning of an era of chronic shortages. Everything, particularly the basics of food, clothing, shoes, and housing, was in short supply.[16]

Let us focus first on food. Recall that one of Rand's criticisms of the film was that it nowhere showed the ubiquitous Russian food lines. Fitzpatrick reports that, "The most serious and widespread recurrence of bread lines occurred in the winter and spring of 1936–37, after the harvest failure of 1936."[17] A woman, in a letter to her husband, describes the lines in one town as follows: "Mama and I stood from 4 in the morning and didn't even get any black bread because they didn't bring any at all to the store and that happened in almost all the stores of the town." A housewife from Volga, in a 1940 letter to Stalin, wrote: "you have to go at two o'clock at night and stand until six in the morning to get two kilograms of ryebread."[18] Bread was not an exception. All other foodstuffs were in short supply in the period that concerns us, the late 1930s and early 1940s.

On the subject of food, how accurate was Ayn Rand's complaint about Moscow restaurants? I again quote Fitzpatrick:

> One of the signs of the times was the revival of Moscow restaurant life in 1934. This followed a four-year hiatus during which restaurants had been open only to foreigners, payment was in hard currency, and the OGPU regarded any Soviet citizens who went there with deep suspicion. Now, all those who could afford it could go to the Metropole Hotel, where "wonderful live starlets swam

in a pool right in the center of the restaurant hall," and hear jazz by Antonin Ziegler's Czech group, or to the National to hear the Soviet jazzman Aleksandr Tsfasman and Leonid Utesov, or to the Prague Hotel on the Arbat where gypsy singers and dancers performed. The restaurants were patronized particularly by theater people and other "new" elite members, and their prices were, of course, out of reach of ordinary citizens.[19]

So, one may argue that Rand is wrong here—that restaurants such as those portrayed in *Song of Russia* did exist in Moscow. This is the line taken by Louis B. Mayer in his HUAC testimony:

Smith: Do you recall scenes in there at the night club where everybody was drinking?
Mayer: They do in Moscow. . . .
Smith: Do you feel it represents Russia in 1943 as conditions were in Russia?
Mayer: This is what I understood, that they go to night clubs there in Moscow. If only the rest of the Russians had a chance to do the same thing, it would be fine, but they don't. This picture was laid in Moscow.[20]

Mayer is too easy on the Russians, and is not entirely accurate about where *Song of Russia* "is laid," but then he was getting heat for making the movie. Nevertheless, the state of restaurants in Moscow did seem to have changed somewhat since 1926, when Rand was last there. But to view this as an objection to her testimony would be pettifogging. For she is right when she says: "Certainly a girl from a village . . . could not afford to enter [such a restaurant], even if she worked ten years." John Meredith, as a foreign celebrity, could have taken Nadya to such a restaurant. But there is *no* indication in the film of how rare such restaurants were, that it was impossible for private citizens to own restaurants, and that the secret police would probably regard Nadya "with deep suspicion."

The issue of housing does not arise in Ayn Rand's critique of *Song of Russia*, except indirectly. Since the film presents the city as prosperous and the citizens as happy, one would assume that the citizens, in general, were not suffering from a severe housing shortage; but such a shortage was in fact the Soviet urban reality. In Moscow in 1940, the average living space was just over four square meters per capita.[21] In one letter to Molotov, a worker from Leningrad begs for "a room or a little apartment where I can build a personal life."[22] Moreover, most rooms lacked running water, and the bathrooms and cooking facilities the residents shared were extremely primitive.[23]

Another of Ayn Rand's complaints about the film is that it shows Moscow and the people in it as clean. Again, the reality was quite different. An

American engineer who worked in the U.S.S.R. in the early 1930s reported: "The physical aspect of the cities is dreadful. Stench, filth, dilapidation batter the senses at every turn."[24] There was little change in the decade that followed. In the mid-1930s, at the recommendation of the government, Soviet citizens (and not merely peasants) were trying to master such practices as washing with soap and brushing their teeth.[25]

The Moscow subway—as Rand points out, "the famous Russian subway out of which they make such propaganda capital"—is no doubt much like what we see in *Song of Russia*. But this is show for foreigners; it is a "Potemkin" subway station, not a reflection of the quality of life in Russian cities.[26] Further, Moscow *did* have streetcars. But the film does not tell the whole story: "Residents and visitors to Moscow and Leningrad have left vivid descriptions of its streetcars and their incredible overcrowding." Other towns lacked even *crowded* streetcars. "In provincial towns, where paved roads were still a comparative rarity at the end of the decade, public transport services of any kind were minimal."[27]

In the tour of Moscow that *Song of Russia* takes us on, we see trains and railway stations, but no crime. In fact, watching the film—seeing John and Nadya strolling through the streets at night—one gets the impression that crime was not a problem. But it certainly was:

> It was dangerous to walk the streets in many Soviet cities in the 1930s. The new industrial towns and the workers' settlements in old ones were the most perilous. Here drink, the congregation of restless single men, inadequate policing, bad living conditions, and unpaved and unlighted streets all contributed to the lawless frontier atmosphere. Robberies, murders, drunken fights, and random attacks on passersby were common.[28]

The *Great Soviet Encyclopedia* (of 1934) predicted that "With the growth of productive forces, luxury items may become necessities."[29] In fact, in the Soviet Union during the period portrayed in *Song of Russia*, the opposite was true: What are normally regarded as basic necessities—bread, running water, a room of one's own, a certain level of protection against crime—had become (for the most part unattainable) luxuries. There is no indication of this in the film.

With conditions in the Soviet Union so miserable, its citizens had little incentive to work. This problem was solved the Soviet way: They were *forced* to work harder. *The Black Book of Communism* reports:

> In the workplace the date of 26 June 1940 remained imprinted on the minds of many because of the decree "on the adoption of the eight-hour working day,

the seven-day working week, and the ban on leaving work of one's own accord." Any unjustified absence, including lateness of more than twenty minutes, was henceforth treated as a criminal offense. Lawbreakers were liable to six months' uninterrupted "corrective work," the loss of 25 percent of their salary, and the possibility of a prison sentence of between two and four months. On 10 August another decree increased the punishments for any act of "hooliganism," shoddy work, or petty theft in the workplace to as much as three years of imprisonment in the camps. In the conditions that then prevailed in Soviet industry, almost any worker could be prosecuted under this severe new law. . . . In the first six months after they came into effect, more than 1.5 million people received sentences; the fact that 400,000 of these were custodial sentences partly explains the huge increase in prison numbers after the summer of 1941. The number of "hooligans" sentenced to the camps rose from 108,000 in 1939 to 200,000 in 1940.[30]

All this took place while protection against real crime was grossly inadequate in Soviet cities.

Another major urban problem was the proliferation of underage vagabonds. Recall that Ayn Rand contrasted the "happy little children in white blouses running around" Moscow in *Song of Russia*, with "the homeless children in rags, such as I have seen in Russia." The problem of vagabond children was also solved the Soviet way:[31]

In 1936 alone more than 125,000 underage vagabonds passed through the special NKVD centers. From 1935 to 1939 more than 155,000 minors were sent to the NKVD work colonies, and 92,000 children aged twelve to sixteen appeared in court from 1936 to 1939. On 1 April 1939 it was calculated that more than 10,000 children were incarcerated in the gulags.[32]

Here, too, Ayn Rand's critique of the portrayal of Soviet city life in *Song of Russia* is well founded.

As a transition to Soviet village life, consider these words of Elinor Lipper, a Swiss woman who spent eleven years in Soviet prison camps. She describes the fate of *ukazniki*, prisoners sent to the camps for violations of the various harsh work laws:

An ukase [labor law] was issued which provided that any worker who left his job in a war plant, no matter for what reasons, was subject to from six to eight years of imprisonment. Hundreds of young girls between the ages of eighteen and twenty were sent to Kolyma for running away to their villages because they could no longer endure the starvation in the cities where they had been forced to work. Some had only gone back home for a few days to visit a sick mother,

but the factory manager would not give them any days off and when they returned they were arrested. They came as adolescents and were instantly trans-
formed by Kolyma into full-fledged prostitutes. . . . These prisoners were given
amnesties when the war ended in 1945, but those who had not been physically
wrecked were morally shattered.[33]

The *ukazniki* began arriving at the camps in 1941, the year in which
Nadya traipses around Russia trying to buttonhole John Meredith. But
Nadya does not come close to ending up in the camps—they don't exist in
Song of Russia—nor do her fellow villagers. Instead, leaving Moscow, she re-
turns home to her village. What was it like—and what was the Soviet rural
reality?

Village Life

The village presented in *Song of Russia* is a Potemkin village—a façade built
to hide the miserable reality of Soviet peasant life.[34] Whether or not the creators of the film were aware of it, they did exactly what the Soviets (who
were aware of the reality) were doing in their presentations—in the press and
in art—of village conditions as infinitely better than they were. The Soviets
called this "socialist realism":

> In its crudest forms, "socialist realism" was hard to distinguish from outright
> deception—the creation of "Potemkin villages" where nothing lay behind the
> façade. During the famine [of 1932–1933], for example, the press depicted col-
> lective farms as happy and prosperous, with merry peasants gathering around
> laden tables in the evening hours to dance and sing to the accordion.[35]

One would be hard pressed to better describe the village in *Song of Russia*.
   Ayn Rand, like any honest observer, could see behind the façade; she rejected this picture of a prosperous Soviet village. Here is the relevant account
from her HUAC testimony:

> The Russian villages are something—so miserable and so filthy. They were
> even before the revolution. They weren't much even then. What they have be-
> come now I am afraid to think. You have all read about the program for the
> collectivization of the farms in 1933, at which time the Soviet Government
> admits that three million peasants died of starvation. Other people claim there
> were seven and a half million, but three million is the figure admitted by the
> Soviet Government as the figure of people who died of starvation, planned by
> the government in order to drive people into collective farms. That is a
> recorded historical fact.

Now, here is the life in the Soviet village as presented in *Song of Russia*. You see the happy peasants. You see they are meeting the hero at the station with bands, with beautiful blouses and shoes, such as they never wore anywhere. You see children with operetta costumes on them and with a brass band which they could never afford. You see the manicured starlets driving tractors and the happy women who come from work singing. You see a peasant at home with a close-up of food for which anyone there would have been murdered. If anybody had such food in Russia in that time he couldn't remain alive, because he would have been torn apart by neighbors trying to get food. But here is a close-up of it and a line where Robert Taylor comments on the food and the peasant answers, "This is just a simple country table and the food we eat ourselves."[36]

Then the peasant proceeds to show Taylor how they live. He shows him his wonderful tractor. It is parked somewhere in his private garage. He shows him the grain in his bin, and Taylor says, "That is wonderful grain." Now, it is never said that the peasant does not own this tractor or this grain because it is a collective farm. He couldn't have it. It is not his. But the impression he gives to Americans, who wouldn't know any differently, is that certainly it is this peasant's private property, and that is how he lives, he has his own tractor and his own grain. Then it shows miles and miles of plowed fields. . . .

Robert Taylor proposes to the heroine. She accepts him. They have a wedding, which, of course, is a church wedding. It takes place with all the religious pomp which they show. They have a banquet. They have dancers, in something like satin skirts and performing ballets such as you never could possibly see in any village and certainly not in Russia. Later they show a peasants' meeting place, which is a kind of a marble palace with crystal chandeliers. Where they got it or who built it for them I would like to be told.[37]

To understand the reality of Soviet rural life in the early 1940s, one must keep in mind two related, key elements of the historical context, neither of which is even hinted at in *Song of Russia*: (1) the collectivization of peasant agriculture and the destruction of the kulaks (i.e., successful peasant farmers) and (2) the Great Famine of 1932–1933.

Fitzpatrick describes the collectivization of peasant agriculture as follows:

Stimulated by Stalin's announcement in December [1930] that it was time to move towards "liquidation of the kulaks as a class," Communists and Komsomols descended on the countryside en masse to get rid of kulaks, collectivize the village, close the churches, and generally kick the backward peasantry into the socialist twentieth century.[38]

The collectivizers employed confiscation of property, humiliation, violence, terror, rape, and murder to bring about collectivization. By 1937, 93 percent of farms were collectivized.[39] *The Black Book of Communism* provides a tally of the damage done:

> Recent research in the newly accessible archives has confirmed that the forced collectivization of the countryside was in effect a war declared by the Soviet state on a nation of smallholders. More than 2 million peasants were deported. . . , 6 million died of hunger, and hundreds of thousands died as a direct result of deportation. Such figures, however, only hint at the size of the human tragedy. Far from being confined to the winter of 1929–30, the war dragged on until the mid-1930s and was at its peak in 1932 and 1933, which were marked by a terrible famine deliberately provoked by the authorities to break the resistance of the peasants.[40]

The results of this are no surprise. First, there was a high degree of resentment on the part of the villagers toward the Soviet state and its representatives. This resentment had certainly not mellowed into the deep respect for Stalin that we find in *Song of Russia*. Fitzpatrick writes that, "Malice, anger, and bitterness were rife in the village in the decade after collectivization."[41]

Further, the peasant economy had not improved much by the late 1930s and early 1940s. As one villager wrote to her husband during this period: "We stand in line for bread from 12 o'clock at night, and they only give one kilogram, even if you're dying of hunger."[42] Where, then, did that "simple peasant fare" dished up to John Meredith in *Song of Russia* come from? One could answer: from Russian tradition.

> One facet of "making fairy tales come true" was particularly dear to Soviet citizens: the promise that socialism would bring abundance. This was literally an excursion into the world of Russian fairy tales, whose furniture included a Magic Tablecloth that, when laid, produced an extravagant array of food and drink of its own accord.[43]

The creators of *Song of Russia* laid the peasant's table with a magic tablecloth; it had nothing to do with reality.

If a Russian peasant managed to lay hold of something like the magic tablecloth meal served up to John Meredith, what would his neighbors think? Ayn Rand suggests that the peasant would not be able to enjoy it for long: "You see a peasant at home with a close-up of food for which anyone there would have been murdered. If anybody had such food in Russia in that time he couldn't remain alive, because he would have been torn apart by neighbors trying to get food."[44]

The peasants in *Song of Russia* are all well groomed and clean—at least until they start fighting Nazis. (Ayn Rand accurately describes two of them as "manicured starlets driving tractors.") The reality was quite different. In the mid-1930s, the *Soviets* reported:

> Until quite recently, people used soap only on big holidays; now 87 percent of kolkhoznik households use soap, while 55 percent of kolkhozniks had individual towels. In the past, bathing was a rarity; now the great majority of kolkhoznik families took baths at least once every two weeks.[45]

Keep in mind that this is an official Soviet boast, and thus should be taken with a handful of salt.

In many other ways, the picture of Soviet peasant life painted by *Song of Russia* is inaccurate or incomplete. Tractors and horses do not seem to be a rarity in Nadya's village, though in reality, they were both rare commodities, and (as Rand points out in the case of tractors) they could not be privately owned. (Recall that Nadya's father had named "his" tractor.) Further, medicine was extremely backward, and only about 4 percent of collective farms had electricity in the period before World War II.[46]

In her HUAC testimony, Ayn Rand complains that there is no sign in *Song of Russia* of the effects of collectivization or the Great Famine, and she is right to object. It is ludicrous to think that by 1941 the villages had gotten over them. In fact, the economic conditions of Soviet villages were not to improve—by *Soviet standards*—until the 1960s.[47]

Religion

During her testimony, Chief Investigator Robert E. Stripling interrupts Ayn Rand: "I saw the picture. At this peasant's village or home, was there a priest or several priests in evidence?" She responds:

> Oh, yes; I am coming to that, too. The priest was from the beginning in the village scenes, having a position as sort of a constant companion and friend of the peasants, as if religion was a natural accepted part of that life. Well, now, as a matter of fact, the situation about religion in Russia in my time was, and I understand it still is, that for a Communist Party member to have anything to do with religion means expulsion from the party. He is not allowed to enter a church or take part in any religious ceremony. For a private citizen, that is a nonparty member, it was permitted, but it was so frowned upon that people had to keep it secret, if they went to church. If they wanted a church wedding they usually had it privately in their homes, with only a few friends present, in order not to let it be known at their place of employment because, even though it was not forbidden, the chances were that they would be thrown out of a job for being known as practicing any kind of religion.[48]

Two days later, Stripling asked Robert Taylor a question about the film's portrayal of religion:

Stripling: Miss Ayn Rand gave the committee a review of the picture several days ago. In the picture there were several scenes, particularly a wedding scene at which a priest officiated; also several other scenes at which clergy was present. When you were making this picture were you under the impression that freedom of religion was enjoyed in Russia?

Taylor: No, sir; I never was under the impression that freedom of religion was enjoyed in Russia. However, I must confess when it got down to that part of the picture the picture was about two-thirds gone and it didn't actually occur to me until you mentioned it just a minute ago.[49]

Whatever did or did not occur to Taylor when he made the film, Rand's testimony is correct. Contrary to the picture painted in *Song of Russia*, freedom of religion was not enjoyed in the Soviet Union. (Recall that Ayn Rand was an atheist. Her concern here is not specifically freedom of religion, but freedom of thought generally.)

There were three periods (before the war) in which the Soviets were particularly oppressive toward religion: 1918–1922, 1929–1930, and 1937–1941. A quick look at statistics—especially from this last period—provides an idea of the level of religious repression in the years prior to and including the action in *Song of Russia*. The *Black Book of Communism* reports:

On 1 April 1936 only 15,835 Orthodox churches remained in service in the U.S.S.R. (28 percent of the re-Revolutionary total), 4,830 mosques (32 percent of the re-Revolutionary figure), and a few dozen Catholic and Protestant churches. The number of registered priests was a mere 17,857, in contrast to 112,629 in 1914 and 70,000 in 1928. The clergy, in official terminology, had become "the debris of a dying class". . . .

The census of January 1937 revealed that approximately 70 percent of the population, despite the pressures placed on them, still replied in the affirmative when asked "Are you a believer?" Hence Soviet leaders embarked on a third and decisive offensive against the church. In April 1937 Malenkov sent a note to Stalin suggesting that legislation concerning religious organizations was outdated. . . . He concluded: "The time has come to finish once and for all with all clerical organizations and ecclesiastical hierarchies." Thousands of priests and nearly all the bishops were sent to the camps, and this time the vast majority were executed. Of the 20,000 churches and mosques that were still active in 1936, fewer than 1,000 were still open for services at the beginning of 1941. In early 1941 the number of officially registered clerics of all religions had fallen to 5,665 . . . from over 24,000 in 1936.[50]

To be sure, there is evidence that this repression led to something of a religious revival among Soviet peasants in the 1930s. For example, the observance of religious holidays was on the rise during this period.[51] There were religious people practicing their religions in Stalinist Russia; Rand does not deny this in her testimony. But their practice of religion is still light-years away from freedom of religion. Religion was not as widespread in the cities as it was in the villages; where it did exist, it was not legal and was tolerated only sporadically, and the practice of religion was risky—that is, religious people were under threat of Soviet terror, especially on the eve of World War II.[52]

Moreover, whatever limited religious toleration did exist, it was not extended to members of the Communist Party, as Rand points out. Fitzpatrick reports that "one of the most common ideological offenses for a party member was to have allowed his wife or other female relative to remain a believer, to christen their children, attend church, or keep icons in the house. Party members were frequently cross-examined on this score."[53]

It is of course possible that there occasionally occurred, in Russian villages, religious weddings held out in the open, such as we see in *Song of Russia* (though I doubt any were as opulent). But to show us churches, with no reference to the number of churches destroyed by the Soviets—to show us priests, with no reference to the number of clergy imprisoned or executed—is to give a false impression of the state of religion in Stalinist Russia. The unsuspecting viewer could not help but conclude—especially since he has been told that this film presents a true picture of Russian life—that Russia is a land where one is free to worship as one pleases. But that is a complete fabrication.

Travel

Earlier in this chapter, we saw the awful state of public transportation in Soviet cities, the harsh penalties for leaving work without permission to return home, and the unsafe nature of Soviet city streets and train stations. This section covers the lack of freedom of travel.

In her HUAC testimony, Ayn Rand comments on travel in the Soviet Union: "[John Meredith] meets a little Russian girl from a village who comes to him and begs him to go to her village to direct concerts there. There are no GPU agents and nobody stops her. She just comes to Moscow and meets him." And a little later: "Certainly a girl from a village . . . would never have been allowed to come voluntarily, without permission, to Moscow." Finally, describing the border with Poland: "You have a very lovely modernistic sign saying 'U.S.S.R.' I would just like to remind you that that is the border where probably thousands of people have died trying to escape out of this lovely paradise."[54] What she says accurately describes travel in *Song of Russia*. More generally, judging by the content of that film, one would conclude that Soviet citizens were free to travel from one city to another, from city to village (and vice versa), and within a city. Further, and perhaps more important, one would tend to conclude that citizens were free to leave the country. For example, whether Nadya stays in Russia or goes to America (she eventually does the latter) is left entirely up to her; similarly, a woman truck driver says that after the war she plans on going to Detroit to meet the men who made her truck.

Once again, Ayn Rand is right: *Song of Russia* is a fraud.

First, there was no freedom of emigration. Millions of people were dying to get out of the country (in many cases literally) but were forbidden to do so. As chance would have it, Rand got out with a travel visa in 1926. Not long after this, however, the window of opportunity shut tight, and her family was unable to leave. And this was before the appearance of Stalin, when leaving the country became even more difficult. For over ten years, until 1937 (when she stopped writing to her family, because she was told by the U.S. Post Office that writing to Soviet citizens could endanger them), Rand tried without success to get the Soviet government to allow her family to leave.

What about travel within the Soviet Union? For many years, Communists had regarded internal passports as a Tsarist tool of oppression. But on December 27, 1932—in large part to control the flow of starving peasants and other undesirables into the cities—the Passport Law was established. All noncriminal townspeople over the age of sixteen automatically received a passport. But the law excluded peasants, who did not receive the automatic right to a passport until 1970.[55]

As part of the new passport system, OGPU inspectors increased their checks on people, especially on trains and in train stations. Further, all cities became classified as "open" or "closed"—that is, closed to anyone without a passport. Moscow was a closed city.

The results of the new passport law were pretty awful. *The Black Book of Communism* reports the following: "within the first week passportization 'discovered' 3,450 'ex-White Guards, ex-kulaks, and other criminal elements.' Nearly 385,000 people were refused passports in the closed cities and forced to vacate their homes within ten days." In total, "420,000 people were expelled from the open cities." During the summer of 1933, 5,470 Gypsies from Moscow were arrested and sent to Siberia.[56]

Here are a couple of examples of individual passport tragedies. K. Vino-gradova, a collective farm worker (like Nadya Stepanova), "was going to visit her brother, the chief of police in the eighth sector in Moscow, when she got picked up by the police after getting off the train at the wrong station. She was deported."[57] In 1938, a twenty-year-old man was arrested and sent to Kolyma because his passport was no longer valid.[58] Such stories are not un-common.

None of this is anywhere to be seen in *Song of Russia*: Nadya—a simple peasant girl—has the right (and the means) to travel freely about the coun-try, and even leave the country if she wishes.

Radios and Telephones

Discussing the portrayal of the Soviet village in *Song of Russia*, Ayn Rand says:

> [T]he peasants all have radios. . . . You see a scene where all the peasants are listening on radios, and one of them says, "There are more than millions lis-tening to the concert."
>
> I don't know whether there are a hundred people in Russia, private individ-uals, who own radios. . . . Such an idea that every farmer, a poor peasant, has a radio, is certainly preposterous. You also see that they have long-distance telephones. Later in the picture Taylor has to call his wife in the village by long-distance telephone. Where they got this long-distance phone, I don't know.[59]

This account is *somewhat* inaccurate—perhaps owing to the fact that lo-cal radio "flourished in the late 1920s and early 1930s,"[60] after Rand left Rus-sia. And in the film, not every peasant is shown with a radio; instead, there seems to be a radio around which several families are gathered. Still, Stepanov does say that millions are listening to the radio broadcast (and we are shown the border guards listening). But that *may* have resembled the So-viet reality right before the war.

On the one hand, the Soviets wanted to make radio broadcasts available to the widest number of people possible, since it was an especially efficient way of spreading propaganda at home and abroad.[61] On the other hand, So-viet economic inefficiency kept the supply of radios much lower than the de-mand. As a result, there were fewer radios in the villages, especially in the more remote ones.[62]

Another reason the Soviet reality here is difficult to determine with pre-cision is that statistics on the number of radios are what Sheila Fitzpatrick calls "Potemkin statistics"—that is, they were part of the Soviet attempt to present a favorable, though false, picture of village life.[63] Here is how Fitzpatrick describes the situation generally:

> If the goods sent for sale to rural cooperatives had been equally distributed among Soviet collective farms, every kolkhoz [collective farm] would have acquired one bicycle and one gramophone, with a reasonable chance of getting a sewing machine and a pocket watch as well. One kolkhoz out of six could have had an alarm clock, and one out of a hundred a motorcycle. In the real world, of course, many of these goods were siphoned off before they ever got to the rural cooperative store or sold to a handful of "millionaire" collective farms in the fertile south. But *in principle*, to use a favorite Soviet phrase, they were available to peasants. It was unlikely, but certainly not impossible, that an ordinary kolkhoznik would become the possessor of a watch, a sewing machine, or an iron bedstead.[64]

Radios definitely played a part in the Potemkin village—in creating "the image of abundance."[65] Radios—like grand pianos—were what Fitzpatrick calls "Potemkin goods."[66] A prize-winning tractor driver from Stalingrad boasted to the Second Congress of Outstanding Kolkhozniks: "We had a cabin for sixteen people in which each tractor-driver had a separate cot. In the cabin there were a radio, a wind-up gramophone, a clock, and music."[67] This was a Soviet boast. What were the actual statistics for the possession of radios in Soviet villages? Fitzpatrick reports that at the end of the 1930s, "only a quarter of all village clubs had their own radio receivers—and the receivers they had were very likely to be out of order."[68]

Vitaly Shentalinsky reports that in 1953, he "lived in a remote, tiny village in the Tartar republic where my father was chairman of the collective farm. Ours was the only radio in the whole village (it worked on batteries, of course, since there was no electricity there yet)."[69] So Rand is probably right about the essential point: Radios were less available than *Song of Russia* suggests.

Radio *transmitters* were, of course, forbidden. *The Black Book of Communism* reports that during the Great Terror, "anyone who had contacts outside the country, no matter how far removed, [was particularly vulnerable]. Such people, including *anyone who owned a radio transmitter*, collected stamps, or spoke Esperanto, stood a very good chance of being accused of espionage."[70]

There is less information available on telephones, though it is likely that Nadya's village would not have possessed one. Fitzpatrick describes one "Potemkin" report on a village telephone: "Vera Pankratova, an outstanding worker in the 'Iskra' kolkhoz, actually had a telephone installed in her izba [peasant hut] in 1935. . . . She was the first (and perhaps the only) peasant in Gorky krai [province] to be so honored."[71]

The Nazi–Soviet Pact

The Nazi–Soviet Pact—also known as the Hitler–Stalin Pact, the German–Soviet Pact and the Ribbentrop–Molotov Pact—was signed on August 23, 1939. In her HUAC testimony, Ayn Rand criticizes "the fact that an American conductor had accepted an invitation to come there and conduct a concert, and this took place in 1941 when Stalin was the ally of Hitler. That an American would accept an invitation to that country was shocking to me."[72]

Rand rejects the idea that the enemy of one's enemy is one's friend (more on this in chapter 7), but she would also maintain that the friend of a friend of Hitler is a friend of Hitler. Visiting Stalin's U.S.S.R. is bad enough. But here Rand is saying that an American visiting Hitler's ally is akin to him visiting Nazi Germany. She understandably finds this shocking—and so, in some sense, did the makers of *Song of Russia*, because they ultimately chose to evade the issue.

They hadn't always, as we saw in chapter 2. An early draft of the "Scorched Earth" screenplay included the following dialogue. In Nadya's presence, John refers to the Nazis as "your friends."

Nadya: Is that what you think—that the Nazis are our *friends?*
John: You signed a pact with them.
Nadya: It is because we have such good friends that sixty percent of our national budget goes for defense?[73]

Paul Jarrico was still offering a defense of the pact in a 1985 interview:

Patrick McGilligan: Do you doubt, historically, that the Pact was sensible?
Jarrico: I think the Pact made sense for the Soviet Union. The Pact was the Soviet Union double-crossing the double-crosser. It was a brilliant coup. It gained them some time, which they didn't use properly. Nevertheless, it achieved the aim of enabling the Soviet Union to deflect Hitler's onslaught or at least to postpone it.[74]

Lionel Stander (best known for his role as the chauffer on the TV series *Hart to Hart*) presents, in a 1983 interview, a rather common "former-Communist defense" of the Pact:

McGilligan: What was your reaction when you first heard of the Hitler-Stalin Pact?

Stander: I was cool. I figured it was a temporary thing, which it was, and that the reasons for the Pact was the inability of the democracies to line up with the Soviet Union against Hitler.[75]

There are, however, two major problems with these defenses of the pact—besides their ignoring the fact that the pact made Hollywood Communists Hitler's allies for a couple of years. First, they are revisionist history. Most significant—a point Ayn Rand emphasizes, and which is covered in the next section—they ignore the Soviet designs on other countries, especially on Poland. (That Jarrico and Stander could choose to ignore this as late as the 1980s is especially damning.) Second, these defenses of the pact ignore political philosophy.

The reason free countries like the United States, Great Britain, and France did not automatically "line up with the Soviet Union" is because the Soviet Union was in no way a free country. The free countries of the West were natural enemies of the Soviet Union. Any country even partially devoted to the conviction that every individual has the right to life, liberty, property, and the pursuit of happiness is the natural enemy of a country devoted to the idea that these are "bourgeois rights," and that every person owes his life, his labor, and the product of his labor to society or the state.

Similarly, the Soviet Union and Nazi Germany were natural allies.[76] The American Communists' führer, Stalin, was well aware of this. In a telegram to Ribbentrop, Stalin refers to the pact as a sign of "friendship, joined in blood."[77] And as Martin Amis points out, after the war, Stalin "was in the habit of repeating: 'Ech, together with the Germans we would have been invincible'."[78] Nazi Germany and Soviet Russia were two different forms of collectivism—more specifically, of socialism. It was perfectly natural that not only Stalin, but also members of the U.S. Communist Party, would support a pact with Hitler. And given collectivism's focus on the group and rejection of the individual, it is also natural that American Communists—all their claims to being antiracist notwithstanding—would disregard the racist nature of Hitler's Germany (just as Paul Robeson and other Communists would later disregard or deny the anti-Semitic nature of the Soviet Union and continue to give it their support[79]). Not only did Stalin, in the spirit of the pact, hand over more than 500 German Communists (many Jewish) to the Gestapo, the pact was in general extremely detrimental to the Jews (and especially Polish Jews). Arkady Vaksberg, in *Stalin Against the Jews*, reports:

German and Polish Jews, knowing nothing about this secret criminal deal be-tween two cannibals, continued to stream into the Soviet Union, hoping to find shelter in the most democratic and most humane state in the world. . . . Like moths drawn to a flame, European Jews flocked to [the Soviet Union], seeking salvation from the bloodthirsty Nazis. . . . Jews from western and cen-tral regions of Poland tried to cross over as quickly as possible to the areas of Soviet military units. Knowing he would be sending them to Germany and not wishing to waste time or money on this unwieldy operation, Stalin gave orders not to allow Jews onto "Soviet territory." They were shot at from both sides.[80]

Lionel Stander was no doubt cool with this, too.

That Hitler in the end attacked Stalin shows only that collectivist countries—like primitive tribes and inner-city gangs—are quite capable of going to war for any number of reasons (so long as war supports the group—the Volk or class). In Hitler's case, this was a turf war, not an indication of a major difference between the Soviet Union and Nazi Germany. He simply wanted to do to Russia what he and Stalin had already done to Poland.

The real surprise is that the United States, Great Britain, etc., became al-lies of the Soviet Union, and that many non-Communists supported such an alliance. (More on this issue in chapter 7.)

The Russian–Polish Border

The caption on a Soviet poster picturing a Young Pioneer with a rifle reads: "Everyone remembers the Stalinist words: 'We don't want the territory of oth-ers, but. . . .' And at that 'but' each one grips his weapon more tightly."[81] This is the foreign policy implicit in *Song of Russia*, where Russians are a free and peaceful people who would not harm anyone, though they are fully prepared to fight hard and make the sacrifices necessary to defeat any aggressor who attacks the Soviet Union. In fact, in an earlier draft of the screenplay, this is made ex-plicit. Much like this Soviet poster, a minor character says during a machine gun demonstration: "remember the words of Comrade Stalin: 'We don't want a foot of any other country's soil, but we won't yield an inch of our own'."[82]

The picture that the Soviet Union and *Song of Russia* paints of Soviet foreign policy is shockingly false, as Ayn Rand points out in her HUAC testimony:

> Now, here comes the crucial point of the picture. In the midst of this concert, when the heroine is playing, you see a scene on the border of the U.S.S.R. . . . It shows the U.S.S.R. sign, and there is a border guard standing. He is listen-ing to the concert. Then there is a scene inside kind of a guardhouse where the

guards are listening to the same concert, the beautiful Tschaikowsky music, and they are playing chess. Suddenly there is a Nazi attack on them. The poor, sweet Russians were unprepared. Now, realize—and that was a great shock to me—that the border that was being shown was the border of Poland. That was the border of an occupied, destroyed, enslaved country which Hitler and Stalin destroyed together. That was the border that was being shown to us—just a happy place with people listening to music.[83]

The Soviet oppression of Finland and the Baltic states is not in the film nor in Ayn Rand's testimony, and so is set aside here. It is Poland's border with the Soviet Union that plays a part in *Song of Russia*, at least implicitly. The detrimental effect of the Nazi–Soviet Pact on Polish Jews has already been noted. What else can be said about the Soviet treatment of Poland?[84]

The Soviet Union's official policy toward Poland is captured in this passage from a letter from Dimitrov to Stalin, dated September 26, 1939 (about a month after the signing of the pact):

The collapse of the reactionary Polish state, which exposed its internal rottenness, its military impotence, its complete political incapacity, is a historic retribution for the entire counterrevolutionary domestic and foreign policy which the Polish landowners and capitalists have been waging since the creation of the state. . . . [I]t was a prison of peoples which took the place of tsarism in oppressing Ukrainians, Belorussians, Jews, Lithuanians, and other nationalities. . . . By its entire reactionary foreign and domestic policy, it generated hatred of itself among the masses.[85]

And so on, ad nauseam. Of course, this is a grotesque and hypocritical rationalization. What the Soviets wanted was to enslave Poland and the rest of Eastern Europe (or as much of it as the Germans would allow).

The Nazi–Soviet Pact was the chance the Soviets were looking for. *The Black Book of Communism* reports:

Eight days after the signing of the pact, Nazi troops marched into Poland. One week later, after all Polish resistance had been crushed, and at the insistence of the Germans, the Soviet government proclaimed its intentions to occupy the territories to which it was entitled under the secret protocol of 23 August. On 17 September the Red Army entered Poland, on the pretext that it was coming to the aid of its "Ukrainian and Belorussian blood brothers," who were in danger because of "the disintegration of the Polish state." Soviet intervention met with little resistance, since the Polish army had been almost completely destroyed. The Soviet Union took 230,000 prisoners of war, including 15,000 officers.[86]

Not long after the Soviets went into Poland, the NKVD began "cleansing" eastern Poland of "hostile elements"—that is, "landowners, industrialists, shopkeepers, civil servants, policemen, and 'military colonists' . . . who had received a parcel of land from the Polish government in recognition of their service in the Soviet-Polish war of 1920."[87]

Over 380,000 Poles were deported to Siberia. After the Nazis attacked Russia, and the Soviets entered the war, amnesty was granted to many (but not all) of these Poles. Many Poles were released, but most of the Polish officers were unaccounted for. Poland demanded an explanation, but none was forthcoming. In April 1943, in the Katyn forest, the German Army discovered a mass grave containing the remains of about 4,500 Polish officers. The Red Cross determined that the Soviets were responsible, but the Soviets blamed the Germans. (Finally, in 1992, on an official visit to Warsaw, Boris Yeltsin admitted that the Soviet Union alone had been responsible for the Katyn massacre, in spring 1940.) Katyn was the largest such massacre, but it was not the only one. In total, nearly 15,000 Polish policemen and officers were murdered.[88]

Katyn is not all that far from where Tschaikowskoye is supposedly located—and yet it is light-years away.

Mother Russia

A major theme of *Song of Russia* is that the people of the Soviet Union—free, cultured, and happy—are willing to do whatever is necessary to defend their motherland. Everyone happily submits to civilian defense exercises; Peter is (unnecessarily) concerned that, as a twelve-year-old, he might not be able to stay behind and fight; Nadya temporarily chooses staying and fighting over going to America. In one scene, John meets up with a soldier who, though wounded, has returned to battle:

> Soldier: There's nothing so brave about [what I've done]. Thousands of others are doing the same thing.
> John: That's what so incredible. You never give up.
> Soldier: What's so incredible about it? Can you give up your mother's love? Can you forget the way she sang to you? The way she nursed you? Give up our land—how can we? It's our mother.[89]

In reality, once the Nazis attacked, and the war got going, many Soviet citizens did seem to forget their woes and support their country. Nevertheless, the mood of the people in *Song of Russia* does not accurately capture the attitude of Soviet citizens *before* the war. Ayn Rand does not deal with this issue directly in her HUAC testimony; but since this is a corollary of the issue of the general unhappiness of the Russian people—an issue that does concern her—this chapter includes a brief discussion of loyalty to the motherland.

In *Song of Russia*, the people are presented as lovers of their country and—to the extent that it is indicated at all—their system of government. But in fact, before the war, people fell into three groups: (1) patriots, (2) ambivalent people, and (3) defeatists, who hoped for a German victory.[90] There were more defeatists in the country than in the cities, and they seem to have consisted of those who were actively pro-Nazi and anti-Semitic, and/or those who longed for the end of Communism and thus of their suffering. Here are three (of many) lines recorded from disgruntled citizens, all of which depict an attitude that was not uncommon:

> If Hitler takes power, it will be better in Russia.
> If only war would start soon, I would be the first to destroy the communists.
> I think that if war comes, not a single [peasant] will go to the defense of Soviet power.[91]

This picture contradicts the one painted in *Song of Russia* and fits the broader picture of life in prewar Soviet Union sketched so far.

Culture

One of the themes of *Song of Russia* is that great music is an important part of Russian culture—or to put it more generally, that the Russians (unlike the Nazis) are a highly cultured people. At the opening of the film, Petrov says: "All hail the cultural achievements of our free people." The music student, Peter, points out to Meredith that Russian children have the opportunity to pursue musical training. During the evacuation of children from the village, as the Nazis approach, Meschkov reassures them that, "The music—the culture—we've been building here will never die."

In her HUAC testimony, Ayn Rand comments on this last line: "What culture? The culture of concentration camps."[92] And in an unpublished note on *Song of Russia*, Ayn Rand writes: "Here we see the Soviet citizens as happy, cultured music lovers—with no mention of any musical, literary or artistic purges, of Soviet celebrities vanishing overnight, of concentration camps loaded with artists and intellectuals."[93] Again, she sees a huge difference between *Song of Russia* and Soviet reality, and again, she is right.

Sheila Fitzpatrick writes: "Music was important in the Potemkin world. . . . In 1933, a photograph captioned 'As the prosperity of the kolkhoz masses grows, so does their cultural level' shows a peasant boy playing the violin."[94] This could be Peter, from *Song of Russia*. But let us contrast Peter—for whom so much had been possible, until his life was cut short by a Nazi's bullet—with an actual young violinist from around the same time, Gita Atlasman:

> In 1944 the brilliant violinist Gita Atlasman graduated from the Moscow Conservatory and her name was placed in gold letters on the marble honor board. (The graduation commission, chaired by Shostakovich, gave her the highest grade.) But she was not allowed to enter international competitions, and that determined her fate, depriving her of any protection.
>
> "You have a horrible [i.e., Jewish] surname," a ministry clerk explained frankly when the violinist tried to find out why she was being refused and denied everything. "Let me give you some friendly advice. Don't go anywhere and don't ask for anything," the kind man concluded.[95]

So much for the opportunities of young violinists. And being Jewish was not the only barrier to actualizing one's talents. Any deviation from Stalinism— that is, both Stalinist ideology and Stalin's whims—was a major (and often fatal) barrier.

Music was not the only field of art to be subjected to such harsh controls and restrictions—to such a lack of opportunity. For example, take the postwar theater. In *Song of Russia*, the only impediment to cultural achievement is the Nazis. But Shostakovich reports that Stalin forbade the presentation of the ghost in performances of *Hamlet* (presumably on Marxist-materialist grounds).[96] More grimly, in the late 1940s, in a frenzy of anti-Semitism, the ranks of Soviet theater critics were purged, and the director Solomon Mikhoels was murdered by the GPU.[97] I will return to the fate of writers shortly.

The arts were not the only realm of human endeavor in which the minds of men were enslaved. *The Black Book of Communism* reports:

> The intelligentsia were another social group who fell victim to the Great Terror. . . . [I]n March and April 1937, a virulent press campaign railed against 'deviationism' in economics, history, and literature. . . . Teachers and professors were especially vulnerable, since their lectures were readily accessible to zealous informers. Universities, institutes, and academicians were all decimated, notably in Belorussia (where 87 of the 105 academics were arrested as "Polish spies") and in Ukraine.

The Black Book of Communism goes on to give examples from astronomy, sta-tistics, genetics, botany, and biology. On this last: "Arrests were made . . . of several hundred biologists who opposed the charlatanism of the 'official' bi-ologist Trofim Lysenko."[98] Robert Conquest, in his study of the Great Terror, remarks on the same phenomena. Here is what he says about philosophy and linguistics:

> Stalin pervaded every sphere. In philosophy, for example, he was celebrated as a profound critic of Hegel, as the first to elucidate certain pronouncements of Aristotle, as the only man to bring out the full significance of Kant's theories. On the tercentenary of Spinoza's birth, *Pravda* had put in several quotations from Stalin, having nothing to do with Spinoza or even philosophy. . . . Stalin happened to say in an aside that the Azerbaijanis were obviously descended from the Medes. Though there is no basis for such a notion, it became estab-lished doctrine among the historians. Linguists spent fifteen years trying to find Median words in Azeri. Eventually thirty-five dubious Median words were found, although the Median language itself is mythical.[99]

In his destruction of the intelligentsia, Stalin is simply following Lenin, who wrote (in a letter to Maxim Gorky) that intellectuals "are not the brains of the nation. They're its shit."[100]

And while Hollywood Communists—many of whom were writers—si-multaneously presented themselves as defenders of the Soviet Union *and* of the First Amendment of the United States Constitution (a classic case of di-alectical thinking), what was happening to writers in the Soviet Union?[101] The numbers are staggering: Shentalinsky, in *Arrested Voices*, says that be-tween 1917 and 1991 (and mostly during the Stalin years), about 2,000 writ-ers were arrested, of whom 1,500 were killed or died as a result of their im-prisonment; *The Black Book of Communism* claims that 2,000 writers were arrested during the years of Stalin's terror. (Jewish writers were a major tar-get.)[102]

Anyone concerned with the memory of these writers should read *Arrested Voices*. Here, I briefly recount the fate of one writer, Isaac Babel. He was born in Odessa in 1894. His most famous collection of stories is *Red Cavalry*, pub-lished in 1926. On May 16, 1939, he was arrested, pretty much for the "crime" of suffering from writer's block—famous Soviet writers were expected to produce—and for not following the Party line completely (though he was fairly pro-Soviet, and seemed to have many Soviet friends and associates). He was held in the infamous Lubyanka, where he was interrogated, physi-cally and mentally tortured (he was most likely beaten with a rubber strap and threatened with the destruction of family and friends), forced to confess that he was a spy (which he was not), and to (falsely) denounce friends and associates. On January 27, 1940, at 1:30 A.M., he was shot.[103] Shentalinsky writes:

> There were a great many executions in early 1940. . . . [T]he bodies were taken away from the prisons at night to the crematorium at the former Donskoi Monastery in central Moscow. The ashes were then tipped into a pit at the cemetery there. . . . [A]mong them, in all probability, lie those of [Isaac Babel]. . . . When the pit was filled to overflowing it was leveled and for many years a modest stone explained that this was "Common grave No. 1" which contained "unclaimed ashes, 1930 to 1942 inclusive." The stone remains there to this day but now it backs on to a monument, formally inaugurated in August 1991, which bears the inscription: "Here lie buried the remains of the innocent tortured and executed victims of the political repressions. May they never be forgotten!"[104]

This was only one possible fate of writers who stayed in the Soviet Union:

> Under the Soviet regime writers suffered from an infinite variety of repressive measures. These went beyond execution and imprisonment, internal exile and expulsion abroad, to cripple the life and work of many others. Marina Tsvetaeva was driven to commit suicide. Others were harassed and not published for years on end. Many were forced to step on the throat of their own song and drown the promise of their first works in feeble praise of the regime. They killed their talent in order to live.[105]

This is what happened to any artist or thinker who fell under Stalin's disfavor. What about those who actively sought his favor and gave him their support?

Ayn Rand, in *Atlas Shrugged*, dramatizes how dictatorship results in what she calls a brain drain—the best minds escaping the dictatorship or being destroyed. This phenomenon is made clear, in the case of writers, in *Arrested Voices*. If the brains are drained, what is left are the brainless. The so-called writers, scientists, artists, etc., who embraced Stalin are what Robert Conquest calls "the old and talentless Communist lumpen-intelligentsia:"[106] party hacks and bootlickers. Not only did such people toe the Party line, they often acted as informers.[107] In some cases their motives might have been simply to stay alive. More often than not, they sought the readily available privileges and honors that went with being an intellectual or artist in Stalin's good graces: higher salaries, better living spaces, better vacations, etc.[108] Envy must have been another powerful motive, many of them no doubt having the attitude: "I can never be a Dostoyevsky (or even an Isaac Babel); but

I can be one of Stalin's favorites, and winner of a Stalin Medal—happy in the knowledge that no genuine writer will be allowed to rise to the level of a Dostoyevsky."

In 1949, Ayn Rand was asked about a Soviet–American "Cultural Conference," held in the United States, and the Soviet delegates to that conference. Her reply presents her opinion of those Russian artists who chose to cooperate with the Soviet government in order to stay alive:

> I do not "understand the tragic dilemma of the Iron Curtain delegates," and I do not "pity these men." I despise them. The men I pity are the ones who preferred to go to a Soviet concentration camp rather than make careers under a totalitarian government and go crawling on their bellies all over the world, glorifying their own slavery and their masters.[109]

Lillian Hellman, a writer and contemporary of Rand's, had a different view. She supported these delegates and, with no threat of a concentration camp or gulag hanging over her head, she freely assisted them in glorifying their slavery and their Stalinist masters.[110]

In *Song of Russia*, Boris, patting his son Peter on the back, says: "We grow many fine things in our country, but the finest crop of all is this." But the reality was that Soviet Russia was producing rotten fruit, having destroyed the best.

At this point, let us take a brief excursion away from Russia and to Hollywood, and explore Communist artists there. For all of their posturing and claims about the freedom of expression, Hollywood Communists were creating the same kind of "culture." In their own Party, they clamped down on any dissent—on any writing that strayed from the Party line and any attempts to defend a writer's freedom of expression. When Albert Maltz called for greater appreciation of writers who did not stick so closely to the Party line, he was, in effect, placed on trial and forced to write a retraction. (The Communists were not in power, so he merely lost his dignity, not his life.) Budd Schulberg was told that his novel *What Makes Sammy Run* deviated from Party ideology and thus had to be changed. Because he was not such a Communist as to be totally lacking in autonomy (and because this was America and not the Soviet Union), he could politely tell his comrades to go to hell.[111] It is not hard to imagine what the reaction of the Party would have been had the Communists been in power.

There would have been no difference between their Soviet America and Stalin's Soviet Union, which American Communists supported with all their hearts and minds and souls.[112] As an indication, consider the fact that *New Masses* published a symposium on the subject, "Should Ezra Pound Be

Shot?" (He broadcast Fascist propaganda during the war, which is arguably treason in wartime.) None of the five symposiasts (including the play-wright Arthur Miller) said no. Here is part of Albert Maltz's contribution: "It is because he is a poet that he should be hanged, not once, but twice— for treason as a citizen, and for his poet's betrayal of all that is decent in civilization."[113]

Many Hollywood Communists—not unlike many Soviet hacks—were in-terested in a bargain: "Give me a Beverly Hills home and swimming pool and salary, and I'll defend the world's poor and exploited." (This is still consid-ered a favorable arrangement among Hollywood leftists.) But Hollywood Communists were no doubt sometimes motivated by envy as well—by the awareness, in effect, "that I can more easily rise in a Soviet America than I can in a capitalist America, and no genuine writer can rise above me."

Consider Bernard Gordon, a blacklisted writer (perhaps best known for his screenplay for *Day of the Triffids*), who—not because of government de-cree, but because studios did not wish to hire Communists (for the same rea-sons they did not want to hire Nazis)—had to go to *Europe* to find work. In his autobiography, he comes across as an unrepentant Marxist, who, puppet-like Communist that he was, disavowed Stalinism when he was told to. By whom? By Khrushchev, the dictator who took Stalin's place. Gordon is in-credibly easy on himself—he supported Stalin because, he claims, at that time anyone who was "a principled, self-respecting person" supported Stalin—and the entire book is written in a whiny and childishly self-centered style. His mawkish concern for the poor notwithstanding, he shows no genuine compassion. He never comes to terms with Stalin's victims, and his and his comrades' role in creating them, or at the very least, muffling their cries. His attitude, in effect, is: 'The hell with Stalin's victims, the U.S. government made life difficult for *me!*'[114]

At most, the blacklist "cost us"—in this case—*Day of the Triffids II*. What did the Stalinism supported by the Hollywood Communists cost us? Shen-talinsky ends his *Arrested Voices* with the following: "For years a soot-stained chimney released a stream of smoke over the Lubyanka and for decades sprin-kled Moscow with the ash of incinerated manuscripts. How many books were consumed by that chimney, never to be read by another person!"[115] In light of what was happening to writers in that country, I confess that I cannot muster one ounce of compassion for the fate of Bernard Gordon and the rest of the blacklisted Communists.

Let us return to culture in *Song of Russia* versus actual Soviet culture. As always, big lies have nasty consequences. Whether or not the creators of *Song of Russia* knew of the falsehood that film presented about Russian culture, and whatever their actual motives, this lie had a negative effect. As Arkady Vaksburg writes:

> The triumphs of young Soviet artists in the international arena were part of the propaganda program to deflect attention from Soviet reality. The enthusiastic shouts for the graceful successes of Soviet polar explorers, pilots, athletes, border patrols, and musicians were designed to drown out the sounds of executioners' bullets and the groans of innumerable victims.[116]

To the extent to which the audience of *Song of Russia* believed the film, they ignored Soviet reality—the concentration camp "culture," the groans of Stalin's victims.

Terror

After Ayn Rand's general statement about *Song of Russia*, John McDowell (Republican congressman from Pennsylvania) asked a question that led to an unusual exchange:

> McDowell: Don't [the Russians] do things at all like Americans? Don't they walk across town to visit their mother-in-law or somebody?
> Rand: Look, it is very hard to explain. It is almost impossible to convey to a free people what it is like to live in a totalitarian dictatorship. I can tell you a lot of details. I can never completely convince you, because you are free. It is in a way good that you can't even conceive of what it is like. Certainly they have friends and mothers-in-law. They try to live a human life, but you understand it is totally inhuman. Try to imagine what it is like if you are in constant terror from morning till night and at night you are waiting for the doorbell to ring, where you are afraid of anything and everybody, living in a country where human life is nothing, less than nothing, and you know it. You don't know who . . . is going to do what to you because you may have friends who spy on you, where there is no law and any rights of any kind.[117]

I find it unfortunate (and bizarre) to have to defend this accurate description of life under Soviet dictatorship; but as we shall see in chapter 8, Congressman McDowell is not the only one who denies the validity of Rand's description—that is, who claims that Stalinist Russia wasn't all that bad. The life of the average Soviet in the period portrayed in *Song of Russia* was miserable. He was also living in terror.[118] (As Fitzpatrick writes: "Terror . . . was so frequently used that it must be regarded as a systemic characteristic of Stalinism in the 1930s."[119]) Here, I'll simply make two additions to what we have seen so far: (1) some statistics that will hopefully project the scope of what happened in the Soviet Union in the 1930s and early 1940s and (2) an account of the effect living under terror had on people.

Here is a "tally" of terror from *The Black Book of Communism*:

- 6 million dead as a result of the famine of 1932–33, a catastrophe that can be blamed largely on the policy of enforced collectivization and the predatory tactics of the central government in seizing the harvests of the *kolkhozy*.
- 720,000 executions, 680,000 of which were carried out in 1937–38, usually after some sort of travesty of justice by a special GPU or NKVD court.
- 300,000 known deaths in the camps from 1934 to 1940. By extrapolating these figures back to 1930–33 (years for which very few records are available), we can estimate that some 400,000 died during the decade, not counting the incalculable number of those who died between the moment of their arrest and their registration as prisoners in one of the camps.
- 600,000 registered deaths among the deportees, refugees, and "specially displaced."
- Approximately 2,200,000 deported, forcibly moved, or exiled as "specially displaced people."
- A cumulative figure of 7 million people who entered the camps and Gulag colonies from 1934 to 1941 (information for the years 1930–33 remains imprecise).

On 1 January 1940 some 1,670,000 prisoners were being held in the 53 groups of corrective work camps and the 425 corrective work colonies. One year later the figure had risen to 1,930,000. In addition, prisons held 200,000 people awaiting trial or a transfer to camp.[120]

What was the nature of Soviet terror? First, who was targeted? The "usual suspects" (as Fitzpatrick calls them) were "former members of other political parties, former priests and nuns, former White Army officers," as well as family members of undesirables, children of kulaks or merchants, socially dangerous university faculty and students, and the list goes on.[121] Of course, one could try to conceal one's social identity—and many did—though the price could be high. If you were caught, the punishment was severe; and, psychologically, you would live in constant anxiety and fear of being caught. As someone who lived through the period put it, "You can, with the help of *blat* [pull], get false documents and work for a few years, but you can never have peace with this kind of affair."[122]

But the usual suspects were not the only suspects. Everyone was a suspect, and anyone could be arbitrarily arrested. In 1935, the writer Pavel Florensky said that "in the Soviet Union they punish people for no reason at all."[123] (He was executed on December 8, 1937.) In 1938, a local official remarked: "[T]hey are putting people in prison for nothing now."[124] Robert Conquest reports that an "American journalist living in a block of about 160 apartments in the summer of 1937 notes that the Secret Police had made arrests in more than half of them."[125] Enemies, the state said, were everywhere.[126]

The reactions of people living under such a system are not difficult to guess. First, there is the initial shock and puzzlement over the arrest on the part of the victim and his family. Conquest writes:

> If experienced politicians felt baffled, the man in the street was even more uncomprehending: "I asked myself and others, why, what for? No one could give me an answer." As for victims, the first words on entering a cell were almost always, we are told, a shaken "But why, why?" The prison and camp literature tells of the same phrase, "Why?", often found written on cell walls, carved into the sides of prison wagons, and on the planks of the transit camps.[127]

Family and friends of those arrested were deeply concerned and anxious about the fate of their loved ones. And given the Soviet penchant for treating children, spouses, friends, and associates as polluted by their connection to an undesirable, such relations also felt increased fear over their own situation and were in many cases ostracized by those who—concerned about their own fates—did not want to be tainted by the tainted. Distrust was rampant during this period. Isaac Babel said that "today a man only talks freely with his wife—at night, with the blanket pulled over his head."[128]

But strongest of all was the fear of the nighttime knock at the door, and eventual execution. Fitzpatrick explains: "Even in terror, there are rituals. Arrests are made at night, so the sound of a car stopping, feet going up the stairs at 2 or 3 A.M., and knocks on doors, are vividly remembered by most memoirists."[129] A classic joke from the period goes as follows:

> 1937. Night. A ring at the door. The husband goes to answer. He returns and says: "Don't worry, dear, it is bandits who have come to rob us."[130]

In 1935, the writer Boris Pilnyak said: "There is not a single thinking adult in this country who has not at some time thought that he might be shot." (He was executed—shot in the head—on December 21, 1938.)[131]

As Ayn Rand said in her HUAC testimony, and as Robert Conquest was to remark later, it is difficult for people who live under freedom to understand life under terror. Here is Conquest:

> It is very hard for the Western reader to envisage the sufferings of the Soviet people as a whole during that time. And in considering the Terror, it is precisely this moral and intellectual effort which needs to be made. . . . It is easy

to speak of the constant fear of the 4 a.m. knock on the door, of the hunger, fatigue and hopelessness of the great labour camps. But to feel how this was worse than a particularly frightful war is not so simple. . . . What is so hard to convey about the feeling of Soviet citizens through 1936–38 is the similar long-drawn-out sweat of fear, night after night, that the moment of arrest might arrive before the next dawn. . . . Fear by night, and a feverish effort by day to pretend enthusiasm for a system of lies, was the permanent condition of the Soviet citizen.[132]

This feeling of fear was at its worst in 1937–1938, but it also existed in the prior decade, and afterwards, until the Nazis attacked and the Soviets went to war (which many regarded as a breath of fresh air compared to the terror).[133] This fear would return after the war and remain at least until Stalin's death in 1952—and to a degree, until the fall of Communism.

But in a sense, in the period immediately following the worst of the terror—the period that most concerns us—the attitude of Soviet citizens was not quite the same as it was in those years. The worst years produced "a terrified level of almost unrelieved conformism." Conquest continues:

In the country as a whole a new public mood had been created. The experience had given the ruled as well as the rulers a new impress. The population had become habituated to silence and obedience, to fear and submission. In the years which remained of Stalin's rule after the Purges, the all-out mass terror was no longer necessary. The machine had been started up, and could now be kept rolling without extraordinary efforts. It is true, in a sense, that the comparative calm which may reign in an autocracy following the elimination of opponents or potential opponents is no less a manifestation of terror than the original killings—is, in fact, merely a product and consolidation of them.[134]

The film historian Fred Lawrence Guiles disagrees. In *Hanging on in Paradise*, he presents Ayn Rand's exchange with McDowell as something rather comical and chastises her for lacking a sense of humor. He wished she had lightened up while talking about Stalinist terror. Commenting on Rand's response to McDowell, he writes: "It was especially difficult for the genial Mr. MacDowell [sic] to imagine over 200,000,000 Russians lying every night in their unhappy beds waiting for doorbells to ring."[135]

In light of what we know about the conditions in the Soviet Union in the 1930s and the 1940s—and what Guiles could certainly have known in 1975—I find his remark morally disgusting. Unfortunately, he is not alone. As we shall see in chapter 8, such a dismissal of Rand and her testimony—coupled with a lack of concern for Stalin's victims—is standard leftist fare.

During the 1940s and 1950s, many leftists in America—and certainly the Communists—dismissed the claims of Rand and others about Stalin's terror. This is not to say they were unconcerned about all "terror." Consider this advertisement from the Freedom from Fear Committee, which appeared in the *Hollywood Reporter* two months after the HUAC hearings:

TIRED? JITTERY? SLEEPING BADLY?
Find out The Reason. Test Yourself! Here Are 10 Questions:
If you score 25, you're in the danger zone! Score 5 for each YES answer.
1. Are you nervous about whom you sit with in the commissary?
2. Are you thinking about changing your name? . . . .
3. Are you haunted by your past? Remember? Your fourth vote for Roosevelt? The ambulance you helped send to Republican Spain? . . .
4. Are you giving up that idea for a story? Or changing a scene—just a little?
5. Are you thinking you'd better drop your subscription to: The Nation? Commonweal? New Republic? . . . . [etc.]
6. Do you think you hear a strange click every time you pick up your phone?
7. Are you thinking of hiding any of your books in your incinerator?
8. Do you think about the future safety of your children—when you lie awake nights?
9. Do you experience mixed feelings at the news that England has offered sanctuary to political refugees from the American motion picture industry?
10. DO YOU THINK THAT *YOU* ARE SAFE FROM BLACKLISTS?[136]

Note point 8, and the concern it expresses for those lying awake at night in fear; then consider Guiles's response to Rand's remarks about terror. At the time of the 1947 HUAC hearings and after, while the Left chattered about such "terror" in the United States, the spiritual brothers of Fred Lawrence Guiles ignored Stalin's very real terror. There are many possible motives for such behavior on the Left during this period; compassion is not one of them.

Notes

1. *Hearings Regarding the Communist Infiltration of the Motion Picture Industry* (Hearings Before the Committee on Un-American Activities, House of Representatives, Eightieth Congress, First Session, October 20, 21, 22, 23, 24, 27, 28, 29, and 30, 1947) (Washington, DC: United States Government Printing Office, 1947), 83. For Rand's views on propaganda generally, see Ayn Rand, *The Romantic Manifesto: A Philosophy of Literature* (New York: Signet, 1975), 22–23; Ayn Rand, *The Art of Fic-*

tion: A Guide for Writers and Readers, ed. Tore Boeckmann (New York: Plume, 2000), 69; Ayn Rand, *The Art of Nonfiction: A Guide for Writers and Readers*, ed. Robert Mayhew (New York: Plume, 2001), 27–40, 116–17, 152; David Harriman, ed., *Journals of Ayn Rand* (New York: Plume, 1997), 57–59; and, "Screen Guide for Americans" (in Harriman, *Journals of Ayn Rand*, 356–67).

2. From her article "Judas Goats," written for the magazine of the Screen Writers Guild, and quoted in Kenneth Lloyd Billingsley, *Hollywood Party: How Communism Seduced the American Film Industry in the 1930s and 1940s* (Rocklin, CA: Prima, 1998), 198. She moves slightly away from this extreme (and extremely inaccurate) position in *Scoundrel Time* (New York: Bantam Books, 1976), 68: "Movie producers knew full well that the Communists of Hollywood had never made a single Communist picture."

3. Jerry Schwartz, "Some Actors Outraged by Kazan Award," *Associated Press*, March 13, 1999.

4. In earlier treatments and versions of the screenplay, there was a heavy dose of "anti-U.S. neutrality" propaganda. But with America in the war, as work on the film progressed the issue of U.S. neutrality or "isolationism" had become passé. As a result, most overt antineutrality propaganda was removed before the film was completed.

5. When Rand quotes dialogue from the film, she is remarkably accurate. (She took notes during her sole viewing of *Song of Russia*.) In the case of substantial quotes, I provide the exact line from the film. In this case it was: "I have a great responsibility, to my family and to my village, and to the way in which I've lived. I don't quite see how I can build a life with you, and then also help to build a better and better life for my country."

6. *Hearings Regarding the Communist Infiltration of the Motion Picture Industry* (1947), 86–87.

7. Little about America is presented in *Song of Russia*; the focus is on the Soviet Union. But the implication throughout is that America is good—just as Russia is good. At one point, however, the film slips. Nadya asks John to tell her about America. It's wonderful, he says. When she asks why, he responds: "I don't know."

8. *Hearings Regarding the Communist Infiltration of the Motion Picture Industry* (1947), 87. The actual quote from Boris is virtually identical: "You can go back to your country and tell them what you have seen here."

9. *Hearings Regarding the Communist Infiltration of the Motion Picture Industry* (1947), 86.

10. The exact line from the film is: "I come from a small town, too. A little place in New England called Lexington. A lot of fools, like you, fought for that once—died for it, right there on the Village Green."

11. *Hearings Regarding the Communist Infiltration of the Motion Picture Industry* (1947), 87.

12. Sheila Fitzpatrick, *Everyday Stalinism: Ordinary Life in Extraordinary Times: Soviet Russia in the 1930s* (New York: Oxford University Press, 1999), 226.

13. Quoted in Stephen Koch, *Double Lives: Spies and Writers in the Secret Soviet War of Ideas Against the West* (New York: The Free Press, 1994), 200.

14. Since I am not a Sovietologist and cannot read Russian, I have tried in every case to rely on secondary sources that themselves rely for the most part on primary sources: archival material, interviews, letters, Soviet newspapers, etc. This explains the high degree of my reliance on, and the numerous quotations from, secondary sources in this chapter.

15. Fitzpatrick, *Everyday Stalinism*, 51, 66, 69, 105.

16. Fitzpatrick, *Everyday Stalinism*, 2. Aleksander Topolski, in his memoirs about his time in Russia just before and during the war, often comments on the lack of basic goods, compared to what was available in Poland. See *Without Vodka: Adventures in Wartime Russia* (South Royalton, VT: Steerforth Press, 2001), 12–13.

17. Fitzpatrick, *Everyday Stalinism*, 43.

18. Both letters quoted in Fitzpatrick, *Everyday Stalinism*, 43.

19. Fitzpatrick, *Everyday Stalinism*, 93. See also Walter Krivitsky's description of Moscow's Hotel Lux, in W. G. Krivitsky, *In Stalin's Secret Service* (New York: Enigma Books, 2000), 59.

20. *Hearings Regarding the Communist Infiltration of the Motion Picture Industry* (1947), 74–76.

21. Fitzpatrick, *Everyday Stalinism*, 46.

22. Quoted in Fitzpatrick, *Everyday Stalinism*, 47.

23. Fitzpatrick, *Everyday Stalinism*, 47.

24. Quoted in Fitzpatrick, *Everyday Stalinism*, 51.

25. Fitzpatrick, *Everyday Stalinism*, 80.

26. Fitzpatrick, *Everyday Stalinism*, 51, 69. On the meaning of "Potemkin," see note 34.

27. Fitzpatrick, *Everyday Stalinism*, 52.

28. Fitzpatrick, *Everyday Stalinism*, 52.

29. Quoted in Fitzpatrick, *Everyday Stalinism*, 105.

30. Stéphen Courtois et al., *The Black Book of Communism: Crimes, Terror, Repression*, trans. Jonathan Murphy and Mark Kramer (Cambridge: Harvard University Press, 1999), 214.

31. On children in Stalin's Russia generally, see Lewis Siegelbaum and Andrei Sokolov, eds., *Stalinism as a Way of Life* (New Haven, CT: Yale University Press, 2000), ch. 6. The chapter title—"Happy Childhoods"—is obviously ironic.

32. Courtois et al., *Black Book of Communism*, 178.

33. Quoted in Robert Conquest, *Kolyma: The Arctic Death Camps* (New York: Viking, 1978), 193–94.

34. "[Prince Gregory] Potemkin made a great effort to populate and develop the newlywon southern lands. The display which Potemkin put up for Catherine the Great, Emperor Joseph II of Austria, and the Polish king Stanislaw Poniatowski when they visited the area in early 1787 gave rise to the expression 'Potemkin villages,' i.e., pieces of stage décor which passed at a distance for real buildings and communities."

Nicholas V. Riasanovsky, A History of Russia, 3rd ed. (Oxford: Oxford University Press, 1977), 294.

35. Fitzpatrick, Everyday Stalinism, 9. See also Sheila Fitzpatrick, Stalin's Peasants: Resistance and Survival in the Russian Village After Collectivization (Oxford: Oxford University Press, 1994), ch. 10.

36. The exact line in the film is: "here you are at a simple, peasant farm table, where we have nothing to offer you but our company, and the country food we eat ourselves."

37. Hearings Regarding the Communist Infiltration of the Motion Picture Industry (1947), 84–87.

38. Fitzpatrick, Stalin's Peasants, 48. See Stalin's Peasants, ch. 2, and Courtois et al., Black Book of Communism, ch. 7.

39. Fitzpatrick, Stalin's Peasants, 52, 153.

40. Courtois et al., Black Book of Communism, 146.

41. Fitzpatrick, Stalin's Peasants, 233. See Stalin's Peasants, chs. 2,5, & 9.

42. Quoted in Fitzpatrick, Everyday Stalinism, 43. Topolski writes: "I knew that 'not everything is perfect in the Soviet Union' but I never thought that it was so bad that free citizens would be buying bread from prisoners," a practice he witnessed. He adds: "And this was in 1940, before the Soviets were at war with Germany." Not Without Vodka, 195.

43. Fitzpatrick, Everyday Stalinism, 89.

44. Hearings Regarding the Communist Infiltration of the Motion Picture Industry (1947), 85.

45. Quoted in Fitzpatrick, Everyday Stalinism, 80.

46. On tractors and horses, see Fitzpatrick, Stalin's Peasants, 136–39, 216–17; on medicine, Stalin's Peasants, 217; on electricity, Stalin's Peasants, 218.

47. Fitzpatrick, Stalin's Peasants, 318.

48. Hearings Regarding the Communist Infiltration of the Motion Picture Industry (1947), 85.

49. Hearings Regarding the Communist Infiltration of the Motion Picture Industry (1947), 168–69.

50. Courtois et al., Black Book of Communism, 172–74, 200. See also Fitzpatrick, Stalin's Peasants, 204; Fitzpatrick, Everyday Stalinism, 119.

51. Fitzpatrick, Stalin's Peasants, 6–7, 207, 213. Note that Article 124 of the new (June 12, 1936) constitution, which describes religious freedom in the Soviet Union, had nothing to do with any religious revival. See Siegelbaum and Sokolov, Stalinism as a Way of Life, 184–86.

52. See, for instance, Fitzpatrick, Stalin's Peasants, 283.

53. Fitzpatrick, Everyday Stalinism, 18.

54. Hearings Regarding the Communist Infiltration of the Motion Picture Industry (1947), 83, 84, 86.

55. On the passport law, see Fitzpatrick, Stalin's Peasants, 92–96, and Courtois et al., Black Book of Communism, 175–77.

56. Courtois et al., *Black Book of Communism*, 176.

57. Courtois et al., *Black Book of Communism*, 176–77. It is true that by the 1940s it was easier to bribe an official and receive a passport. But this is travel by permission, not by right. One could still be caught by the secret police.

58. Vitaly Shentalinsky, *Arrested Voices: Resurrecting the Disappeared Writers of the Soviet Regime*, trans. John Crowfoot (New York: Free Press, 1996), 136.

59. *Hearings Regarding the Communist Infiltration of the Motion Picture Industry* (1947), 86.

60. James von Geldern, "Radio Moscow: The Voice from the Center," in *Culture and Entertainment in Wartime Russia*, ed. Richard Stites, 45 (Bloomington: Indiana University Press, 1995).

61. In prison in the Soviet Union, Topolski met a number of "Ukrainians who had been living in the Bukovina area of Romania and, hearing incessant Soviet radio propaganda, decided to escape from Romania to the Soviet workers' paradise "where 'sausages hang on fences for the picking and wells are filled with beer'." *Without Vodka*, 40.

62. See von Geldern, "Radio Moscow."

63. Fitzpatrick, *Stalin's Peasants*, 271.

64. Fitzpatrick, *Stalin's Peasants*, 266.

65. Fitzpatrick, *Everyday Stalinism*, 90–92.

66. Fitzpatrick, *Stalin's Peasants*, 268.

67. Quoted in Fitzpatrick, *Stalin's Peasants*, 264.

68. Fitzpatrick, *Stalin's Peasants*, 271.

69. Shentalinsky, *Arrested Voices*, 1.

70. Courtois et al., *Black Book of Communism*, 188 (emphasis added).

71. Fitzpatrick, *Stalin's Peasants*, 264.

72. *Hearings Regarding the Communist Infiltration of the Motion Picture Industry* (1947), 86.

73. Paul Jarrico and Richard Collins, 10/30 – 11/24/42 (MHL 2996f.2928–29).

74. Patrick McGilligan and Paul Buhle, eds., *Tender Comrades: A Backstory of the Hollywood Blacklist* (New York: St. Martin's Griffin, 1997), 335.

75. McGilligan and Buhle, *Tender Comrades*, 617.

76. See Krivitsky, *In Stalin's Secret Service*, ch. 1, and Koch, *Double Lives*, chs. 2–5.

77. Arkady Vaksberg, *Stalin Against the Jews*, trans. Antonina W. Bouis (New York: Alfed A. Knopf, 1994), 103.

78. Martin Amis, *Koba the Dread: Laughter and the Twenty Million* (New York: Hyperion, 2002), 193.

79. For a brief account of Paul Robeson's betrayal of Soviet Jews, see David Horowitz, *Radical Son: A Generational Odyssey* (New York: Simon & Schuster, 1997), 73–74. Lillian Hellman too was aware of anti-Semitism in Soviet Russia, but said nothing. See Joan Mellen, *Hellman and Hammett: The Legendary Passion of Lillian Hellman and Dashiell Hammett* (New York: HarperCollins, 1996), 231.

80. Vaksberg, *Stalin Against the Jews*, 105. For more on the pact's negative effect on Jews, see *Stalin Against the Jews*, ch. 6.

81. Fitzpatrick, *Everyday Stalinism*, 71.

82. "Scorched Earth," screenplay, Paul Jarrico and Richard Collins, 9/11/42 (MHL 2996–f.2925–26).

83. *Hearings Regarding the Communist Infiltration of the Motion Picture Industry* (1947), 86. Otto Friedrich comments: "Miss Rand was sufficiently an ideologue to point out that the border station where the Nazis attacked the . . . guards must have been located in central Poland, where Stalin had established them at the time of his alliance with Hitler." *City of Nets: A Portrait of Hollywood in the 1940s* (New York: Harper & Row, 1986). This is a bizarre remark. If one can make sense of it at all, Friedrich is criticizing Rand for pointing out the truth—a truth that supports her "ideological" (and correct) critique of this aspect of the film. The German attack on Minsk and Smolensk (supposedly twenty miles from the village in *Song of Russia*), which was headed for Moscow, originated in Poland. See John Keegan, *The Second World War* (New York: Penguin, 1989), 182–83.

84. On the Soviet treatment of Poland generally, see *Black Book of Communism*, ch. 19: "Poland: 'Enemy Nation'."

85. Alexander Dallin and F. I. Firsov, eds., *Dimitrov and Stalin, 1939–1943: Letters from the Soviet Archives* (New Haven, CT: Yale University Press, 2000), 156.

86. Courtois et al., *Black Book of Communism*, 208.

87. Courtois et al., *Black Book of Communism*, 209.

88. Courtois et al., *Black Book of Communism*, 211, 367–69.

89. This kind of story was standard fare in wartime Russia. See Louise McReynolds, "Dateline Stalingrad: Newspaper Correspondents at the Front," in Stites, ed., *Culture and Entertainment in Wartime Russia*, 36.

90. I use the terminology employed in Courtois et al., *Black Book of Communism*, 215.

91. Quoted in Fitzpatrick, *Everyday Stalinism*, 171, Fitzpatrick, *Stalin's Peasants*, 289. Topolski reports that in the remote villages near the Afghanistan border, as a result of effective German propaganda, "The locals whispered among themselves that Hitler was a good Muslim and the German Army would free them from the Soviet yoke." *Without Vodka*, 337.

92. *Hearings Regarding the Communist Infiltration of the Motion Picture Industry* (1947), 87.

93. From "Some Film Reviews," in the Ayn Rand Archives.

94. Fitzpatrick, *Stalin's Peasants*, 264.

95. Vaksberg, *Stalin Against the Jews*, 146.

96. *Testimony: The Memoirs of Dmitri Shostakovich*, as related to and edited by Solomon Volkov, translated by Antonina W. Bouis (New York: Limelight Editions, 1990), 85–86.

97. Vaksberg, *Stalin Against the Jews*, ch. 8.

98. Courtois et al., *Black Book of Communism*, 199–200.

99. Robert Conquest, *The Great Terror: Stalin's Purge of the Thirties* (New York: Macmillan, 1968), 497–98.

100. Amis, *Koba the Dread*, 15. Lillian Hellman visited Russia in 1944, and wrote in her diary of "the deep reverence & respect that even intellectuals have for Stalin." Mellen, *Hellman and Hammett*, 231. Bizarre as always. But then, when it came to American writers describing Stalinist Russia, to paraphrase Lenin, Hellman was not the brains of the nation but its shit.

101. It is worth mentioning that at the same time writers were being oppressed, libraries were being purged of books. See Siegelbaum and Sokolov, *Stalinism as a Way of Life*, 77–84.

102. Shentalinsky, *Arrested Voices*, 6; Courtois et al., *Black Book of Communism*, 200; Vaksberg, *Stalin Against the Jews*, passim.

103. Shentalinsky, *Arrested Voices*, ch. 2. I chose Babel, not because he was the most heroic of the murdered writers (he was not opposed—or at least not sufficiently opposed—to the Soviet regime), and not because I am fond of his writing style (I dislike the gritty realism of his short stories). Babel is a good example, because he is relatively well known in the West, and as a (lukewarm) friend of the regime, his fate underscores what happened to writers who did not become *complete* puppets.

104. Shentalinsky, *Arrested Voices*, 70.

105. Shentalinsky, *Arrested Voices*, 284.

106. Robert Conquest, in his introduction to Shentalinsky, *Arrested Voices*, vii.

107. Fitzpatrick, *Everyday Stalinism*, 166–67.

108. Fitzpatrick, *Everyday Stalinism*, 102, 109, 111–12.

109. Michael S. Berliner, ed., *Letters of Ayn Rand* (New York: Dutton, 1995), 435.

110. See Mellen, *Hellman and Hammett*, 267.

111. On the Maltz affair, see Kenneth Lloyd Billingsley, *Hollywood Party: How Communism Seduced the American Film Industry in the 1930s and 1940s* (Rocklin, CA: Prima Publishing, 1998), ch. 11, "Hollywood Inquisition." On Budd Schulberg and *What Makes Sammy Run*, see *Hollywood Party*, 48–49.

112. As Harvey Klehr, John Earl Haynes, and Kyrill M. Anderson document in *The Soviet World of American Communism* (New Haven, CT: Yale University Press, 1998), 215–51, American Communists in Russia collaborated "with the Comintern and the Soviet state in decisions about whether an American should be allowed to return to the United States" (216). The authors conclude: "Of the shameful episodes in the history of American communism recounted thus far, the CPUSA's abandonment of at least several hundred and probably more than a thousand of its own to Stalin's Terror is surely one of the worst" (251). I see no reason to assume that the Hollywood Communists who stuck with the Party through the Great Terror and the Nazi–Soviet Pact would have behaved much differently from their American comrades in Russia.

113. *New Masses*, December 25, 1945, quoted in Victor Navasky, *Naming Names* (New York: Viking Press, 1980), 300.

114. Bernard Gordon, *Hollywood Exile, or How I Learned to Love the Blacklist: A Memoir* (Austin: University of Texas Press, 1999). He writes: "What about Stalin? What we knew then, what we knew for certain, was that he was heading the most

ferocious, bloody, and heroic fight against Hitler. . . . Viewed from the perspective of that time, the question for me then became *not* why join the party, but how can a principled, self-respecting person refuse?" (3–4). On when he became certain of the nature of Stalin: "In early 1956, Khrushchev spoke publicly about Stalin's atrocities. This was quite different from Henry Luce of *Time* magazine or the Chandlers of the *Los Angeles Times* unfurling their anti-communist propaganda. This news could not be ignored" (71). Thoughts like this may have, at least subconsciously, urged him to tell his readers early on: "We [members of the Communist Party] were not just unthinking sheep" (5). Yes, they were, and Gordon perhaps most of all (or at least of all those who have written their memoirs). Finally, on the "suffering" he endured:

> During the worst of those years, I was fortunate to earn big Hollywood dollars in Europe when the dollar was absolute king in France, England, Italy, and Spain; to live in the finest hotels on "the company"; to become familiar with the Michelin Guide when looking for three-star restaurants; to enjoy off-time in resorts from Monaco to St. Moritz; and to work on films of greater and lesser importance as both a writer and producer. (xi)

Recall that he says next to nothing about the suffering of the citizens of the Soviet Union he so unthinkingly supported. He writes, for example: "Today most of us feel that the party made grievous mistakes in its uncritical support for the Stalinist regime" (5), and that's about it.

115. Shentalinsky, *Arrested Voices*, 285.

116. Vaksberg, *Stalin Against the Jews*, 69.

117. *Hearings Regarding the Communist Infiltration of the Motion Picture Industry* (1947), 90.

118. See Conquest, *Great Terror*, and Courtois et al., *Black Book of Communism*, chs. 10–13.

119. Fitzpatrick, *Everyday Stalinism*, 7.

120. Courtois et al., *Black Book of Communism*, 206–207.

121. Fitzpatrick, *Everyday Stalinism*, 203–204.

122. Quoted in Fitzpatrick, *Everyday Stalinism*, 136. See also p. 138.

123. Shentalinsky, *Arrested Voices*, 118.

124. Quoted in Fitzpatrick, *Everyday Stalinism*, 190.

125. Conquest, *Great Terror*, 285; see also Fitzpatrick, *Everyday Stalinism*, 211.

126. Krivitsky, *In Stalin's Secret Service*, writes: "The Soviet government became one gigantic madhouse. . . . Everyone was a traitor, until he proved the contrary by exposing someone else as a traitor. Men of prudence sought obscurity, demotion to a clerical position if possible—anything to avoid importance and get out of the limelight" (131).

127. Conquest, *Great Terror*, 479.

128. Conquest, in Shentalinsky, *Arrested Voices*, x.

129. Fitzpatrick, *Everyday Stalinism*, 209.

130. Fitzpatrick, *Everyday Stalinism*, 185.

131. Shentalinsky, *Arrested Voices*, 152. On fear under Stalin, see also Shostakovich's memoirs, *Testimony*, 116–18.

132. Conquest, *Great Terror*, 276–78. Krivitsky, *In Stalin's Secret Service*, writes: "When I say that the Soviet government became a gigantic madhouse, I mean it literally. Americans laugh when I recount to them some of these preposterous things that happened—and I could fill volumes with them—but it was not a laughing matter to us. It is not funny when your lifelong friends are disappearing in the night and dying all around you. Please remember that I was an inmate in that gigantic madhouse" (138).

133. Conquest, *Great Terror*, 278.

134. Conquest, *Great Terror*, 331, 481. On the terror continuing after the war, see Courtois et al., *Black Book of Communism*, 228.

135. Fred Lawrence Guiles, *Hanging on in Paradise* (New York: McGraw-Hill, 1975), 249–50.

136. *Hollywood Reporter*, 15 December 1947.

~

CHAPTER SEVEN

Noble Lies: Rejecting the Standard Defense of *Song of Russia*— An Analysis of Ayn Rand's HUAC Testimony, Part 2

The idea that it is proper for a government to lie to its citizens for the good of the country is at least as old as Plato. In the *Republic*, he writes that "it's appropriate for the rulers, if for anyone at all, to lie for the benefit of the city in cases involving enemies or citizens, while all the rest must not put their hands to anything of the sort." He later calls this a "noble lie."[1]

Noble lies are a favorite tool of Communists and Fascists. What is surprising, however, is that in defense of films like *Song of Russia*, noble lies are accepted by non-Communists and non-Fascists as well, on supposedly pragmatic grounds.

For example, at the 1947 HUAC hearings, Jack Warner thought it sufficient to defend Warner Bros.' *Mission to Moscow* (which is more pro-Soviet than *Song of Russia*) by pointing out that the film supported the war effort:

[Mission to Moscow] was made when our country was fighting for its existence, with Russia as one of our allies. It was made to fulfill the same wartime purpose for which we made such other pictures as Air Force, This Is the Army, Objective Burma, Destination Tokyo, Action in the North Atlantic, and many more. If making Mission to Moscow in 1942 was a subversive activity, then the American Liberty ships which carried food and guns to Russian allies and the American naval vessels which conveyed them were likewise engaged in subversive activities. The picture was made only to help a desperate war effort and not for posterity.[2]

Louis B. Mayer took a similar position, though he denied *Song of Russia* was any kind of lie.

Toward the end of her statement to the HUAC, Ayn Rand challenges the noble lie defense of such films:

Now, here is what I cannot understand at all: if the excuse that has been given here is that we had to produce the picture in wartime, just how can it help the war effort? If it is to deceive the American people, if it were to present to the American people a better picture of Russia than it really is, then that sort of an attitude is nothing but the theory of the Nazi elite—that a choice group of intellectual or other leaders will tell the people lies for their own good. That I don't think is the American way of giving people information. We do not have to deceive the people at any time, in war or peace.[3]

Congressman John Wood (Democrat from Georgia) later said to her:

[Song of Russia] portrayed the people of Russia in a better economic and social position than they occupied . . . . And it would also leave the impression in the average mind that they were better able to resist the aggression of the German Army than they were in fact able to resist.[4]

Wood believed such a noble lie was justified, because it gave the impression that Russia was a good ally, which in turn (he claimed) helped the war effort. Wood's dialogue with Rand next turns to whether it was wise to have Russia as an ally at all. (More on this shortly.) Wood then asks Rand a question, and in the ensuing discussion, he never confronts the issue of lying head on, and does not get her point:

Wood: What do you interpret, then, the picture as having been made for?
Rand: I ask you: what relation could a lie about Russia have with the war effort. I would like to have somebody explain that to me, because I really don't understand it, why a lie would help anybody or why it would keep Russia in or out of the war. How?
Wood: You don't think it would have been of benefit to the American people to have kept them in?
Rand: I don't believe the American people should ever be told any lies, publicly or privately. . . .
Wood: Do you think it would have had as good an effect upon the morale of the American people to preach . . . that Russia was on the verge of collapse?
Rand: I don't believe that the morale of anybody can be built up by a lie. If there was nothing good that we could truthfully say about Russia, then it would have been better not to say anything at all. . . . You don't have to come out and denounce Russia during the war; no. You can keep quiet. There is no moral guilt in not saying something if you can't say it, but there is in saying the opposite of what is true.
Wood: Thank you. That is all.[5]

Wood's "thank you" is perfunctory; he is not convinced. Nor have commentators been since these hearings. Ayn Rand's position here has not received much attention in the years since the hearings (as we'll see in chapter 8). After all, how does one successfully challenge the claim that a government should not lie to its citizens—without accepting some fundamental principles of Fascism and Communism?

And yet the attention her position *has* received—indirectly, for her critics never directly confront the issue of lying—has been negative. The typical reaction to Rand's attitude, and to those on the HUAC who objected to the dishonesty of such films, is, in effect, a dismissive "quit complaining, these films supported the war effort." The implication is that lying in such cases is appropriate. What's more, this position is presented as obvious—as not requiring a defense.

Fred Lawrence Guiles criticizes Ayn Rand's "critique of *Song of Russia*" and describes the film as

> made by Metro in 1944 during our alliance with the Soviet Union against the Axis war machine that by the end of the European war had crushed out the lives of some seventeen million of her former countrymen. She called it a completely naïve propaganda film that had not helped Soviet-American relations.[6]

Similarly, in the early 1980s, coscreenwriter Paul Jarrico said—without regret or embarrassment—that the purpose of *Song of Russia* was "to celebrate our alliance with Russia."[7] More recently, Gary Wills has written: "Even the few films that praised the Soviet Union— . . . 'Song of Russia' and 'Mission to Moscow'—were patriotic efforts, encouraged by the government (President Roosevelt requested the filming of the second of those movies) when Moscow was a wartime ally."[8] Otto Friedrich, in *City of Nets*, writes that "Congressman John Wood . . . tried to get Miss Rand to admit that the United States had a strategic interest in keeping the Soviets at war against Germany, but she disputed even that."[9] Charles Higham, in his biography of Louis B. Mayer, writes that Mayer, in his HUAC testimony,

> mentioned that *Song of Russia* was "an opportunity for a pat on the back of our then ally, Russia," noted that Secretary of the Navy Frank Knox had recalled Robert Taylor for the film, mentioned the U.S. Signal Corps' pro-Soviet *The Battle for Stalingrad* and expressed pride in the picture. This was an entirely correct approach by any standard and should have humiliated the committee.[10]

No, this was an entirely incorrect approach by any proper moral standard—that is, by any nonpaternalistic standard that upholds the importance of honesty and respects the intelligence of Americans.

Clearly, Guiles, Wills, et al. accept Wood's justification of the film: It was a noble lie; lying to American citizens in such cases is justified, because our alliance with the Soviet Union is part of a "patriotic effort" for the good of the country. Leftists are capable of taking a "my country, right or wrong" approach when it's convenient.

To fully understand the point of Ayn Rand's testimony here, we must investigate more deeply her conviction that dishonesty is wrong.

According to Rand, telling the truth is not a Kantian duty divorced from reality and from every possible context. That is not why she opposes a government lying—or urging the film industry to lie—about the nature of one of our "allies." For example, she would—quite rationally—have no objections to lying to the Gestapo or the KGB to protect one's life; lying in such cases is the only moral option. But neither does she believe that whether one lies or not is a purely arbitrary issue, or one to be determined by some kind of utilitarian moral calculus: The end does not justify the means. Leonard Peikoff provides a superb explanation of Rand's position:

> The principle of honesty, in the Objectivist view, is not a divine commandment or a categorical imperative. It does not state that lying is wrong "in itself" and thus under all circumstances, even when a kidnapper asks where one's child is sleeping (the Kantians do interpret honesty in this way). But one may not infer that honesty is therefore "situational," and that every lie must be judged "on its own merits," without reference to principle. This kind of alternative, which we hear everywhere, is false. . . . Lying is absolutely wrong—under certain conditions. It is wrong when a man does it in the attempt to obtain a value. But, to take a different kind of case, lying to protect one's values from criminals is not wrong. If and when a man's honesty becomes a weapon that kidnappers or other wielders of force can use to harm him, then the normal context is reversed; his virtue would then become a means serving the ends of evil. In such a case, the victim has not only the right but also the obligation to lie and to do it proudly. The man who tells a lie in this context is not endorsing any antireality principle. On the contrary, he is now the representative of the good and the true; the kidnapper is the one at war with reality (with the requirements of man's life). Morally, the con man and the lying child-protector are opposites. The difference is the same as that between murder and self-defense.[11]

The U.S. government lying to Nazi Germany or Soviet Russia to protect American citizens is justified; lying to American citizens in the name of our alliance with the Soviet Union is not. But the issue here is precisely lying to American citizens—supposedly for their own good. Given Rand's moral philosophy, how would she approach such an issue?

First, there is the issue of justice. The American people—unlike the Gestapo, say—deserve the truth. Rand rejects paternalism—the idea that a government may lie to its citizens the way a parent might lie to a child, for his or her own good. Americans deserve better treatment and more respect. By contrast, there is an implied paternalism embraced by those who reject Rand's position and see nothing wrong with such noble lies.

But there is more to Ayn Rand's rejection of such lies than this. Her longest statement on the virtue of honesty comes from *Atlas Shrugged*:

> Honesty is the recognition of the fact that the unreal is unreal and can have no value, that neither love nor fame nor cash is a value if obtained by fraud— that an attempt to gain a value by deceiving the minds of others is an act of raising your victims to a position higher than reality, where you become a pawn of their blindness, a slave of their non-thinking and their evasions, while their intelligence, their rationality, their perceptiveness become the enemies you have to dread and flee—that you do not care to live as a dependent, least of all a dependent on the stupidity of others, or as a fool whose source of values is the fools he succeeds in fooling—that honesty is not a social duty, not a sacrifice for the sake of others, but the most profoundly selfish virtue that man can practice: his refusal to sacrifice the reality of his own existence to the deluded consciousness of others.[12]

Honesty is the refusal to fake reality. It is a corollary of rationality, the primary virtue according to Rand's moral philosophy. As Leonard Peikoff explains: "If rationality, as we may say, is the commitment to reality, then honesty is the obverse: it is the rejection of unreality. The exponent of the first acknowledges that existence exists; of the second, that *only* existence exists."[13]

The problem with dishonesty—and why it should be rejected on principle— is that it leads a person to clash with reality and to have to invent an alternative to reality. Quoting Peikoff again:

> The man who traffics in unreality, seeking to make it his ally, thereby makes reality his enemy. All facts are interconnected. Thus the first step of faking, like a man's first act of evasion, leads to the next; neither practice can be contained. Ultimately, the dishonest individual comes into conflict not merely with an isolated datum, but with the realm of existence as such. His policy commits him to the invention of a competitor to existence, a growing world of unreality, like a supernatural dimension that clashes at every point with the actual world. The latter, therefore, becomes his nemesis. It becomes a time bomb waiting to explode in his face.[14]

This is one reason Ayn Rand said, in her testimony: "I don't think the American people should ever be told any lies, publicly or privately. I don't believe that lies are practical. I think the international situation now rather supports me. I don't think it was necessary to deceive the American people about the nature of Russia."[15] The kind of big and noble lies represented by *Song of Russia* necessitated the creation of an alternative reality: the Soviet Union as seen—or claimed to be seen—by the American Left of the 1930s, 1940s, and beyond. Contrary to the claims of the defenders of noble lies, the creation of such lies was unnecessary; far from helping this country, they were destructive.

Putting aside the question of whether deceiving the Americans about Russia could actually help the war effort, what was the effect of this distorted picture of Russia being sold to the American people—not simply by *Song of Russia*, but by other such films, and by many politicians on the Left, and by much of the media? One immediate result was to earn not the friendship, but the contempt, of the Soviets after the war, a point Rand makes in her testimony:

> If it [the purpose of making such a film] was to please the Russians, I don't see how you can please the Russians by telling them that we are fools. To what extent we have done it, you can see right now. You can see the results right now. If we present a picture like that as our version of what goes on in Russia, what will they think of it. We don't win anybody's friendship. We will only win their contempt, and as you know the Russians have been behaving like this [i.e., treating America with contempt].[16]

But the long-term effects were much worse. After the war, the Soviet Union remained an enormous totalitarian evil (as it had been since its creation) and a significant military threat. But the alternative reality created by films like *Song of Russia*, and more so by leftists stretching back to 1917 and forward to the present, was the Soviet Union as a country deserving of our respect, a noble ally who had sacrificed much for the freedom of Europe and the world, a potentially productive partner in rebuilding the postwar world, if only America would stop its saber-rattling and strive for peace—if only America would try to understand the Soviet Union, stop moralizing, and exchange enough physicists, ballerinas, and pianists.[17]

The American public, during the war and in the decades to follow, was presented with a monstrous contradiction—with both the reality and its alternative. There were voices telling us of the Soviet evil and military threat, and there were other, often louder, voices—usually on the Left—proclaiming an alternative reality. For example, this alternative was present at Yalta, where an American president known for his concern for humanity—ignoring Soviet reality and pretending Russia was what it clearly was not—proceeded to join with a mass-murderer in dividing up Europe.[18] The results were devastating for Eastern Europe and for American security in the years following the war. As Slavomir Rawicz writes, describing the suffering of Poles during the twentieth century: "Then came Yalta with its humiliating sale of great parts of Europe to the bastardly, inhuman treatment by Stalin, the KGB, and the Moscow-trained puppets and paid stooges—and this for half a century."[19]

Ayn Rand is right: Lies are impractical.

Even since the fall of Communism, the alternative to Soviet reality continues to be peddled. Here is Maurice Rapf, in an interview about the Hollywood blacklist:

> As for all the revelations about the atrocities that took place in the Soviet Union—the so-called exposé of Stalin—by the time it began, I was no longer a member of the Party, anyway—and I don't believe half of it, either. I tend to be pro-Soviet—and I don't like what Yeltsin is doing—but I've come to recognize that human nature is the big stumbling block and that it's very difficult to get people to adhere to the noble principles that stand behind the Communist ideal.[20]

Howard Koch, in a similar sort of interview (published in 1995), said the following about his writing of the screenplay for *Mission to Moscow*:

> It's funny, not too many years ago, the *New Yorker* film critic, Pauline Kael, was here for lunch. And to my amazement, she said, "Aren't you embarrassed now, that you once wrote *Mission to Moscow*?" I said, "Look. It's the thing I value most in my life—that I was able to stand for something that needed to be said." And she shut up and didn't say anything more! [Laughs.][21]

Keep in mind that *Mission to Moscow* is more pro-Soviet than *Song of Russia*—that it whitewashes or defends the Great Terror and the purge trials; the Nazi–Soviet Pact; the Soviet invasion of Finland and the Baltics; and, in general, Stalin and Stalinism. That Koch many years ago and at the request of Roosevelt wrote the screenplay for a film that is the essence of Stalinist propaganda is bad enough, but to be proud of it *now* is despicable, and—like Rapf's rejection of "the so-called exposé of Stalin"—a paradigm of leftist Holocaust denial.

Note that Koch was *amazed* that Pauline Kael asked the question she did. This is significant. Another consequence of the peddling of the alternative reality is that whereas Nazis are properly denounced, and former Nazis are expected to renounce their views and apologize for them or at least explain themselves, Communists and former Communists who supported the Soviet Union are under no such pressure, though the Soviet Union succeeded in destroying even more lives than the Nazis did. As Eric Breindel explained, it has become "virtually impossible, in polite company, to call a Communist a Communist";[22] anyone who inquires into a person's pro-Soviet Communist past—or at least anyone who does not do so sympathetically—is treated with disdain and encounters the clichés about Red-baiting, witch hunts, inquisitions, and Communist paranoia.

In 1999, during the Kazan affair, Kazan was requested to apologize for naming names—and he was asked this by unrepentant old (ex-) Communists who were not expected to apologize for having supported Stalin for all those years, and who, like Koch, would have been amazed at the request.

Song of Russia made a small contribution toward (and is an excellent example of) the destructive alternative reality that was created in America, Europe, and around the world—a consequence of the idea that it was proper to lie about the nature of the Soviet Union since it helped defeat Nazi Germany.

Hand-in-hand with the alternative reality, supported by it, and equally destructive, was the idea that we should do anything to keep the Soviet Union as our ally against Hitler. Aside from the impropriety and impracticality of lying to do so, was this in fact a good idea? This is a complicated issue that cannot be sufficiently discussed here; instead, I'll simply present Ayn Rand's position, which unfortunately she did not share with the HUAC in 1947. But first, the relevant exchange with Congressman Wood:

> Rand: But if you want me to answer, I can answer, but it will take me a long time to say what I think, as to whether we should or should not have had Russia on our side in the war. I can, but how much time will you give me?
> Wood: Well, do you say that it would have prolonged the war, so far as we were concerned, if they had been knocked out of it at that time?
> Rand: I can't answer that yes or no, unless you give me time for a long speech on it.
> Wood: Well, there is a pretty strong probability that we wouldn't have won it at all, isn't there?
> Rand: I don't know, because on the other hand I think we could have used the lend-lease supplies that we sent there to much better advantage ourselves.
> Wood: Well, at that time—
> Rand: I don't know. It is a question.

Wood: We were furnishing Russia with all the lend-lease equipment that our industry would stand, weren't we?
Rand: That is right.
Wood: And continued to do it?
Rand: I am not sure it was at all wise. Now, if you want to discuss my military views—I am not an authority, but I will try.[23]

Congressman Wood did not take her up on her offer. But in the mid-1970s, Ayn Rand was asked about Lillian Hellman's *Scoundrel Time* and the resurgence of interest in the Hollywood blacklist. As part of her answer, she gave a brief account of what she thought the American policy toward the Soviet Union should have been:

How many people died in this country, and in Russia or in Russian-occupied countries, because of Miss Hellman's ideas, God only knows.[24] Nobody could compute the evil of what those Communists in the 1930s did. To begin with, they pushed this country into World War II. What would have been a better policy? Let Hitler march into Russia, as he had started to. Let the two dictatorships fight each other, then the West—England, France, and the United States—should finish off the winner. Then maybe, today, the world would be safe. (Except, of course, the ultimate safety of the world depends on philosophy, and nobody has the right ideas.) People like Lillian Hellman were pushing the policy of this country to the left and in support of only one country—not the United States, but Soviet Russia.[25]

It made no difference whether one supported our alliance with the Soviet Union because one admired the Soviets, as Hellman did, or on pragmatic grounds. This policy, Rand believed, was wrong and destructive; it required that one accept or pretend to accept the alternative Soviet "reality." The result was that Stalin and the Soviets were the big winners in World War II, whereas the people of Russia and Eastern Europe were the big losers. This would not have been possible were it not for those who presented and pushed the Soviet Union—à la *Song of Russia* and Lillian Hellman—as a noble ally and savior.

But wherever one stands on the issue of the Soviet Union as an ally, Rand argued in 1947, lying to the American people is not justified:

We are discussing the fact that our country was an ally of Russia, and the question is: what should we tell the American people about it—the truth or a lie? If we had good reason, if that is what you believe, all right, then why not tell the truth? Say it is a dictatorship, but we want to be associated with it. Say it is worthwhile being associated with the devil, as Churchill said, in order to defeat another evil which is Hitler. There might be some good argument made for that. But why pretend that Russia was not what it was?[26]

This is a point that both the Left and the Right still do not get, namely, that neither the government nor anyone else should attempt to whitewash evil. In the years since World War II, the Left has been willing to ignore the evils of leftist regimes around the world (in the Soviet Union and Eastern Europe, until the end, and in China and Cuba today, to give a few examples)—to pretend that they are what they are not—while supposedly being concerned about the suffering of humanity in places like South Africa, El Salvador, and the Philippines. Similarly, the Right has been willing to ignore reality and whitewash dubious or evil regimes—to pretend that they are what they are not—in the name of combating Communism. (A relevant example is President Reagan's support of the anti-Soviet Islamic "freedom fighters" in Afghanistan.[27])

But one might argue that it is silly to claim that films like *Song of Russia* are presenting lies; rather, they are simply typical Hollywood productions. Hollywood presents Russia in its films, the objection runs, the same way it presents New York City, the Wild West, or medieval France, namely, romantically and unrealistically. So why call it propaganda or dishonest?

Fred Lawrence Guiles presents such an objection in *Hanging on in Paradise*:

Miss Rand asserted that the "Moscow" of the film showed beautiful restaurants and lakes with swans. "The streets are clean and prosperous-looking . . . . There is a park where you see happy little children in white blouses running around. . . . They are not homeless children in rags. . . . Then they attend a luxurious dance. I don't know where they got the idea of the clothes and the settings that they used at the ball. . . ." No one thought to question her about the Hollywood view of life, as shown upon the screen, even though she had worked at a studio for some months adapting *The Fountainhead* into a movie and then seeing it through production.[28]

Similarly, Otto Friedrich writes in *City of Nets*:

What Miss Rand could not seem to understand, what the House committee could not seem to understand, was that *Song of Russia* was rubbish not because of any political purpose, subversive or otherwise, but because M-G-M was in the business of producing rubbish. That was its function, its nature, its mission. It hardly knew that political purposes existed. M-G-M was the home of Andy Hardy, of Judy Garland and Esther Williams, and no Communist ideology could ever penetrate or take root in such a playland. When Louis B. Mayer of Minsk decided to make a movie about Russia, he would inevitably make it the Russia of Andy Hardy, accompanied by Tchaikovsky.[29]

It is true that Hollywood was and is capable of departures from realism that are frankly quite stupid, and *Song of Russia* is no exception. Here are three (further) indications of this: First, Richard Collins reported that "one of the criticisms that came up about *Song of Russia* . . . was that the peasants' cottages were ridiculous. And they were. But it wasn't that we wrote them as ridiculous, it's that the MGM art department can't make an ugly set."[30] Second, an account of Susan Peters's preparations for her role as Nadya Stepanova reports: "for her new assignment as a peasant girl in 'Song of Russia,' Susan Peters . . . was requested by Director Gregory Ratoff to put on ten pounds."[31] But owing to conditions in Russia at the time, it is unlikely that any peasant women were gaining weight. Finally, John Wexley tells the following story about an experience he had working on *Song of Russia*:

> There was a beautiful Russian girl, played by a contract player [Susan Peters], who in fleeing the scorched earth dares to get dirt on her face. I remember when Mayer saw the rushes. I was there with Joe Pasternak. Mayer screamed at me. "The heroine! In all the pictures we have ever made the heroines never have any dirt on their faces! I won't have my lead actress shown with dirt on her face, and by the way, her hair should be dressed properly!" I said, "Your heroine is running through bombs. How can she look like she just came up from the hairdresser?" He took me outside and said, "Look, I built this studio on this policy. So don't tell me what to do. You're only a writer." That was MGM. Edicts came down from on high.[32]

Of course, *Song of Russia* as a whole is as unrealistic as these small touches, which contributed to making the movie what it was. And clearly, such attitudes were not reserved by MGM for movies portraying the Soviet Union. Nevertheless, the objection leveled by Guiles, Friedrich, and others does not withstand scrutiny.

Ayn Rand did recognize the "Hollywood" nature of *Song of Russia*; but she argued that this does nothing to rescue it from the charge of propaganda, for to make a film about *Soviet Russia* and make it "Hollywood"—to make it Andy Hardy's Russia, as Friedrich puts it—is itself a form of propaganda, whether Louis B. Mayer was aware of it or not:

> My whole point about the picture is this: I fully believe Mr. Mayer when he says that he did not make a Communist picture. To do him justice, I can tell you I noticed, by watching the picture, where there was an effort to cut propaganda out. I believe he tried to cut propaganda out of the picture, but the terrible thing is the carelessness with ideas, not realizing that the mere presentation of that kind of happy existence in a country of slavery and horror is

terrible because it is propaganda. You are telling people that it is all right to live in a totalitarian state.

Now, I would like to say that nothing on earth will justify slavery. In war or peace or at any time you cannot justify slavery. You cannot tell people that it is all right to live under it and that everybody there is happy.[33]

Further, there is a difference between art—which is selective and thus omits certain details, and can be stylized and should not be a mere journalistic presentation—and a piece of propaganda, which (in the case of *Song of Russia*) tells *us* that it presents the truth.[34] For example, a glamorous, romanticized love story set in New York is not dishonest or propagandistic if it fails to show its audience union corruption or the housing problems of the poor. A romantic, happy existence is possible to people in New York City; moreover, such films do not normally claim to be "about New York City." This is not the case with *Song of Russia*. But most important, New York City (or the Wild West, or even medieval France—or any other romantic setting that Hollywood regularly makes use of) is *not* the equivalent of the Soviet Union or Nazi Germany. That there is a difference between presenting a glamorized picture of New York City or the Wild West and presenting such a picture of Nazi Germany or Soviet Russia should be obvious. Ayn Rand makes this point in her HUAC testimony:

Visualize a picture in your own mind as laid in Nazi Germany. If anybody laid a plot just based on a pleasant little romance in Germany and played Wagner music and said that people are just happy there, would you say that that was propaganda or not, when you know what life in Germany was and what kind of concentration camps they had there. You would not dare to put just a happy love story into Germany, and for every one of the same reasons you should not do it about Russia.[35]

Leftist commentators *never* mention this part of Rand's testimony, for the same reason they ignore her insistence that it is improper to lie for the good of the country: There is no rational reply to make.

The part of her testimony they instead focus on is interesting and quite revealing, as we shall see in the next chapter.

Notes

1. Allan Bloom, trans., *The Republic of Plato*, 2nd ed. (New York: Basic Books, 1991), 67, 93 (389b-c, 414b-c).

2. *Hearings Regarding the Communist Infiltration of the Motion Picture Industry* (Hearings Before the Committee on Un-American Activities, House of Representa-

tives, Eightieth Congress, First Session, October 20, 21, 22, 23, 24, 27, 28, 29, and 30, 1947) (Washington, DC: United States Government Printing Office, 1947), 10.

3. *Hearings Regarding the Communist Infiltration of the Motion Picture Industry* (1947), 87.

4. *Hearings Regarding the Communist Infiltration of the Motion Picture Industry* (1947), 88.

5. *Hearings Regarding the Communist Infiltration of the Motion Picture Industry* (1947), 89–90.

6. Fred Lawrence Guiles, *Hanging on in Paradise* (New York: McGraw-Hill, 1975), 249. Guiles's apparent feelings of remorse for the seventeen million crushed Russians are in fact crocodile tears. See his comments on the Great Terror, which I discuss in chapter 6, pp. 135–36.

7. Patrick McGilligan and Paul Buhle, eds., *Tender Comrades: A Backstory of the Hollywood Blacklist* (New York: St. Martin's Griffin, 1997), 339.

8. Garry Wills, "The Truth About the Blacklist," *Outrider* (March 19,1999), at http://archive.bibalex.org/web/20001201185000/uexpress.com/ups/ opinion/column/gw/ archive.html.

9. Otto Friedrich, *City of Nets: A Portrait of Hollywood in the 1940s* (New York: Harper & Row, 1986), 318.

10. Charles Higham, *Merchant of Dreams: Louis B. Mayer, M.G.M., and the Secret Hollywood* (New York: Donald I. Fine, Inc., 1993), 367.

11. Leonard Peikoff, *Objectivism: The Philosophy of Ayn Rand* (New York: Meridian, 1993), 275–76.

12. Ayn Rand, *Atlas Shrugged* (New York: Random House, 1957; paperback ed., Dutton, 1992), 945.

13. Peikoff, *Objectivism*, 268.

14. Peikoff, *Objectivism*, 268; see also 270–72.

15. *Hearings Regarding the Communist Infiltration of the Motion Picture Industry* (1947), 89.

16. *Hearings Regarding the Communist Infiltration of the Motion Picture Industry* (1947), 87.

17. This is not to say that everyone on the Left was pro-Soviet. For example, at the time, the philosopher John Dewey was actively anti-Soviet.

18. On FDR and Stalin, see, for example, Thomas Fleming, *The New Dealers' War: F.D.R. and the War Within World War II* (New York: Basic Books, 2001), chs. 12, 13, and 19.

19. Slavomir Rawicz, *The Long Walk: The True Story of a Trek to Freedom* (New York: Lyons Press, 1997), xi.

20. McGilligan and Buhle, *Tender Comrades*, 539.

21. Griffin Fariello, ed., *Red Scare: Memories of the American Inquisition: An Oral History* (New York: W. W. Norton, 1995), 276.

22. John Podhoretz, ed., *Passion for Truth: The Selected Writings of Eric Breindel* (New York: HarperCollins, 1999), 18.

23. *Hearings Regarding the Communist Infiltration of the Motion Picture Industry* (1947), 88–89.

24. Consider this passage from Irving Howe's review of Hellman's *Scoundrel Time*, wherein he replies to Hellman's claim that she and her Communist friends never caused any harm: "Dear Lillian Hellman, you could not be more mistaken. Those who supported Stalinism and its political enterprises, either here or abroad, helped befoul the cultural atmosphere, helped bring totalitarian methods into trade unions, helped perpetuate one of the great lies of our century." *Dissent* (Fall 1976): 382.

25. From the Q&A period (in which Rand took part) following lecture 6 of Leonard Peikoff's 1976 "Philosophy of Objectivism" course (tapes and transcripts in the Ayn Rand Archives).

26. *Hearings Regarding the Communist Infiltration of the Motion Picture Industry* (1947), 89.

27. As Leonard Peikoff writes in "End States Who Sponsor Terrorism," *New York Times*, October 2, 2001:

> Conservatives are equally responsible for today's crisis, as Reagan's record attests. Reagan not only failed to retaliate after 241 U.S. marines in Lebanon were slaughtered; he did worse. Holding that Islamic guerrillas were our ideological allies because of their fight against the atheistic Soviets, he methodically poured money and expertise into Afghanistan. This put the U.S. wholesale into the business of creating terrorists. Most of them regarded fighting the Soviets as only the beginning; our turn soon came.

28. Guiles, *Hanging on in Paradise*, 250–51.

29. Friedrich, *City of Nets*, 318.

30. Interview with author, January 10, 2001, Los Angeles.

31. Publicity Service, "Song of Russia," 10 (in the MHL files on *Song of Russia*).

32. McGilligan and Paul Buhle, *Tender Comrades*, 715–16.

33. *Hearings Regarding the Communist Infiltration of the Motion Picture Industry* (1947), 87.

34. This is what Paul Buhle and Dave Wagner fail to see in *Radical Hollywood: The Untold Story Behind America's Favorite Movies* (New York: The New Press, 2002), when they write, in part with *Song of Russia* in mind, that American films "not at all infrequently romanticiz[ed] human rights violations in the name of progress. . . . *Gone with the Wind*, Hollywood's biggest film for a decade, would be hard to beat as a historic justification of a system vastly more widespread, brutal, and lasting than Stalinism" (240). It is refreshing to find leftists admitting that *Song of Russia* romanticized human rights violations. But their comparison of the film to *Gone with the Wind* is off, for (without defending the accuracy of *Gone with the Wind*), viewed objectively, *Gone with the Wind* is not "a historical justification" of slavery, whereas *Song of Russia* was certainly meant to justify the Soviet way of life. Further, although I dislike discussions about different rungs of hell, I think Buhle and Wagner's comparison of nineteenth-century Southern slavery with Stalinist tyranny is flawed.

35. *Hearings Regarding the Communist Infiltration of the Motion Picture Industry* (1947), 88.

~

CHAPTER EIGHT

Russian Smiles: The Leftist Response to Ayn Rand's HUAC Testimony

Ayn Rand's HUAC testimony covers a broad range of topics. The focus of her testimony is *Song of Russia* and its false portrayal of conditions in the Soviet Union. She comments on the absence of any signs of terror in the film, the easy access to food and other goods, the freedom of travel, the freedom of religion, the flourishing of culture, and the general happiness of people. She also discusses the nature of propaganda, why a government should not lie to its own citizens, and the attitude the United States should have taken toward the Soviet Union in World War II.

At one point during her testimony, Ayn Rand mentions smiles: "Incidentally, I have never seen so much smiling in my life, except on the murals of the world's fair pavilion of the Soviets. . . . It is one of the stock propaganda tricks of the Communists, to show these people smiling."[1] Following the body of her testimony, Republican Senator John McDowell comments: "You paint a very dismal picture of Russia. You made a great point about the number of children who were unhappy. Doesn't anybody smile in Russia any more?"

> Rand: Well, if you ask me literally, pretty much no.
> McDowell: They don't smile?
> Rand: Not quite that way; no. If they do, it is privately and accidentally. Certainly, it is not social. They don't smile in approval of their system.

Clearly, Ayn Rand's incidental mention of smiles is simply one point among many; it is connected to a larger point, namely, that to show Russians as happy and cheerful when in fact they were miserable, hungry, and terrified is a grotesque distortion. And of course, Soviet citizens had little to smile about. As one (rather charitable) Australian visitor to a *carnival* in Moscow in the 1930s reported: "There is no doubt that they 'take their pleasure sadly'; among the many thousands there *we scarcely saw a smile*, though we assumed that they were enjoying themselves."[2]

Why give any attention to Ayn Rand's incidental remark about smiles? Because leftist commentators have focused on the smiles, and what they say—and what they ignore—is revealing. Nearly everyone on the Left who has commented on Rand's testimony proceeds as if her sole (or at least primary) complaint was that *Song of Russia* showed people smiling.

What follows are several examples, presented chronologically. Note that I did not sort through comments on Rand's testimony and extract remarks about Russian smiles. Her mention of smiles is pretty much the *only* subject leftists have thought noteworthy. They treat these remarks, in effect, as the whole of her testimony. This alone is an indication of their lack of accuracy and objectivity.

The "review" of Ayn Rand's HUAC testimony that may have set the tone for future leftist comment on it is Joseph North's "Torquemada in Technicolor," which appeared in *New Masses* (a Communist rag) a couple of weeks after the hearings:

> On this latter movie [*Song of Russia*], they hauled up a strange character by the name of Ayn Rand (a White Guard Russian) who had been shown the picture over again by the FBI as recently as October 10 and had written a review of it for this session. Then came a hysterical outburst that surprised even these jaded Washingtonians. She flatly contradicted the *New York Times* and *Herald Tribune* reviews that called the film "innocuous," "pleasant." Miss Rand regarded the film as the quintessence of Communist propaganda. She railed at the night club depicted in the film, at the collective farm, at the tractor on the collective farm, at a modernistic sign on the Soviet border where two Red Guards were quietly playing chess, at the wedding ceremony (which showed priests in Russia!) and, what seemed to her the ultimate in perfidy, the telephone on which Mr. Taylor makes a long-distance call. Then, in crescendo, she shouted: "The children are always portrayed smiling, smiling, smiling!" And, with absolute finality, she concluded, "In Russia, children never smile, except *accidentally*."[3]

This passage is riddled with errors and distortions—for example, "White Guard Russian," "a hysterical outburst"—and both lines attributed to Rand are misquotes. Further, note the "conservatism" of radicals, dragged out when it's convenient: North cites her disagreement with the mainstream press as a sign that something is off. Finally, the first few points that North criticizes— about the night club, the Soviet border, religion—were completely war- ranted, as we have seen.

Later commentators may have realized this, because they skip these points, instead seemingly taking their cue from the last distortion in the ar- ticle, namely, the obvious ridiculousness—to North—of Rand's claims about smiling in Russia.

Gordon Kahn, in *Hollywood on Trial*—published a year after the hearings— wrote that in Rand's view, "Louis B. Mayer was not much better than an agent of a foreign government inasmuch as the film he produced showed the Rus- sians smiling."[4] Alvah Bessie, one of the Hollywood Ten, reported that

> Ayn Rand . . . testified that she had escaped from the Soviet Union and claimed that *Song of Russia* (MGM) was Red propaganda because, among other equally cogent reasons, "There is a park where you see happy little children in white blouses running around. . . ." She said she had never seen such children around the time she escaped (1926), and when asked, "Doesn't anybody smile in Russia any more?" she replied, "Well . . . pretty much no."

Bessie goes on to call all of this "fantastic."[5]

Stefan Kanfer, in *A Journal of the Plague Years*, writes that Ayn Rand

> had weighed *Song of Russia* and found it wanton. True, Rand had not returned to Russia since 1926, but she had read about it and learned of the disease of collectivism. She knew propaganda when she saw it. Perhaps the most flagrant of the film's distortions, in her view, was the evidence of not miserable people.

Kanfer then quotes her exchange with McDowell about smiles, and con- cludes: "Thus, with impenetrable sequiturs and rambling dialogues, the Com- mittee ended its first day's revelations."[6]

Gary Wills, in his introduction to Lillian Hellman's *Scoundrel Time*, writes:

> They called for expert testimony on [*Song of Russia*] from novelist Ayn Rand, and she quickly identified the work's major flaw: it showed Russians smiling. "It is one of the stock propaganda tricks of the Communists, to show these peo- ple smiling." Since Russian propaganda shows Russians smiling, and this American film showed Russians smiling, this American film was part of the Russians' propaganda effort. . . . Richard Nixon . . . had no questions to ask about her Syllogism of the Smiles. Only Representative John McDowell had some reservations.[7]

Wills misrepresents Rand's testimony when he suggests that she thought "the work's major flaw" was that "it showed Russians smiling." Her comment about smiles was clearly incidental. Further, his remark about the "Syllogism of the Smiles" is an obviously inaccurate account of what Rand says.[8] She nowhere claims that *Song of Russia* was "part of the Russians' propaganda effort." She said the film contained pro-Soviet propaganda, which is not the same thing, though she surely thought the Soviets would approve of the film, which they did. The Soviet Embassy's review of the screenplay for the Office of War Information, and Aram Khachaturyan's Soviet review of the film, were both positive; further, *Song of Russia* was one of only two MGM films ordered by the Soviets in 1944 for release in Russia.[9] Ayn Rand mentions that the Soviets used the same kind of propaganda employed in *Song of Russia*, because this supports her case—it shows that smiles can be used as propaganda.

Over twenty years later, writing *John Wayne's America*, the smiles were still on Wills's mind: "Ayn Rand resented the fact that Russians smiled in the 1943 *Song of Russia*, a favorable treatment of the Soviet ally." A few pages later, he writes: "Ayn Rand . . . hated the fact that Communists smiled in *Song of Russia*."[10]

David Platt, in his slanted review of Hellman's *Scoundrel Time*—though no longer a reviewer for the *Daily Worker*, he continued to write like one—presents the "official" leftist position on Ayn Rand and Russian smiles: "Typical of the idiocies of the time was . . . Ayn Rand's assertion that MGM's wartime anti-Nazi film, *Song of Russia*, was propaganda for communism because it showed 'smiling' Russians, 'a stock (Kremlin) propaganda trick'."[11] Brother-in-spirit to Platt, Victor Navasky, writes in *Naming Names* that: "The [HUAC] proceedings had comic overtones. . . . Ayn Rand found Communist propaganda . . . in the smiling faces of Russian children in *Song of Russia*." Later he writes: "Ayn Rand had told HUAC [*Song of Russia*] was pro-Soviet propaganda because it showed so many smiling Russian children."[12]

Lester Cole, another of the Hollywood Ten, complained in *Hollywood Red* that "Ayn Rand, self-styled expert on the Soviets, testified that the MGM film, *Song of Russia*, was clearly Communist propaganda because in it the performers playing Russians often smiled. 'In Russia,' she testified smiling [sic], 'nobody smiles.' Nobody smiled at her joke either."[13] (Cole was bothered by Rand's presumptuousness, as he saw it, in claiming to know about Soviet Russia, though she had lived there until 1926, and corresponded with her parents and sisters—who were not permitted to leave—until 1937. Elsewhere Cole calls her a "self-acknowledged expert on Soviet Communism."[14] This is a common mistake about Rand's credentials as a witness; if anything, conditions in Russia were *worse* in the 1930s and early 1940s than they were in the 1920s.[15])

Russian smiles even make an occasional appearance in accounts that do not mention Ayn Rand by name. Dan Georgakas, in "Hollywood Blacklist," one of his contributions to the *Encyclopedia of the American Left*, writes: "Evidence of leftist images and dialog in Hollywood films was extremely thin. HUAC had to resort to citing the smiling children in *Song of Russia* (1944) and noticing that Russian workers shouted 'tovarich' (comrade) [to] American merchant ships . . . in *Action in the North Atlantic*."[16]

I did encounter one leftist commentator on the 1947 HUAC hearings who actually comes across as objective, namely, Nancy Lynn Schwartz. She writes: "Next [of the friendly witnesses] came Ayn Rand, author of the bestselling novel *The Fountainhead*, who testified to the horrors of Russia, which, as a Russian immigrant, she knew to be true, and to the dangers of propaganda in such films as *Song of Russia*, which painted the false portrait of happy, smiling Russians."[17] Yet she, too, mentions only the smiles.

As evidence that the standard leftist conception of Ayn Rand's testimony is no longer confined to the Left, consider a 1999 article on Rand in *The Economist*, entitled "Still Spouting." The author writes: "It was Rand who told the [HUAC] that a film showing Russians smiling was inaccurate, because no one smiled in the Soviet Union." The article includes a photo of her testifying, with the caption: "Rand says Soviets don't smile."[18]

William Tripplett dished out the same old stuff, with sarcasm, in a recent article in *Salon*:

> HUAC's ostensible purpose was to root out Communist subversion of the movies, specifically in the form of Red propaganda flickering on screens across the country. The evidence? Ayn Rand cited an image of smiling Russians in a then-contemporary movie, and she, a Russian immigrant, knew that Russians had no reason to smile under communism.[19]

Recently, Arthur Laurents, with an utter lack of originality, follows the "official story" in his autobiography, *Original Story By*: "Ayn Rand could point to smiles on the faces of the peasants in *Song of Russia* as proof that Louis B. Mayer had made a Communist movie, but the Committee knew she was absurd even as they thanked her."[20]

In an interview published in 1995, Ring Lardner, Jr.—until recently the last surviving member of the Hollywood Ten—reported: "Rand said that the film *Song of Russia* gave a distorted picture of how things were in Russia. It showed Russian children smiling. She had been there until 1929 [sic], I think, and said children never smiled there."[21] Similarly, in an interview on February 13, 1997, he said:

> She had been born in Russia and lived there until she was a young woman. And she testified that she had seen a picture MGM made called "The Song of Russia" and that it showed Russian children smiling, which was a phenomenon she had never observed during her years in the Soviet Union.[22]

And like a fish-that-got-away story gone out of control, Rand's testimony, as Lardner misremembered it, became even more bizarre. In his autobiography, he claims that she "testified that she had never once seen a smiling child in the Soviet Union from the time of the Revolution in 1917 until her departure in 1926."[23] This time Lardner got her year of departure right, but the rest is a distortion.

I cannot be certain of the historical connection among the above claims, but it is uncanny how close they are in focus and content. It is as if some of the Hollywood Ten, and their friends and admirers, remembered solely what was underscored in the original *New Masses* article, and kept repeating it—without any additional thinking—for more than fifty years. Whether or not these commentators remained or ever were Communists, they continued to analyze the world with a rigid, narrow, Party mentality.

They are guilty of ignoring or evading most of Ayn Rand's HUAC testimony and focusing on (and distorting) one minor point of hers. But what about that point? Was she wrong in saying what she did about smiling Russians?

As Rand points out, the Soviets themselves used smiles (and laughter) as propaganda devices. In 1935, Stalin declared: "Life has become better, comrades; life has become more cheerful."[24] Since this was clearly not the case, steps were taken to make the people *appear* more cheerful. Officially scripted speeches were written declaring how good life was. For instance, one peasant woman, making just such a speech, stated: "Thank you comrade Stalin, our leader, our father, for a happy, merry kolkhoz [collective farm] life!"[25] But peasant life under Stalin was miserable.

In fact, so lacking in merriment were the Soviet people that the government had to encourage laughter. As Sheila Fitzpatrick explains: "Laughter was much emphasized: as *Krokodil* reported, carnival slogans proposed by 'individual enthusiasts' included 'He who does not laugh, does not eat,' and 'Make fun of those who fall behind!'"[26] The government did not have much success.

The ubiquitous smiling in *Song of Russia* is an attempt to create the same thing the Soviets wanted: a lie—a picture of Russian people as happy, when in fact they were not. Whether the creators of the film were consciously following, or even knew about, this Soviet form of propaganda is beside the point. The goal—and morality—of the propaganda is the same.

Putting aside the Soviets, imagine the effect of a film that presented life in Nazi Germany as happy and filled with smiles. Ayn Rand makes this point in her testimony (as discussed at the end of chapter 7). It is simply absurd to think that smiling—in a certain context—cannot be used as propaganda. It can be, and it was.

However, one might respond that whether or not smiles can be used as propaganda, and whether or not it was normal for people to smile in Nazi Germany, it is mistaken to think that people *never* smiled in the Soviet Union under Stalin.

In fact, Ayn Rand does *not* say that no one ever smiled in Stalinist Russia. (Even if she had, given the conditions under Stalin, it would be pettifogging to challenge her on it.) What she said was that Soviet citizens do not smile *openly and in approval of their system*. And she was right.

Similarly, the laughter that existed in the Soviet Union was not laughter in approval of their system. On the contrary, even government-sanctioned jokes—the only ones allowed to be published—attacked problems the Party wanted to fix: "The stupidity, rudeness, inefficiency, and venality of Soviet bureaucrats constituted the main satirical targets of the Soviet humorous journal, *Krokodil*."[27] But as a more typical example of the laughter of disapproval, consider this funny and unofficial reply to the official slogan, "Catch up and overtake the West!": "When we catch the capitalist countries, can we stay there?"[28]

But Rand did make one remark that perhaps requires an explanation: She says that if Soviet citizens smile, they do so *accidentally*. Garry Wills couldn't resist taking a shot: "Miss Rand, a screenwriter, must have put some odd directions in her scripts—like 'Smile accidentally, not socially.'"[29] But putting Wills aside, and for the sake of those actually interested in knowing what she meant, let me quote the opening of her essay "Art and Sense of Life":

If one saw, in real life, a beautiful woman wearing an exquisite evening gown, with a cold sore on her lips, the blemish would mean nothing but a minor affliction, and one would ignore it.

But a painting of such a woman would be a corrupt, obscenely vicious attack on man, on beauty, on all values—and one would experience a feeling of immense disgust and indignation at the artist. (There are also those who would feel something like approval and who would belong to the same moral category as the artist.)[30]

According to her esthetics, all art is selective. She defines art as "a selective re-creation of reality according to an artist's metaphysical value-judgments" (i.e., according to his basic view of reality and man's relation to it).[31] In life, she maintains, a cold sore is accidental, that is, inessential; it is unimportant in one's evaluation of reality, life, and in this case, human beauty. In life, the accidental, as she uses the term, is ignored. In art, however, the accidental—what the artist regards as inessential—is *excluded*. An artist selects only what is essential and important, given his view of reality and his theme—the point he is trying to make.

If one witnessed life in the Soviet Union in the 1930s and early 1940s, Ayn Rand claims, one might well have seen an occasional smile. But occasional smiles should be of no importance in—they should be excluded from—one's assessment of life under Stalin. This is what she meant when she said that if Russians smiled, they did so *accidentally*. Smiling was not an essential part of the Russians' appraisal of life. Nor would smiling be a regular occurrence in one's observations of Russians. So when a filmmaker chooses to include an abundance of smiling faces in his portrayal of life under Stalin, those smiles become enormously significant; they tell the audience something about the film's theme—its view of life under Stalin, namely, that Stalin's Russia is good. And that evaluation is false.

Besides being remarkably unoriginal—that is, characterized by an unthinking devotion to something like a Party line—the leftist commentators are completely wrong about Ayn Rand's HUAC testimony.

What else do their comments reveal about them? First, on the whole, they are dishonest: Not only are they unconcerned with the true nature of Soviet Russia, they ignore much of what Ayn Rand said—the bulk of her HUAC testimony—and distort what they do not ignore. They employ the same methodology as the Soviets; that is, they assume that one may properly ignore and distort the facts if it promotes a leftist end, in this case, smearing the HUAC and a well-known anti-Communist and pro-capitalist.

Second, for all the Left's claims about its concern for the suffering of humanity, the remarks of these commentators reveal an utter lack of compassion, not only for Ayn Rand—who personally experienced the horrors of the Soviet Union (directly, when she lived there, and indirectly, through her parents and sisters, who were not permitted to leave)—but also for the millions of Stalin's victims. Gary Wills, Victor Navasky, Arthur Laurents, Ring Lardner Jr. and the rest couldn't give a damn.

There is *one* sense, however, in which these leftist commentators are right: Ayn Rand did overstate her case. There was *some* smiling and laughing in approval of Stalinist Russia. For some people, to quote Stalin again, "Life *had* become better. . . , more cheerful." Arkady Vaksberg, in *Stalin Against the Jews*, reports:

[Karl] Pauker had a wonderful way of rolling his R's, and did a small-town Jewish accent that made the usually affectless Stalin roar with laughter. . . . After a late party, Pauker did an imitation of Zinoviev being dragged away to his execution by two guards, and with a Jewish accent (which Zinoviev did not have), moaning as he grabbed hold of the guards' legs, 'For God's sake, comrades, call Joseph Vissarionovich [Stalin]. Josif Vissarionovich promised to save our lives!' Delighted, Stalin choked with laughter and demanded a reprise.[32]

On a single day—December 12, 1938—Stalin signed the death warrants of 5,000 people, "following which he went to his private Kremlin movie theater to enjoy two films, one of them a comedy called *Merry Fellows*."[33]

But Stalin was not the only happy Soviet citizen.

Slavomir Rawicz, a former Polish cavalry officer who managed to escape from his Siberian prison, writes of the smiles and laughter of the prison guards in the Lubyanka. For example: "It was a callous public stripping, the preliminary to my first interrogation. The Russian officers lolled around smiling as I was forced to strip. . . . I stood before them robbed of my dignity. . . . [They] looked me over and laughed."[34]

There was also laughing and smiling in Kolyma, the notorious Siberian labor camp. Reports from former prisoners reveal that many in Kolyma were "killed for fun." One prisoner said: "when [we were] going to or coming back from work in the usual columns of five, [the guards] would sometimes stop us in the middle of the road, unleash their dogs, and laugh uproariously as the dogs sank their fangs into the prisoners' legs."[35] A female prisoner—a trained midwife—asked if she might get work commensurate with her training. "The overseer gave a nasty smile and replied: 'There are two tasks for people with your sentence: breaking the [frozen] soil and felling [trees]'."[36]

So, Fred Lawrence Guiles can sleep peacefully, knowing he was right: Not *all* 200 million Soviet citizens were lying every night in their unhappy beds waiting for doorbells to ring. But for the other 199.9 million, *this* was the Soviet reality—not the fantasy presented in *Song of Russia* and still lodged in the minds of many American leftists. For these millions, there was nothing to smile about.

Song of Russia—however inept and typically "Hollywood"—is a fraud that dishonors these millions. But much worse than *Song of Russia* are the leftists who also dishonor these millions, while smearing a great mind for her attempt to set the record straight.

Notes

1. For this mural and similar posters, see the photo insert in Lewis Siegelbaum et al., *Stalinism as a Way of Life* (New Haven, CT: Yale University Press, 2000).

2. Quoted in Sheila Fitzpatrick, *Everyday Stalinism: Ordinary Life in Extraordinary Times: Soviet Russia in the 1930s* (Oxford: Oxford University Press, 1999), 95 (emphasis added).

3. Joseph North, "Torquemada in Technicolor," *New Masses* 65 (November 4, 1947).

4. Gordon Kahn, *Hollywood on Trial: The Story of the 10 Who Were Indicted* (New York: Boni & Gaer, 1948), 32.

5. Alvah Bessie, *Inquisition in Eden* (New York: Macmillan, 1965), 201.

6. Stefan Kanfer, *A Journal of the Plague Years* (New York: Atheneum, 1973), 50.

7. Lillian Hellman, *Scoundrel Time*, introduction by Gary Wills (Boston: Little Brown, 1976), 1–2.

8. Wills is clearly not concerned with accuracy here; but then this is from his laudatory introduction to an "autobiographical" work of Lillian Hellman's, and I imagine that when writing in such a context, a concern for the truth is an obstacle.

9. Federal Bureau of Investigation, Freedom of Information and Privacy Acts File (Communist Infiltration-Motion Picture Industry), File Number: 100-138754, Serial: 157x1, Part 3 of 15.

10. Garry Wills, *John Wayne's America* (New York: Simon & Schuster, 1998), 194–95, 200.

11. David Platt, "The Hollywood Witchhunt of 1947: A Thirtieth Anniversary," in *Jewish Currents* (December 1977), reprinted in David Platt, ed., *Celluloid Power: Social Film Criticisms from The Birth of a Nation to Judgment at Nuremberg* (Metuchen, NJ: Scarecrow Press, 1992), 436.

12. Victor Navasky, *Naming Names* (New York: Penguin), 80, 225.

13. Lester Cole, *Hollywood Red: The Autobiography of Lester Cole* (Palo Alto, CA: Ramparts Press, 1981), 275.

14. Cole, *Hollywood Red*, 274.

15. See Richard Pipes, *Communism: A History* (New York: The Modern Library, 2001), 57–60.

16. Dan Georgakas, "Hollywood Blacklist," in *Encyclopedia of the American Left*, ed. Mari Jo Buhle, Paul Buhle, and Dan Georgakas, 326 (Urbana and Chicago: University of Illinois Press, 1992).

17. Nancy Lynn Schwartz, *The Hollywood Writers' Wars* (New York: Alfred A. Knopf, 1982), 267.

18. "Still Spouting," *The Economist*, November 27, 1999, 12–13.

19. William Triplett, "Busting Heads and Blaming Reds: How Movie Producers Used the Blacklist to Crack Down on Hollywood Unions," *Salon* (January 11, 2000), at http://dir.salon.com/ent/movies/feature/2000/01/11/blacklist/index.html.

20. Arthur Laurents, *Original Story By: A Memoir of Broadway and Hollywood* (New York: Alfred A. Knopf, 2000), 304.

21. Griffin Fariello, *Red Scare: Memories of the American Inquisition: An Oral History* (New York: W. W. Norton, 1995), 261.

22. The National Security Archive, from the section created by CNN for its documentary, *Cold War* (see www.gwu.edu/~nsarchiv/coldwar/interviews/episode-6/lardner1.html).

23. From Lardner's posthumously published autobiography—he died in December 2000—*I'd Hate Myself in the Morning: A Memoir* (New York: Thunder's Mouth Press, 2000), 120.

24. Fitzpatrick, *Everyday Stalinism*, 90.

25. Fitzpatrick, *Everyday Stalinism*, 277.

26. Fitzpatrick, *Everyday Stalinism*, 95.

27. Fitzpatrick, *Everyday Stalinism*, 29.

28. Fitzpatrick, *Everyday Stalinism*, 184. (See also pp. 3, 184–88.)

29. Introduction, Hellman, *Scoundrel Time*, 2.

30. Ayn Rand, *The Romantic Manifesto: A Philosophy of Literature* (New York: Signet, 1975), 34.

31. Rand, *Romantic Manifesto*, 19.

32. Arkady Vaksberg, *Stalin Against the Jews*, trans. Antonina W. Bouis (New York: Alfred A. Knopf, 1994), 41–42.

33. Pipes, *Communism*, 65.

34. Slavomir Rawicz, *The Long Walk: The True Story of a Trek to Freedom* (New York: The Lyons Press, 1956; reprint ed., 1997), 5. See also pp. 8, 11, 97.

35. Robert Conquest, *Kolyma: The Arctic Death Camps* (New York: Viking, 1978), 173.

36. Conquest, *Kolyma*, 191. See also pp. 31, 54, 82, 185.

~

Conclusion

What does this case study reveal about the influence of Hollywood Communists on the content of films? This was, after all, supposed to be the focus of Ayn Rand's HUAC testimony. And where is further study—other case studies—necessary?

Recall the standard outlook on Communist propaganda in Hollywood films: Either Communists put no propaganda in films, or they did so in rare cases to praise America's wartime ally, the Soviet Union.

What reasons are given in support of the standard view? First, we often hear that even if Communists *wanted* to insert propaganda into films, they could never get it past the conservative studio heads. Second, the most that Communists could do, we are told, was help to glorify the Soviet Union when she was our ally. That is, Communists could push their ideas only when and to the extent that those ideas followed the policies of the U.S. government. Richard Collins offers a succinct summary of these two reasons in his 1951 HUAC testimony:

> [S]ince the basic policy isn't in the hands of the writer or the director but in the hands of the owners of the studio, who are not at all interested in this propaganda, the chances of any real presentation of Communist material . . . [is] I think extremely unlikely. . . .
>
> [I]n 1943 what Song of Russia said about Russia was far less glowing than what Winston Churchill was saying or Douglas MacArthur or President Roosevelt or General Eisenhower or anybody else.[1]

A third reason given for the standard view is that sticking propaganda into Hollywood films was not a high priority of the Soviet Union, which was ultimately running the show. Jonathan Foreman asserts this in his review of Billingsley's *Hollywood Party*.[2] Soviet Russia was interested in Hollywood exclusively as a cash cow, according to this line of reasoning, not as a source for change in America through propaganda.[3]

There are ample reasons to question all of these claims.

As we have seen, a truly amazing number of Communist Party members (or perhaps in a couple of cases, fellow travelers) were at work on the writing of *Song of Russia*: Paul Jarrico, Richard Collins, Leo Mittler, Viktor Trivas, Guy Endore, John Wexley, Guy Trosper, Michael Blankfort, Boris Ingster, Paul Trivers, and Anna Louise Strong. Was this a fluke—a rare alignment of Red planets that never occurred again—or was this typical for MGM? Was this typical for Hollywood? Such questions need to be answered if we are to understand fully what the Communists in Hollywood tried to accomplish.

Further, there is evidence that the Communists in Hollywood, aside from trying to get propaganda in films, helped each other to get work. Richard Collins explains:

> One of the things the Party did was to get people jobs. That, in a strange way, worked. So, if a writer came in and suggested to a producer that so and so would be a good writer, the secretary would say, "Oh, yes, I hear he's wonderful." And it could work the other way. Leo Townsend told me that he was with Phil Yordan, and a communist came in and said: "To whom are you going to give the story?" And the producer [Yordan] said: "I thought I'd give it to Richard Collins," and the man said, "you can't do that, he'll steal your money, he can't write at all." I figured that's the way it is.[4]

How widespread such a network was, and how effective it was at getting Communists jobs and keeping non-Communists out, ought to be the object of serious study.

The history of *Song of Russia* makes it clear that inserting propaganda into the film *was* an obvious *aim* of the Communists who worked on it. As we have seen, passages were written that presented the Party line on Soviet foreign policy (and the Soviets' supposed love of peace); the Nazi-Soviet Pact; "extreme individualism" as the source of unhappiness; and most of all, the absence of any signs of famine, repression, or terror in the U.S.S.R.

Further, we have had a glimpse—in the case of Louis B. Mayer and Robert Taylor—of the inefficacy of conservatives as obstacles to the insertion of propaganda, because *Song of Russia* is clearly a work of propaganda. Part of the problem, as Ayn Rand pointed out, is that too many Hollywood film-makers did not know what to look for:

> If you wish to protect your pictures from being used for Communistic purposes, the first thing to do is to drop the delusion that political propaganda consists of political slogans. . . . The purpose of the Communists in Hollywood is *not* the production of political movies openly advocating Communism. Their purpose is *to corrupt non-political movies*—by introducing small, casual bits of propaganda into innocent stories—and to make people absorb the basic premises of Collectivism *by indirection and implication.*[5]

Louis B. Mayer and Robert Taylor thought that by objecting to and removing the obvious propaganda and suspicious terminology, the resulting film would be clean. They were wrong.

The same kind of study of preliminary treatments and scripts that I undertook for *Song of Russia* needs to be applied to many other films. For each film, the following questions must be asked: Was there an attempt to insert propaganda? Is there evidence that the studio heads or anyone else tried to remove it? If so, how successful were they? Such studies have not been made, unfortunately, because most scholars who have worked in this area begin with the assumption that, in the words of Jonathan Foreman, "Besides *Song of Russia* and *Mission to Moscow* . . . , one [cannot] detect any ideological taint in the movies these people [i.e., the Hollywood Communists] made."[6] But this assumption is *not* obviously correct. Further, a proper investigation will involve taking a fresh look at a number of films to which Hollywood Communists contributed, while dropping, as Rand advised, "the delusion that political propaganda consists of political slogans."

A good place to begin is with the list of films that Ayn Rand compiled in preparation for her HUAC testimony. She believed these films showed evidence of Communist propaganda, though without employing political slogans or openly advocating Communism. At the top of her list was *The Best Years of Our Lives.*[7] And there were many other films that she claimed had "communist themes." For example (in each case, her statement of the theme is provided first): "The capitalist portrayed as the villain" (*It's a Wonderful Life, Little Foxes, It Happened One Night*); "Idealization of the Soviet Union" (*Mission to Moscow, Song of Russia, Christmas in Connecticut, North Star*); "Idealization of Communists" (*Watch on the Rhine, Blockade, Gung-Ho*); "Idealization of Communist organizations" (*Action in the North Atlantic*); "Propaganda pictures on behalf of Loyalist Spain" (*Blockade*); "Propaganda pictures on behalf of Chinese communists" (*Gung-Ho*).[8] Many will no doubt scoff at this list, but only because they accept the false assumption that Rand warns against, namely, that inserting Communist propaganda into films entails sticking in bold pro-Communist pronouncements, which most of these films lack.

Returning to the contention that there could not be Communist propaganda in films because of the vigilance of conservative studio heads: this is hardly a strong defense of the actions of Hollywood Communists. What's being said is, in effect: "You can't chastise Hollywood communists for secretly propagandizing for communism, because they weren't fully successful." But if we were discussing the attempts of Nazis to influence the content of American films (assuming there were such people attempting such things), we would properly be unsatisfied with the assertion, "You can't condemn Nazis for trying to influence films, because they didn't succeed." This simply does not hold up. The same is true for Hollywood Communists (especially considering that they *did* have some success).

Next, what of the claim that we cannot criticize Communists for making pro-Soviet films, or consider such films Soviet propaganda, because the U.S. government itself was at that time pro-Soviet (Russia being our ally)? Again, this is a weak defense. A neo-Nazi arguing against racial quotas for minorities is still a neo-Nazi, whatever apparent similarities may exist between his views and those of conservatives and moderate liberals who oppose racial quotas. And a Stalinist is still a Stalinist, whatever his foreign policy of the moment. *What* is being put into films is not the only issue. The Communists *wanted* to do more than sell Russia as an ally: They wanted to sell Communism, and particularly Stalinism. We see traces of this in *Song of Russia*. It does not count in the Communists' favor that FDR and the New Dealers (and conservatives at MGM and other studios) were too misguided to oppose them.

Motives matter, even when the Left pretends they don't. In the 1930s, Ayn Rand (and many conservatives) were against the United States becoming entangled in a foreign war. Since Italy and Germany liked the idea of America staying out of the war, such "isolationist" Americans were unjustly labeled fascists. Similarly, the Left considers American Communists during World War II basically the same as moderate liberals or conservatives who thought we needed Russia as an ally; but that's a mistake. Hollywood Communists must be judged differently, because however mistaken such moderate liberals and conservatives were, the Communists were acting primarily and consciously in the interest of the Soviet Union, and that is a crucial difference.

Finally, asserting that the Soviets, to whom the U.S. Communist Party answered, were not that interested in Hollywood Communists inserting propaganda into films, does not make for a strong defense of Hollywood Communists. Again, if American Nazis working in Hollywood had tried to influence the content of films, it would hardly count in their favor if Goebbels was not confident about their chances of success. Whether the Hollywood Communists succeeded or not, whether they had the full support of the Soviet Union or not, we have every right to condemn them for attempting to insert pro-Soviet propaganda into films, as a means to their ends.

But in fact the Soviets *were* interested in getting Communist propaganda into American films. They were—via the Comintern, for example—certainly interested in Hollywood generally, and part of their interest concerned the content of films.[9] For example, Willi Muenzenberg, a major power in the Comintern, wrote an article for the *Daily Worker* (in 1925) that included this quote from Lenin: "You must powerfully develop film production, taking especially the proletarian kino (motion picture theaters) to the city masses and still a much greater extent to the villages. You must always consider that of all the arts, the motion picture is for us the most important." Muenzenberg continued in his own words: "One of the most pressing tasks confronting Communist Parties on the field of agitation and propaganda is the conquest of this supremely important propaganda weapon, until now the weapon of the ruling class. We must wrest it from them and turn it against them."[10] John Howard Lawson, a higher-up among Hollywood Communists, followed this line. Addressing a group of young actors at a "Party Line Indoctrination Center," he gave them the following "advice":

> Unless you portray any role given you in a manner to further the Revolution and the Class War, you have no right to call yourself an artist or an actor. . . . You must do this regardless of what the script says and what the director tells you. Even if you are nothing more than an extra, you can portray a society woman in a manner to make her appear a villainess and a snob. And you can portray a working girl in such a way so as to make her seem a sympathetic victim of the capitalist system.[11]

What was the connection between the Comintern and the Hollywood Communists? There clearly was *some* connection, and the former clearly had *some* interest in the actions of the latter.[12] What is needed is a scholarly investigation into this connection—but not one that begins with the assumption that the Hollywood Communists were harmless saints, nor with the assumption that it is absurd to think that they used films for propaganda purposes.

Ayn Rand was generally very disappointed with the HUAC hearings. Nevertheless, she did not deny that they had accomplished something:

> The good that that hearing accomplished is that that was the turning point for Red propaganda on the screen. It vanished after that completely. . . . And there I take credit, for the "Screen Guide for Americans" did it. Now the best thing was that that "Screen Guide" in condensed form—the most important highlights—was reproduced in the drama section of *The Sunday Times*, on the front page, which [only happened because of] this hearing. . . . When the Screen Guide [first] came out, the major studios generally ignored it. Progressively [after it appeared in *The Times*], I began hearing one studio after another ordering it from the MPA [by the] dozens. And all the points I made in it, particularly about the attacks on businessmen as villains, disappeared—certainly in the form in which they had been. If you watch old movies on TV you'll see the difference.[13]

This is a fascinating claim, one that a careful study of American films from the period following the HUAC hearings should be able to confirm or refute.

Whatever questions remain regarding the effects of the 1947 HUAC hearings on film in America, the following is clear: In the battle between the Communists and the anti-Communists *in Hollywood*, the anti-Communists lost.[14] First, if Ayn Rand is right about films no longer portraying "businessmen as villains" in the years following the hearings, such a trend did not last long. Today, businesspeople in the movies and on television are regularly presented as swine. But more directly, Communists are the winners in the two areas that I mentioned in the introduction: the portrayal of Communist countries (and especially the Soviet Union) and the portrayal of Hollywood Communists.

On this latter point, in films like *The Way We Were* (1973), *The Front* (1976), *Guilty by Suspicion* (1991), and most recently, *The Majestic* (2001), the Hollywood Ten and people like them continue to be cleaned up and presented as heroes. As for the presentation of countries like the Soviet Union, Hollywood can no longer get away with the sort of portrayal offered by *Song of Russia*. Instead, Hollywood does not make films about them at all. But that too is a victory for the Hollywood Communists.[15]

Viktor Kravchenko, who left the Soviet Union and later wrote *I Chose Freedom*, complained before the HUAC in May 1947: "Today few companies in Hollywood want to make a picture that shows the Soviet Union as it really is. . . . Why don't they make a picture on Russia which would show what it means to live there . . . , and show the concentration camps? Show everything as it really is?"[16] The answer, then as now, is Hollywood Communism and its legacy. Here is Dalton Trumbo, one of the Hollywood Ten, bragging in 1946 about what Communists in Hollywood were able to accomplish:

Hollywood [has not] produced anything so untrue or so reactionary as [the anti-communist works] *The Yogi and the Commissar*, *Out of the Night*, *Report on the Russians*, *There Shall Be No Night*, or *Adventures of a Young Man*. Nor does Hollywood's forthcoming schedule include such tempting items as James T. Farrell's *Bernard Clare*, Victor Kravchenko's *I Chose Freedom*, or the so-called biography of Stalin by Leon Trotsky.[17]

This is the ultimate injustice: The Hollywood Ten are regarded as saints, Ayn Rand is vilified, and the Lubyanka Thousand and other victims of Communist terror are—owing to the influence of the Hollywood Ten and their sympathizers—left on the cutting-room floor.

Notes

1. *Communist Infiltration of Hollywood Motion-Picture Industry-Part 1* (Hearings Before the Committee on Un-American Activities, House of Representatives, Eighty-Second Congress, First Session, March 8 and 21; April 10, 11, 12 and 13, 1951) (Washington, DC: United States Government Printing Office, 1951), 234, 236. Similarly, William Triplett writes: "Even the studio heads . . . testified repeatedly to the committee that despite an infrequent 'pro-Communist' passage turning up in a script, no such material ever made it past the editing hatchet of the producer, who still wielded control over content." "Busting Heads and Blaming Reds: How Movie Producers Used the Blacklist to Crack Down on Hollywood Unions," *Salon* (January 11, 2000), at http://dir.salon.com/ent/movies/feature/2000/01/11/blacklist/index.html.

2. Jonathan Foreman, "Blacklist Whitewash," *National Review*, March 22, 1999, 53. Foreman is followed slavishly by Gary Wills in "The Truth About the Blacklist," *Outrider* (March 19, 1999), at http://archive.bibalex.org/web/20001201185000/uexpress.com/ups/ opinion/column/gw/ archive.html.

3. On Hollywood as a source of funds for the Communists, which it certainly was, see Kenneth Lloyd Billingsley, *Hollywood Party: How Communism Seduced the American Film Industry in the 1930s and 1940s* (Rocklin, CA: Prima, 1998), 52–53.

4. Interview with author, January 10, 2001, Los Angeles.

5. Ayn Rand, "Screen Guide for Americans," in *Journals of Ayn Rand*, ed. David Harriman, 356 (New York: Plume, 1999) (emphasis in original).

6. Foreman, "Blacklist Whitewash," 53. Foreman states this in the form of a question, but with the certainty that the answer is obvious.

7. Her brief notes on *Best Years of Our Lives* can be found in *Journals of Ayn Rand*, 367–69.

8. This is a partial list, from Ayn Rand's unpublished "Communist Themes in Motion Pictures" (Ayn Rand Archives).

9. On the Comintern's interest in film in general, and Hollywood in particular, see Stephen Koch, *Double Lives: Spies and Writers in the Secret War of Ideas against the West* (New York: Free Press, 1994), 27–28, 78–80, 220–28.

10. Quoted in Federal Bureau of Investigation, Freedom of Information and Privacy Acts File (Communist Infiltration-Motion Picture Industry), File Number: 100-138754, Serial: 1003 (pt. 2), Part 9 of 15. On Stalin's interest in film, see Peter Kenez, "Black and White: The War on Film," in *Culture and Entertainment in Wartime Russia*, ed. Richard Stites, 157 (Bloomington: Indiana University Press, 1995).

11. From the *Hollywood Reporter*, August 20, 1946, quoted in Federal Bureau of Investigation, Freedom of Information and Privacy Acts File (Communist Infiltration-Motion Picture Industry), File Number: 100-138754, Serial: 251x1, Part 7 of 15.

12. When asked whether the Communist Party in Hollywood had any connection with the Comintern, Richard Collins replied:

> We had a comrade who used to come out occasionally and who obviously outranked everybody out here. He was Comrade Albert. That's the only way I knew him. I have no idea who it was. I think he was Yugoslavian, but I'm not sure. He was from somewhere in Eastern Europe. I had the feeling from what he used to say that that's where he came from. He was really the principal person.

Interview with author, January 10, 2001, Los Angeles.

13. Biographical interview (Ayn Rand Archives).

14. The emphasis on "in Hollywood" is important. Outside of that context, and in general, Communism and Communists are the big losers. They are the big losers existentially, because Communism has been thoroughly repudiated by the twentieth century. And whether present-day academia recognizes it or not, Communism has been utterly repudiated philosophically as well. Simply compare the *Communist Manifesto* and *Das Kapital* with Ayn Rand's *Capitalism: the Unknown Ideal* and *Atlas Shrugged*.

15. See Billingsley, *Hollywood Party*, 273–82. In this sense, Hollywood is far behind the rest of the culture, which has made *some* progress in recognizing the Soviet Union for what it was. As Martin Amis puts it: "But progress has been made. The argument, now, is about whether Bolshevik Russia was 'better' than Nazi Germany. In the days when the New Left dawned, the argument was about whether Bolshevik Russia was better than America." *Koba the Dread: Laughter and the Twenty Million* (New York: Hyperion, 2002), 25.

16. Quoted in Federal Bureau of Investigation, Freedom of Information and Privacy Acts File (Communist Infiltration-Motion Picture Industry), File Number: 100-138754, Serial: 157x1, Part 3 of 15. Ayn Rand was quite critical of Viktor Kravchenko's *I Chose Freedom*—see Michael S. Berliner, ed., *Letters of Ayn Rand* (New York: Plume, 1995), 296-97—but that does not affect the point I am making.

17. Dalton Trumbo, "Getting into Focus," *The Worker*, May 5, 1946, quoted in Billingsley, *Hollywood Party*, 92–93.

~

Ayn Rand's HUAC Testimony

The following is the full and unedited transcript of Ayn Rand's testimony before the House Un-American Activities Committee (October 20, 1947) as reported in the official Government Printing Office record ("Hearings Regarding Communist Infiltration of the Motion Picture Industry"). The Committee's chairman was J. Parnell Thomas; Robert Stripling was Chief Investigator.

The Chairman: Raise your right hand, please, Miss Rand. Do you solemnly swear the testimony you are about to give is the truth, the whole truth, and nothing but the truth, so help you God?
Miss Rand: I do.
The Chairman: Sit down.
Mr. Stripling: Miss Rand, will you state your name, please, for the record?
Miss Rand: Ayn Rand, or Mrs. Frank O'Connor.
Mr. Stripling: That is A-y-n?
Miss Rand: That is right.
Mr. Stripling: R-a-n-d?
Miss Rand: Yes.
Mr. Stripling: Is that your pen name?
Miss Rand: Yes.
Mr. Stripling: And what is your married name?
Miss Rand: Mrs. Frank O'Connor.
Mr. Stripling: Where were you born, Miss Rand?
Miss Rand: In St. Petersburg, Russia.

Mr. Stripling: When did you leave Russia?

Miss Rand: In 1926.

Mr. Stripling: How long have you been employed in Hollywood?

Miss Rand: I have been in pictures on and off since late in 1926, but specifically as a writer this time I have been in Hollywood since late 1943 and am now under contract as a writer.

Mr. Stripling: Have you written various novels?

Miss Rand: One second. May I have one moment to get this in order?

Mr. Stripling: Yes.

Miss Rand: Yes, I have written two novels. My first one was called *We the Living*, which was a story about Soviet Russia and was published in 1936. The second one was *The Fountainhead*, published in 1943.

Mr. Stripling: Was that a best seller—*The Fountainhead*?

Miss Rand: Yes; thanks to the American public.

Mr. Stripling: Do you know how many copies were sold?

Miss Rand: The last I heard was 360,000 copies. I think there have been some more since.

Mr. Stripling: You have been employed as a writer in Hollywood?

Miss Rand: Yes, I am under contract at present.

Mr. Stripling: Could you name some of the stories or scripts you have written for Hollywood?

Miss Rand: I have done the script of *The Fountainhead*, which has not been produced yet, for Warner Brothers, and two adaptations for Hal Wallis Productions, at Paramount, which were not my stories but on which I did the screen plays, which were *Love Letters* and *You Came Along*.

Mr. Stripling: Now, Miss Rand, you have heard the testimony of Mr. [Louis B.] Mayer?

Miss Rand: Yes.

Mr. Stripling: You have read the letter I read from Lowell Mellett?

Miss Rand: Yes.

Mr. Stripling: Which says that the picture *Song of Russia* has no political implications?

Miss Rand: Yes.

Mr. Stripling: Did you at the request of Mr. Smith, the investigator for this committee, view the picture *Song of Russia*?

Miss Rand: Yes.

Mr. Stripling: Within the past two weeks?

Miss Rand: Yes, on October 13, to be exact.

Mr. Stripling: In Hollywood?

Miss Rand: Yes.

Mr. Stripling: Would you give the committee a breakdown of your summary of the picture relating to either propaganda or an untruthful account or distorted account of conditions in Russia?

Miss Rand: Yes. First of all I would like to define what we mean by propaganda. We have all been talking about it, but nobody—

Mr. Stripling: Could you talk into the microphone?

Miss Rand: Can you hear me now? Nobody has stated just what they mean by propaganda. Now, I use the term to mean that Communist propaganda is anything which gives a good impression of communism as a way of life. Anything that sells people the idea that life in Russia is good and that people are free and happy would be Communist propaganda. Am I not correct? I mean, would that be a fair statement to make—that that would be Communist propaganda?

Now, here is what the picture *Song of Russia* contains. It starts with an American conductor, played by Robert Taylor, giving a concert in America for Russian war relief. He starts playing the American national anthem and the national anthem dissolves into a Russian mob, with the sickle and hammer on a red flag very prominent above their heads. I am sorry, but that made me sick. That is something which I do not see how native Americans permit, and I am only a naturalized American. That was a terrible touch of propaganda. As a writer, I can tell you just exactly what it suggests to the people. It suggests literally and technically that it is quite all right for the American national anthem to dissolve into the Soviet. The term here is more than just technical. It really was symbolically intended, and it worked out that way. The anthem continues, played by a Soviet band. That is the beginning of the picture.

Now we go to the pleasant love story. Mr. Taylor is an American who came there apparently voluntarily to conduct concerts for the Soviets. He meets a little Russian girl from a village who comes to him and begs him to go to her village to direct concerts there. There are no GPU agents and nobody stops her. She just comes to Moscow and meets him. He falls for her and decides he will go, because he is falling in love. He asks her to show him Moscow. She says she has never seen it. He says, "I will show it to you."

They see it together. The picture then goes into a scene of Moscow, supposedly. I don't know where the studio got its shots, but I have never seen anything like it in Russia. First you see Moscow buildings—big, prosperous-looking, clean buildings, with something like swans or sailboats in the foreground. Then you see a Moscow restaurant that just never existed there. In my time, when I was in Russia, there was only one such restaurant, which was nowhere as luxurious as that and no one could enter it except commissars and profiteers. Certainly a girl from a village, who in the first place would never have been allowed to come voluntarily, without permission, to Moscow, could not afford to enter it, even if she worked ten years. However, there is a Russian restaurant with a menu such as never existed in Russia at all and which I doubt even existed before the revolution. From this restaurant they go on to this tour of Moscow. The streets are clean and prosperous-looking. There are no food lines anywhere. You see shots of the marble subway—the famous Russian subway out of which they make such propaganda capital. There is a marble statue of Stalin thrown in. There is a park where you see happy little children in white blouses running around. I don't know whose children they are, but they are really happy kiddies. They are not homeless children in rags, such as I have seen in Russia. Then you see an excursion boat, on which the Russian people are smiling, sitting around very cheerfully, dressed in some sort of satin blouses such as they only wear in Russian restaurants here.

Then they attend a luxurious dance. I don't know where they got the idea of the clothes and the settings that they used at the ball and—

Mr. Stripling: Is that a ballroom scene?

Miss Rand: Yes; the ballroom—where they dance. It was an exaggeration even for this country. I have never seen anybody wearing such clothes and dancing to such exotic music when I was there. Of course, it didn't say whose ballroom it is or how they get there. But there they are—free and dancing very happily.

Incidentally, I must say at this point that I understand from correspondents who have left Russia and been there later than I was and from people who escaped from there later than I did that the time I saw it, which was in 1926, was the best time since the Russian revolution. At that time conditions were a little better than they have become since. In my time we were a bunch of ragged, starved, dirty, miserable people who had only two thoughts in our mind. That was our complete terror—afraid to look at one another, afraid to say anything for fear of who is listening and would report us—and where to get the next meal. You have no idea what it means to live in a country where nobody has any concern except food, where all the conversation is about food because everybody is so hungry that that is all they can think about and that is all they can afford to do. They have no idea of politics. They have no idea of any pleasant romances or love—nothing but food and fear.

That is what I saw up to 1926. That is not what the picture shows.

Now, after this tour of Moscow, the hero—the American conductor—goes to the Soviet village. The Russian villages are something—so miserable and so filthy. They were even before the revolution. They weren't much even then. What they have become now I am afraid to think. You have all read about the program for the collectivization of the farms in 1933, at which time the Soviet Government admits that three million peasants died of starvation. Other people claim there were seven and a half million, but three million is the figure admitted by the Soviet Government as the figure of people who died of starvation, planned by the government in order to drive people into collective farms. That is a recorded historical fact.

Now, here is the life in the Soviet village as presented in *Song of Russia*. You see the happy peasants. You see they are meeting the hero at the station with bands, with beautiful blouses and shoes, such as they never wore anywhere. You see children with operetta costumes on them and with a brass band which they could never afford. You see the manicured starlets driving tractors and the happy women who come from work singing. You see a peasant at home with a close-up of food for which anyone there would have been murdered. If anybody had such food in Russia in that time he couldn't remain alive, because he would have been torn apart by neighbors trying to get food. But here is a close-up of it and a line where Robert Taylor comments on the food and the peasant answers, "This is just a simple country table and the food we eat ourselves."

Then the peasant proceeds to show Taylor how they live. He shows him his wonderful tractor. It is parked somewhere in his private garage. He shows him the grain in his bin, and Taylor says, "That is wonderful grain." Now, it is never said that the peasant does not own this tractor or this grain because it is a collective farm. He couldn't have it. It is not his. But the impression he gives to Americans, who wouldn't know any differently, is that certainly it is this peasant's private property, and that is how he lives, he has his own tractor and his own grain. Then it shows miles and miles of plowed fields.

The Chairman: We will have more order, please.

Miss Rand: Am I speaking too fast?

The Chairman: Go ahead.

Miss Rand: Then—

Mr. Stripling: Miss Rand, may I bring up one point there?

Miss Rand: Surely.

Mr. Stripling: I saw the picture. At this peasant's village or home, was there a priest or several priests in evidence?

Miss Rand: Oh, yes; I am coming to that, too. The priest was from the beginning in the village scenes, having a position as sort of a constant companion and friend of the peasants, as if religion was a natural accepted part of that life. Well, now, as a matter of fact, the situation about religion in

Russia in my time was, and I understand it still is, that for a Communist Party member to have anything to do with religion means expulsion from the party. He is not allowed to enter a church or take part in any religious ceremony. For a private citizen, that is a nonparty member, it was permitted, but it was so frowned upon that people had to keep it secret, if they went to church. If they wanted a church wedding they usually had it privately in their homes, with only a few friends present, in order not to let it be known at their place of employment because, even though it was not forbidden, the chances were that they would be thrown out of a job for being known as practicing any kind of religion.

Now, then, to continue with the story, Robert Taylor proposes to the heroine. She accepts him. They have a wedding, which, of course, is a church wedding. It takes place with all the religious pomp which they show. They have a banquet. They have dancers, in something like satin skirts and performing ballets such as you never could possibly see in any village and certainly not in Russia. Later they show a peasants' meeting place, which is a kind of a marble palace with crystal chandeliers. Where they got it or who built it for them I would like to be told. Then later you see that the peasants all have radios. When the heroine plays as a soloist with Robert Taylor's orchestra, after she marries him, you see a scene where all the peasants are listening on radios, and one of them says, "There are more than millions listening to the concert." I don't know whether there are a hundred people in Russia, private individuals, who own radios. And I remember reading in the newspaper at the beginning of the war that every radio was seized by the Government and people were not allowed to own them. Such an idea that every farmer, a poor peasant, has a radio, is certainly preposterous. You also see that they have long-distance telephones. Later in the picture Taylor has to call his wife in the village by long-distance telephone. Where they got this long-distance phone, I don't know.

Now, here comes the crucial point of the picture. In the midst of this concert, when the heroine is playing, you see a scene on the border of the U.S.S.R. You have a very lovely modernistic sign saying "U.S.S.R." I would just like to remind you that that is the border where probably thousands of people have died trying to escape out of this lovely paradise. It shows the U.S.S.R. sign, and there is a border guard standing. He is listening to the concert. Then there is a scene inside kind of a guardhouse where the guards are listening to the same concert, the beautiful Tschaikowsky music, and they are playing chess. Suddenly there is a Nazi attack on them. The poor, sweet Russians were unprepared. Now, realize—and that was a great shock to me—that the border that was being shown was the border of Poland. That was the border of an occupied, destroyed, enslaved country which Hitler and Stalin destroyed together. That was the border that was being shown to us—just a happy place with people listening to music.

Also realize that when all this sweetness and light was going on in the first part of the picture, with all these happy, free people, there was not a G.P.U. agent among them, with no food lines, no persecution—complete freedom and happiness, with everybody smiling. Incidentally, I have never seen so much smiling in my life, except on the murals of the world's fair pavilion of the Soviets. If any one of you have seen it, you can appreciate it. It is one of the stock propaganda tricks of the Communists, to show these people smiling. That is all they can show. You have all this, plus the fact that an American conductor had accepted an invitation to come there and conduct a concert, and this took place in 1941 when Stalin was the ally of Hitler. That an American would accept an invitation to that country was shocking to me, with everything that was shown being proper and good and all those happy people going around dancing, when Stalin was an ally of Hitler.

Now, then, the heroine decides that she wants to stay in Russia. Taylor would like to take her out of the country, but she says no, her place is here, she has to fight the war. Here is the line, as nearly exact as I could mark it while watching the picture: "I have a great responsibility to my family, to my village, and to the way I have lived." What way had she lived? This is just a polite way of saying the Communist way of life. She goes on to say that she wants to stay in the country because otherwise, "How can I help to build a better and better life for my country." What do you mean when you say better and better? That means she has already helped to build a good way. That is the Soviet Communist way. But now she wants to make it even better. All right.

Now, then, Taylor's manager, who is played, I believe, by Benchley, an American, tells her that she should leave the country, but when she refuses and wants to stay, here is the line he uses: he tells her in an admiring friendly way that "You are a fool, but a lot of fools like you died on the village green at Lexington."

Now, I submit that that is blasphemy, because the men at Lexington were not fighting just a foreign invader. They were fighting for freedom and what I mean—and I intend to be exact—is they were fighting for political freedom and individual freedom. They were fighting for the rights of man. To compare them to somebody, anybody fighting for a slave state, I think is dreadful.

Then, later the girl also says—I believe this was she or one of the other characters—that "the culture we have been building here will never die." What culture? The culture of concentration camps.

At the end of the picture one of the Russians asks Taylor and the girl to go back to America, because they can help them there. How. Here is what he says, "You can go back to your country and tell them what you have seen and you will see the truth both in speech and in music." Now, that is plainly saying that what you have seen is the truth about Russia. That is what is in the picture.

Now, here is what I cannot understand at all: if the excuse that has been given here is that we had to produce the picture in wartime, just how can it help the war effort. If it is to deceive the American people, if it were to present to the American people a better picture of Russia than it really is, then that sort of an attitude is nothing but the theory of the Nazi elite—that a choice group of intellectual or other leaders will tell the people lies for their own good. That I don't think is the American way of giving people information. We do not have to deceive the people at any time, in war or peace.

If it was to please the Russians, I don't see how you can please the Russians by telling them that we are fools. To what extent we have done it, you can see right now. You can see the results right now. If we present a picture like that as our version of what goes on in Russia, what will they think of it. We don't win anybody's friendship. We will only win their contempt, and as you know the Russians have been behaving like this.

My whole point about the picture is this: I fully believe Mr. Mayer when he says that he did not make a Communist picture. To do him justice, I can tell you I noticed, by watching the picture, where there was an effort to cut propaganda out. I believe he tried to cut propaganda out of the picture, but the terrible thing is the carelessness with ideas, not realizing that the mere presentation of that kind of happy existence in a country of slavery and horror is terrible because it is propaganda. You are telling people that it is all right to live in a totalitarian state.

Now, I would like to say that nothing on earth will justify slavery. In war or peace or at any time you cannot justify slavery. You cannot tell people that it is all right to live under it and that everybody there is happy.

If you doubt this, I will just ask you one question. Visualize a picture in your own mind as laid in Nazi Germany. If anybody laid a plot just based on a pleasant little romance in Germany and played Wagner music and said that people are just happy there, would you say that that was propaganda or not, when you know what life in Germany was and what kind of concentration camps they had there. You would not dare to put just a happy love story into Germany, and for every one of the same reasons you should not do it about Russia.

Mr. Stripling: That is all I have, Mr. Chairman.

The Chairman: Mr. Wood.

Mr. [John S.] Wood: I gather, then, from your analysis of this picture your personal criticism of it is that it overplayed the conditions that existed in Russia at the time the picture was made; is that correct?

Miss Rand: Did you say overplayed?

Mr. Wood: Yes.

Miss Rand: Well, the story portrayed the people.

Mr. Wood: It portrayed the people of Russia in a better economic and social position than they occupied?

Miss Rand: That is right.

Mr. Wood: And it would also leave the impression in the average mind that they were better able to resist the aggression of the German Army than they were in fact able to resist?

Miss Rand: Well, that was not in the picture. So far as the Russian war was concerned, not very much was shown about it.

Mr. Wood: Well, you recall, I presume—it is a matter of history—going back to the middle of the First World War when Russia was also our ally against the same enemy that we were fighting at this time and they were knocked out of the war. When the remnants of their forces turned against us, it prolonged the First World War a considerable time, didn't it?

Miss Rand: I don't believe so.

Mr. Wood: You don't?

Miss Rand: No.

Mr. Wood: Do you think, then, that it was to our advantage or to our disadvantage to keep Russia in this war, at the time this picture was made?

Miss Rand: That has absolutely nothing to do with what we are discussing.

Mr. Wood: Well—

Miss Rand: But if you want me to answer, I can answer, but it will take me a long time to say what I think, as to whether we should or should not have had Russia on our side in the war. I can, but how much time will you give me?

Mr. Wood: Well, do you say that it would have prolonged the war, so far as we were concerned, if they had been knocked out of it at that time?

Miss Rand: I can't answer that yes or no, unless you give me time for a long speech on it.

Mr. Wood: Well, there is a pretty strong probability that we wouldn't have won it at all, isn't there?

Miss Rand: I don't know, because on the other hand I think we could have used the lend-lease supplies that we sent there to much better advantage ourselves.

Mr. Wood: Well, at that time—

Miss Rand: I don't know. It is a question.

Mr. Wood: We were furnishing Russia with all the lend-lease equipment that our industry would stand, weren't we?

Miss Rand: That is right.

Mr. Wood: And continued to do it?

Miss Rand: I am not sure it was at all wise. Now, if you want to discuss my military views—I am not an authority, but I will try.

Mr. Wood: What do you interpret, then, the picture as having been made for?

Miss Rand: I ask you: what relation could a lie about Russia have with the war effort. I would like to have somebody explain that to me, because I really don't understand it, why a lie would help anybody or why it would keep Russia in or out of the war. How?

Mr. Wood: You don't think it would have been of benefit to the American people to have kept them in?

Miss Rand: I don't believe the American people should ever be told any lies, publicly or privately. I don't believe that lies are practical. I think the international situation now rather supports me. I don't think it was necessary to deceive the American people about the nature of Russia.

I could add this: if those who saw it say it was quite all right, and perhaps there are reasons why it was all right to be an ally of Russia, then why weren't the American people told the real reasons and told that Russia is a dictatorship but there are reasons why we should cooperate with them to destroy Hitler and other dictators. All right, there may be some argument to that. Let us hear it. But of what help can it be to the war effort to tell people that we should associate with Russia and that she is not a dictatorship?

Mr. Wood: Let me see if I understand your position. I understand, from what you say, that because they were a dictatorship we shouldn't have accepted their help in undertaking to win a war against another dictatorship.

Miss Rand: That is not what I said. I was not in a position to make that decision. If I were, I would tell you what I would do. That is not what we are discussing. We are discussing the fact that our country was an ally of Russia, and the question is: what should we tell the American people about it—the truth or a lie? If we had good reason, if that is what you believe, all right, then why not tell the truth? Say it is a dictatorship, but we want to be associated with it. Say it is worthwhile being associated with the devil, as Churchill said, in order to defeat another evil which is Hitler.

There might be some good argument made for that. But why pretend that Russia was not what it was?

Mr. Wood: Well—

Miss Rand: What do you achieve by that?

Mr. Wood: Do you think it would have had as good an effect upon the morale of the American people to preach a doctrine to them that Russia was on the verge of collapse?

Miss Rand: I don't believe that the morale of anybody can be built up by a lie. If there was nothing good that we could truthfully say about Russia, then it would have been better not to say anything at all.

Mr. Wood: Well—

Miss Rand: You don't have to come out and denounce Russia during the war; no. You can keep quiet. There is no moral guilt in not saying something if you can't say it, but there is in saying the opposite of what is true.

Mr. Wood: Thank you. That is all.

The Chairman: Mr. Vail.

Mr. [Richard B.] Vail: No questions.

The Chairman: Mr. McDowell.

Mr. [John] McDowell: You paint a very dismal picture of Russia. You made a great point about the number of children who were unhappy. Doesn't anybody smile in Russia any more?

Miss Rand: Well, if you ask me literally, pretty much no.

Mr. McDowell: They don't smile?

Miss Rand: Not quite that way; no. If they do, it is privately and accidentally. Certainly, it is not social. They don't smile in approval of their system.

Mr. McDowell: Well, all they do is talk about food.

Miss Rand: That is right.

Mr. McDowell: That is a great change from the Russians I have always known, and I have known a lot of them. Don't they do things at all like Americans? Don't they walk across town to visit their mother-in-law or somebody?

Miss Rand: Look, it is very hard to explain. It is almost impossible to convey to a free people what it is like to live in a totalitarian dictatorship. I can tell you a lot of details. I can never completely convince you, because you are free. It is in a way good that you can't even conceive of what it is like. Certainly they have friends and mothers-in-law. They try to live a human life, but you understand it is totally inhuman. Try to imagine what it is like if you are in constant terror from morning till night and at night you are waiting for the doorbell to ring, where you are afraid of anything and everybody, living in a country where human life is nothing, less than nothing, and you know it. You don't know who or when is going to do what to you because you may have friends who spy on you, where there is no law and any rights of any kind.

Mr. McDowell: You came here in 1926, I believe you said. Did you escape from Russia?

Miss Rand: No.

Mr. McDowell: Did you have a passport?

Miss Rand: No. Strangely enough, they gave me a passport to come out here as a visitor.

Mr. McDowell: As a visitor?

Miss Rand: It was at a time when they relaxed their orders a little bit. Quite a few people got out. I had some relatives here and I was permitted to come here for a year. I never went back.

Mr. McDowell: I see.

The Chairman: Mr. Nixon.

Mr. [Richard] Nixon: No questions.

The Chairman: All right.

The first witness tomorrow morning will be Adolph Menjou.

~

Files on *Song of Russia* at the Margaret Herrick Library

Note: Nothing—punctuation, parentheses, brackets, etc.—has been added to this list.

2995-f.2915   Treatment (SCORCHED EARTH) by Leo Mittler, Viktor Trivas and Guy Endore; no date (copied 3/31/42); 59 pages and 55 pages [2 copies, original and retyped version].

2995-f.2916   Outline (SCORCHED EARTH) by Leo Mittler and Viktor Trivas; no date (copied 5/12/42); 11 pages.

2995-f.2917   Treatment (SCORCHED EARTH) by Guy Trosper and Irmgard von Cube; 6/8/42, through 6/29/42; approximately 150 pages [original; revised; also 3-page section by Guy Trosper, 6/17/42].

2995-f.2918   Treatment section (SCORCHED EARTH) by Irmgard von Cube and Guy Trosper; 6/25/42, through 6/26/42; 16 pages.

2995-f.2919   Guerrilla anecdotes from Anna Louise Strong; 7/6/42 (copied 9/21/42); 16 pages and 24 pages [2 copies, original and retyped version].

2995-f.2920   Composite script of treatment (SCORCHED EARTH) by Anna Louise Strong and Guy Trosper; 7/7/42, through 7/23/42; approximately 190 pages [also 4-page new sequence arrangement by Anna Louis Strong, 7/10/42].

2995-f.2921   Notes by Guy Trosper, Laslo Benedek and Michael Blankfort; 7/31/42 and 8/15/42; 8 pages total [2 items].

2995-f.2922 Last half of treatment (SCORCHED EARTH) by Anna Louis Strong; 8/18/42, through 8/31/42; approximately 80 pages and 69 pages [2 copies, original and retyped version; original annotated; also 2-page section, 7/31/42].

2995-f.2923 Notes ("An American Visits the U.S.S.R.") by Paul Jarrico and Richard Collins; 8/31/42; 11 pages.

2995-f.2924 Treatment (SCORCHED EARTH) by Anna Louis Strong; 9/3/42, through 9/14/42; approximately 70 pages [original; annotated].

2996-f.2925 Screenplay sections (SCORCHED EARTH) by Paul Jarrico and Richard Collins; 9/11/42, through 9/26/42; approximately 220 pages [mostly handwritten original].

2996-f.2926 Screenplay sections (SCORCHED EARTH) by Paul Jarrico and Richard Collins; 9/11/42, through 9/26/42; 45 pages.

2996-f.2927 Treatment (SCORCHED EARTH) by Guy Trosper and Michael Blankfort; 9/14/42; 43 pages.

2996-f.2928 Temporary complete screenplay (SCORCHED EARTH) by Paul Jarrico and Richard Collins; 10/30/42, through 12/14/42; approximately 160 pages [original; annotated and many pages handwritten].

2996-f.2929 Temporary complete composite screenplay (SCORCHED EARTH) by Paul Jarrico and Richard Collins; 10/30/42, through 12/14/42; approximately 140 pages.

2996-f.2930 Miscellaneous notes (SCORCHED EARTH) by Paul Jarrico and Richard Collins; 1/7/43; 11 pages.

2996-f.2931 Complete OK screenplay (RUSSIA) by Paul Jarrico and Richard Collins; 1/15/43, through 7/1/43; approximately 140 pages [original; annotated and many pages are handwritten; part 1 of 2].

2997-f.2932 Complete OK screenplay (RUSSIA) by Paul Jarrico and Richard Collins; 1/15/43, through 7/1/43; approximately 140 pages [part 2 of 2].

2997-f.2933 Complete composite OK screenplay (RUSSIA) by Paul Jarrico and Richard Collins; 1/15/43, through 7/1/43; approximately 160 pages [part 1 of 2].

2997-f.2934 Complete composite OK screenplay (RUSSIA) by Paul Jarrico and Richard Collins; 1/15/43, through 7/1/43; approximately 160 pages [part 2 of 2].

2997-f.2935	Screenplay sections, notes and retakes (RUSSIA) by Paul Jarrico, Richard Collins and David Hertz; 1/30/43, through 6/12/43; approximately 50 pages total [6 items, 8 copies, two sets of originals and retyped versions; also 3-page dialogue by David Hertz, 6/2/43].
2997-f.2936	Notes and speeches (RUSSIA) by Laslo Benedek and John Wexley; 4/7/43, through 10/20/43; 24 pages total [4 items, 6 copies, two sets of originals and retyped versions; also 4 page dialogue by John Wexley, 7/8/43].
2997-f.2937	Screenplay sections and notes (RUSSIA) by John Hoffman; 4/10/43, through 6/7/43; approximately 60 pages total [7 items, 8 copies, one set of original and retyped version; also 2-page dialogue by Fitzroy Davis, 6/15/43].
2997-f.2938	Montage (RUSSIA) by Peter Ballbusch; 4/29/43; 3 pages [2 copies, original and retyped version].
2998-f.2939	Screenplay sections (RUSSIA) by Boris Ingster; 6/16/43, through 7/7/43; approximately 80 pages total [2 copies, original and retyped version; original annotated and most pages are handwritten].
2998-f.2940	Retakes (RUSSIA) by Richard Collins; 8/31/43, through 9/9/43; approximately 70 pages total [4 items, 6 copies, originals and retyped version; originals annotated and most pages are handwritten; also 11 old pages, dated 9/7/43–9/11/43].
2998-f.2941	Added scenes (RUSSIA) by Richard Collins and Paul Trivers; 10/13/43, through 10/22/43; 12 pages and 19 pages [2 copies, original and retyped version; original annotated and a few pages are handwritten].
2998-f.2942	Dialogue cutting continuity by George Hively (Editor), footage and music; 12/17/43; 105 pages and 18 pages.
2998-f.2943	Trailer dialogue cutting continuity and trailer footage; 1/11/44; 3 pages and 1 page.
2998-f.2944	Revised dialogue cutting continuity (for Portuguese, French, British and Spanish versions) by George Hively (Editor) and footage for reels #1 and #4; 5/9/44; 79 pages total [5 items].

APPENDIX THREE

~

From the FBI Files: Schedule for the October 1947 HUAC Hearings

Federal Bureau of Investigation, Freedom of Information and Privacy Acts
Subject: Communist Infiltration-Motion Picture Industry
File Number: 100-138754, Serial: 251x1, Part 7 of 15. (See foia.fbi.gov/
compic.htm)

Prior to the excerpt that constitutes the bulk of this appendix, there is a list of twenty-seven "possible unfriendly witnesses" and another of eighteen "possible friendly witnesses." Ayn Rand's name is on the latter list. An "Investigator for the House Committee on Un-American Activities confidentially furnished Special Agent in Charge R.B. Hood of the Los Angeles Office" with these lists. Surrounding documents indicate that the material that follows these lists—what I provide below—most likely dates from early September 1947.

In connection with this pending hearing, [name crossed out] has confidentially advised Mr. Hood of a recent telephonic conversation he had with Robert Stripling of the House Committee on Un-American Activities. According to [name crossed out], he was advised that a tremendous amount of pressure had been put on the Committee by all sources, including Congressional, to call off or otherwise influence the Committee's action on this pending hearing into Communism in the motion picture industry. [Name crossed out] related that in his conversation with Stripling he proposed that the witnesses be called approximately as he has included in the schedule prepared by [name crossed out] for the hearing; however, Stripling was not in complete accord with [name crossed out] desire in this regard.

Investigator [name crossed out] has informed Mr. Hood that he is concerned over the procedure and method of operations to be utilized by the Committee in handling the pending hearing. [Name crossed out] has related that he has definitely promised the witnesses from California that they are going to testify along the lines which he has discussed with them. [Name crossed out] related that a great number of the witnesses are worried that the Committee in an effort to create publicity will go off on some tangent. He related that he has tried to point out to Stripling that he wants to give the impression that the inquiry is not one to attack the industry but rather to show that the motion picture industry is being attacked by the Communists. [Name crossed out] related that it is his desire to show that the House Committee on Un-American Activities is endeavoring to expose this Communist activity and thus strengthen the position of the industry.

[Name crossed out] has indicated that he intended to proceed by air to New York on September 15, 1947, and on the following day meet with Mr. J. Parnell Thomas, Chairman of the Committee, as well as other members of the Committee in order to make plans for the hearing. Prior to leaving California, [name crossed out] furnished Special Agent in Charge Hood of the Los Angeles Office with a copy of a schedule of witnesses which he hopes will be used at the hearing. This schedule is set out in its entirety hereinafter:

"After several discussions between [name crossed out], [name crossed out], [name crossed out], and [name crossed out] the following tentative schedule of witnesses has been arranged:

1. Jack L. Warner,   Time allowed: ½ day
   Co-Owner, Warner Brothers. . . .[1]
2. Louis B. Mayer,   Time allowed: ½ day
   Metro-Goldwyn-Mayer
   Comments: Mayer can testify regarding 'Song of Russia,' 'Tennessee Johnson,' and the fact that there is no law and until there is a law, he does not feel there is anything particular he can do to Communists. . . .[2]

3. Leo Cherne   Time allowed: 1 hour. . . .
4. Roy E. Brewer,   Time allowed: 1 day
   Internat'l Representative, IATSE. . . .

** Two unfriendly Communist witnesses should be called at this point, their names to be selected later.

5. Robert Montgomery)
6. George Murphy), All actors   Time allowed: 1 day
7. Ronald Reagan). . . .

** Two or three more Communists, to be selected later, should be called at this point.

8. Robert Taylor,   Time allowed: 2 hours
    Actor
9. Sam Wood,   Time allowed: 2 hours
    Director, Producer

** We should call Lowell Millett [sic, Mellett] here.

** A couple more Communists, to be selected later, should be called here: Possibly Richard J. Collins, if we have sufficient information, as he was a writer on 'Song of Russia,' regarding which incidents Taylor and Wood will discuss from the Millett [sic] angle.[3]

10. Adolphe Menjou,   Time allowed: ½ day
    Actor
11. James K. McGuiness,   Time allowed: ½ day
    Vice President, MGM. . . .
12. Morrie Ryskind,   Time allowed: 1½ hours
    Writer
13. Borden Chase   Time allowed: 1½ hours. . . .

** Call a couple more Communists, who should be writers, at this point.

14. John Charles Moffett   Time allowed: ¾ day. . . .
15. Rupert Hughes,   Time allowed: 2 hours
    Author
16. Lela E. Rogers   Time allowed: 1 hour. . . .
17. Cedric Gibbons   Time allowed: 1 hour. . .

** Call a couple of Communist directors and actors at this point.

18. Gary Cooper,   Time allowed: 1 hour
    Actor
19. Walt Disney   Time allowed: 1 hour. . . .
20. Leo McCarey   Time allowed: 1 hour. . . .

Note:[4]

From the above schedule, we have first the studio heads, followed by the labor and technical experts, followed by actors from the Screen Actors Guild standpoint; then the special incidents of Robert Taylor, 'Song of Russia,' Wood, Lowell Millett [sic]; followed by general witnesses; then the Screen Writers Guild, the picture analysis, and the closing with three witnesses who are very pro-American."

For purposes of comparison with the above, I here list, in chronological order, the witnesses who testified before the HUAC in Washington D.C. in October 1947:

Oct. 20: H.A. Smith, A.B. Leckie, Louis J. Russell,[5] Jack Warner, Sam Wood, Louis B. Mayer, Ayn Rand.

Oct. 21: Adolphe Menjou, John Charles Moffitt, Rupert Hughes.

Oct. 22: James McGuinness, Robert Taylor, Howard Rushmore, Morrie Ryskind.

Oct. 23: Fred Niblo, Jr., Richard Macaulay, Robert Montgomery, George Murphy, Ronald Reagan, Gary Cooper, Leo McCarey.

Oct. 24: Lela Rogers, Oliver Carlson, Walt Disney.

Oct. 27: John Howard Lawson, Louis J. Russell, Eric Allen Johnston.

Oct. 28 Dalton Trumbo, Louis J. Russell, Roy Brewer, Albert Maltz, Robert Kenny, Louis J. Russell, Alvah Bessie, Louis J. Russell, Roy Brewer (resumed).

Oct. 29: Samuel Ornitz, Louis J. Russell, Herbert Biberman, Louis J. Russell, Emmet Lavery, Edward Dmytryk, Louis J. Russell, Adrian Scott, Louis J. Russell, Dore Schary.

Oct. 30: Ring Lardner, Jr., Louis J. Russell, Lester Cole, Louis J. Russell, Berthold Brecht, Louis J. Russell.

Postscript: For the purposes of the present study, two related points are especially interesting: (1) Ayn Rand is not on the original schedule of witnesses (though she was on the list of possible friendly witnesses), which might suggest that contrary to what anyone told her, her only purpose—as far as the HUAC was concerned— was to refute Louis B. Mayer's testimony on Song of Russia, if it wasn't what the Committee hoped to hear; and (2) a great deal of importance is placed on Song of Russia in the original schedule of witnesses.

Notes

1. I have not included their comments on what they expected from Warner's testimony.

2. I cut the rest of the comments on what they expected from Mayer's testimony, as it is not relevant. There is nothing about the possibility that what he says about *Song of Russia* might have to be refuted.

3. I have no idea what Wood could say about *Song of Russia* or Lowell Mellett; perhaps he had had some experiences with the latter. He was later asked about Lowell Mellett by the HUAC but had nothing to say.

4. I omit the first two paragraphs of this note, which are not relevant here.

5. Louis J. Russell appears here more than any other person. He was a former FBI agent who did investigative work for the HUAC. In many cases, what happened was this: An unfriendly witness was asked whether he was a member of the Communist Party; he refused to answer; after he stepped down, Louis J. Russell was called up, and then presented evidence (e.g., a Communist Party membership card) that the former witness was in fact a member of the Party.

~

From the FBI Files:
The Motion Picture Alliance and
the "Other Blacklist"

Federal Bureau of Investigation, Freedom of Information and Privacy Acts
Subject: Communist Infiltration-Motion Picture Industry
File Number: 100-138754, Serial: 1003 (pt. 2), Part 9 of 15. (See
foia.fbi.gov/compic.htm)

The two excerpts included here come from FBI reports on anti-Communist activities in Hollywood, February 1948 to July 1949, under the subhead: The Motion Picture Alliance for the Preservation of American Ideals.

From February 6, 1948, to September 15, 1948

As previously set forth, the Motion Picture Alliance was an organization set up by a number of motion picture executives, directors and producers in 1944 for the announced purpose of combating Communism and any other subversive elements within the film industry. Those individuals who originated and controlled the policies of this group were all anti-Communists and the new organization immediately drew the fire and counteraction on the part of the Communist elements in Hollywood.

In February of 1948, Confidential Informant [name crossed out] stated that the effectiveness of the Motion Picture Alliance was then on the decline due particularly to pressure being brought against it since the hearings in Washington by the House Committee on Un-American Activities in October of 1947. The informant reported that an important meeting of the group was held on February 12, 1948, and at the meeting a number of very significant statements and charges were made. Inasmuch as the organization was originally set up to combat Communist activities in the motion picture industry, that question was the main subject of discussion at the meeting. The members of the Executive Board, who were present, included James K. McGuinness, Ralph Clare, Ken Martinez, Borden Chase, Morrie Ryskind, Fred Niblo, Jr., Adolphe Menjou, James Grant and several others.

During the meeting, it was brought out that the heads of the motion picture industry were apparently lined up to protect the Communists working for them because the fact that the House Committee on Un-American Activities' hearings and the activities of the Motion Picture Alliance had brought the whole industry into disrepute with the American public.

The informant reported that during the meeting, Adolphe Menjou stated that since he had appeared before the House Committee on Un-American Activities, he was feeling the pressure of the producers and had already lost three parts in forthcoming pictures and felt that this was still not the end of the penalty which he might incur for his antagonism toward Communism.

Mr. McGuinness, an executive at Metro-Goldwyn-Mayer Studios, stated that as a result of his opposition to Communism, he had already been demoted to a lesser position. The informant reported that McGuinness stated the Louis Mayer, head of MGM, had told him that his attitude on the Communist question had caused too much dissension within the studios, thus indirectly warning him to stop his activity. McGuinness told those present that he would like to stay away from the Alliance for approximately three months because of the strain which was becoming too much for him.

Mr. Ryskind also told the meeting that he could not afford to be active in the organization because he felt that all employment for him would be affected and he intimated that it had been some time since he had been employed.

Mr. Clare, President of the Teamsters Union, Local 399, told the gathering that he has been harassed unduly by the producers-executives in dealing with the studios wherein the employment of his union members is concerned. Clare was of the opinion that his difficulties were the result of his activities within the Motion Picture Alliance and his well-known opposition to the Communist elements.

One member of the Executive Board, not identified by the informant, reportedly made the statement at this meeting that Dore Schary had stated that he would never employ at RKO Studios a member of the Motion Picture Alliance and that anyone else who took the same attitude as the Alliance would not be employed. It was also alleged that Schary had told the Screen Writer's Guild to disregard any statements he made regarding the discharging of known Communists and that he had to do this at the present time but that his sympathies were still with that organization in its political leanings.

Mr. McGuiness, according to the informant, also quoted Mr. Mayer as stating that anyone who testified against the Communists or took part in any hearing or investigation as witnesses friendly to Government action against Communists was rendering a distinct disservice to the motion picture industry.

According to the informant, other individuals present at the meeting volunteered information to the effect that anti-Communist writers and employees, not members of the Alliance, had also been discriminated against in obtaining employment.

September 15, 1948, to July 15, 1949

During the fall of 1948, Los Angeles Informant [name crossed out], who has been close to the leaders of the Motion Picture Alliance advised that due to pressure from the motion picture industry this group had dwindled down to a very small organization and was rapidly becoming more and more ineffective. According to the informant, the organization had been attacked since its formation, even by the motion picture producers themselves on the grounds that by raising the Communist issue it would cause a split in the motion picture industry.

According to this same informant, as an indication of the recession of the Alliance, at a meeting held on September 13, 1948, only nine persons were present. At this meeting several of the members related how they had been discriminated against by the studios due to their activity in the Alliance. One of the members, Borden Chase, stated that he had been told by Harry Cohn of Columbia Studios that he would like to employ Chase but that Chase would be unable to get along with the studio personnel, presumably because of Chase's anti-Communist testimony before the House Committee. Another member, Fred Niblo, Jr., stated that he had been forced to obtain employment with one of the Los Angeles newspapers although previously he had been a high priced writer in the film industry. James K. McGuinness, an executive at MGM Studios, advised an Agent of the Los Angeles Offices in the fall of 1948 that he had experienced considerable antagonism within the industry and in his own studio since testifying before the House Committee on Un-American Activities.

In December of 1948, informants advised that the influence of the Motion Picture Alliance was still becoming more and more ineffective. Among the other members of the Alliance who have experienced difficulty due to their anti-Communist stand have been Dick Macauley, who had been able to obtain only two weeks work since appearing before the House Committee in October of 1947, and James McGuinness who terminated his relationship with MGM only three months prior to the time he would have been eligible for a lifetime pension. It was reported that his contract was being dissolved by "mutual consent." Morrie Riskind [sic], a Pulitzer prize winner who had previously been much in demand by the studios, was told in the fall of 1948 by his agent that he was "all through" and that his agent had been unable to place Riskind [sic] in the motion picture industry. Riskind [sic] advised that this situation was having its effect upon the younger talent in Hollywood inasmuch as they would not "stick their necks out" to fight Communism believing that if they did so, it meant that they would get nowhere in the picture business. . . .

However, in the spring of 1949 Los Angeles Informant [name crossed out] advised that the general situation in the motion picture industry had resulted in a considerable amount of favorable public opinion toward the Alliance and that it was now being recognized and appreciated.

Postscript: Despite the optimism expressed in this last paragraph, there is no indication in these FBI files that the situation improved for the friendly witnesses who had suffered for testifying before the HUAC in October 1947.

Select Bibliography

Amis, Martin. *Koba the Dread: Laughter and the Twenty Million.* New York: Hyperion, 2002.

Berliner, Michael S., ed. *Ayn Rand: Russian Writings on Hollywood.* Marina del Rey, CA: Ayn Rand Institute Press, 1999.

———. *Letters of Ayn Rand.* New York: Dutton, 1995.

Bessie, Alvah. *Inquisition in Eden.* New York: Macmillan, 1965.

Billingsley, Kenneth Lloyd. *Hollywood Party: How Communism Seduced the American Film Industry in the 1930s and 1940s.* Rocklin, CA: Prima, 1998.

Bogdanovich, Peter. *Who the Devil Made It.* New York: Alfred A. Knopf, 1997.

Buhle, Mari Jo, Paul Buhle, and Dan Georgakas, eds. *Encyclopedia of the American Left.* Urbana and Chicago: University of Illinois Press, 1992.

Buhle, Paul, and Dave Wagner. *Radical Hollywood: The Untold Story Behind America's Favorite Movies.* New York: The New Press, 2002.

Cole, Lester. *Hollywood Red: The Autobiography of Lester Cole.* Palo Alto, CA: Ramparts Press, 1981.

Conquest, Robert. *The Great Terror: Stalin's Purge of the Thirties.* New York: Macmillan, 1968.

———. *Kolyma: The Arctic Death Camps.* New York: Viking, 1978.

Courtois, Stéphen, et al. *The Black Book of Communism: Crimes, Terror, Repression.* Translated by Jonathan Murphy and Mark Kramer. Cambridge: Harvard University Press, 1999.

Dallin, Alexander, and F. I. Firsov, eds. *Dimitrov and Stalin, 1939–1943: Letters from the Soviet Archives.* New Haven, CT: Yale University Press, 2000.

Dmytryk, Edward. *Odd Man Out: A Memoir of the Hollywood Ten.* Carbondale: Southern Illinois University Press, 1996.

Fariello, Griffin. *Red Scare: Memories of the American Inquisition: An Oral History.* New York: W. W. Norton, 1995.

Fitzpatrick, Sheila. *Everyday Stalinism: Ordinary Life in Extraordinary Times: Soviet Russia in the 1930s.* New York: Oxford University Press, 1999.

Fitzpatrick, Sheila. *Stalin's Peasants: Resistance and Survival in the Russian Village after Collectivization.* Oxford: Oxford University Press, 1994.

Fleming, Thomas. *The New Dealers' War: F.D.R. and the War Within World War II.* New York: Basic Books, 2001.

Friedrich, Otto. *City of Nets: A Portrait of Hollywood in the 1940s.* New York: Harper & Row, 1986.

Gordon, Bernard. *Hollywood Exile, or How I Learned to Love the Blacklist: A Memoir.* Austin: University of Texas Press, 1999.

Guiles, Fred Lawrence. *Hanging on in Paradise.* New York: McGraw-Hill, 1975.

Harriman, David, ed. *Journals of Ayn Rand.* New York: Plume, 1997.

Haynes, John Earl, and Harvey Klehr. *In Denial: Historians, Communism and Espionage.* San Francisco: Encounter Books, 2003.

———. *Venona: Decoding Soviet Espionage in America.* New Haven: Yale University Press, 2000.

Hellman, Lillian. *Scoundrel Time.* Introduction by Garry Wills. Boston: Little Brown, 1976.

Higham, Charles. *Merchant of Dreams: Louis B. Mayer, M.G.M., and the Secret Hollywood.* New York: Donald I. Fine, 1993.

Horowitz, David. *Radical Son: A Generational Odyssey.* New York: Simon & Schuster, 1997.

Kahn, Gordon. *Hollywood on Trial: The Story of the 10 Who Were Indicted.* New York: Boni & Gaer, 1948.

Kanfer, Stefan. *A Journal of the Plague Years.* New York: Atheneum, 1973.

Keegan, John. *The Second World War.* New York: Penguin, 1989.

Klehr, Harvey, John Earl Haynes, and Kyrill M. Anderson, eds. *The Soviet World of American Communism.* New Haven, CT: Yale University Press, 1998.

Klehr, Harvey, John Earl Haynes, and Fridrikh Igorevich Firsov, eds. *The Secret World of American Communism.* New Haven, CT: Yale University Press, 1995.

Koch, Howard. *As Time Goes By: Memoir of a Writer.* New York: Harcourt Brace Jovanovich, 1979.

Koch, Stephen. *Double Lives: Spies and Writers in the Secret Soviet War of Ideas Against the West.* New York: The Free Press, 1994.

Koppes, Clayton R., and Gregory D. Black. *Hollywood Goes to War: How Politics, Profits and Propaganda Shaped World War II Movies.* Berkeley: University of California Press, 1990.

Krivitsky, W.G. *In Stalin's Secret Service.* New York: Enigma Books, 2000.

Lardner, Ring, Jr. *I'd Hate Myself in the Morning: A Memoir.* New York: Thunder's Mouth Press, 2000.

Laurents, Arthur. *Original Story By: A Memoir of Broadway and Hollywood.* New York: Alfred A. Knopf, 2000.

Mayhew, Robert, ed. *Essays on Ayn Rand's We the Living.* Lanham, MD: Lexington Books, 2004.

McGilligan, Patrick, and Paul Buhle, eds. *Tender Comrades: A Backstory of the Hollywood Blacklist.* New York: St. Martin's Griffin, 1997.

Mellen, Joan. *Hellman and Hammett: The Legendary Passion of Lillian Hellman and Dashiell Hammett.* New York: HarperCollins, 1996.

Murray, Bruce. *Film and the German Left in the Weimar Republic.* Austin: University of Texas Press, 1990.

Navasky, Victor. *Naming Names.* New York: Viking Press, 1980.

Orwell, George. *Essays.* Selected and introduced by John Carey. New York: Everyman Library, 2002.

Peikoff, Leonard, ed. *The Early Ayn Rand: A Selection from Her Unpublished Fiction.* New York: Signet, 1986.

Peikoff, Leonard. *Objectivism: The Philosophy of Ayn Rand.* New York: Dutton, 1991.

Pipes, Richard. *Communism: A History.* New York: The Modern Library, 2001.

Pipes, Richard, ed. *The Unknown Lenin: From the Secret Archives.* New Haven, CT: Yale University Press, 1998.

Podhoretz, John, ed. *A Passion for Truth: The Selected Writings of Eric Breindel.* New York: HarperCollins, 1999.

Rawicz, Slavomir. *The Long Walk: The True Story of a Trek to Freedom.* New York: Lyons Press, 1997.

Rand, Ayn. *Anthem.* 50th anniversary paperback ed. New York: Signet, 1996.

———. *The Art of Fiction: A Guide for Writers and Readers.* Edited by Tore Boeckmann. New York: Plume, 2000.

———. *The Art of Nonfiction: A Guide for Writers and Readers.* Edited by Robert Mayhew. New York: Plume, 2001.

———. *Atlas Shrugged.* New York: Random House, 1953; paperback ed., New York: Dutton, 1992.

———. *Night of January 16th.* Rev. ed. New York: Plume, 1987.

———. *Return of the Primitive: The Anti-Industrial Revolution.* Edited by Peter Schwartz. New York: Meridian, 1999.

———. *The Romantic Manifesto: A Philosophy of Literature.* New York: Signet, 1975.

———. *The Voice of Reason: Essays in Objectivist Thought.* Edited by Leonard Peikoff. New York: New American Library, 1988.

———. *We the Living.* New York: Macmillan, 1936; rev. ed., New York: Random House, 1959; 60th anniversary paperback ed., New York: Signet, 1996.

Riasanovsky, Nicholas V. *A History of Russia.* 3rd ed. Oxford: Oxford University Press, 1977.

Platt, David, ed. *Celluloid Power: Social Film Criticisms from* The Birth of a Nation *to* Judgment at Nuremberg. Metuchen, NJ: Scarecrow Press, 1992.

Schrecker, Ellen. *Many Are the Crimes: McCarthyism in America.* Boston: Little, Brown, 1998.

Schwartz, Nancy Lynn. *The Hollywood Writers' Wars.* New York: Alfred A. Knopf, 1982.

Shentalinsky, Vitaly. *Arrested Voices: Resurrecting the Disappeared Writers of the Soviet Regime.* Translated by John Crowfoot. New York: Free Press, 1996.

Shostakovich, Dmitri. *Testimony: The Memoirs of Dmitri Shostakovich.* Edited by Solomon Volkov. Translated by Antonina W. Bouis. New York: Limelight Editions, 1990.

Siegelbaum, Lewis, and Andrei Sokolov, eds. *Stalinism as a Way of Life.* New Haven, CT: Yale University Press, 2000.

Stites, Richard, ed. *Culture and Entertainment in Wartime Russia.* Bloomington: Indiana University Press, 1995.

Strong, Anna Louise. *I Changed Worlds.* New York: Holt, 1935.

Topolski, Aleksander. *Without Vodka: Adventures in Wartime Russia.* South Royalton, VT: Steerforth Press, 2001.

Vaksberg, Arkady. *Stalin Against the Jews.* Translated by Antonina W. Bouis. New York: Alfred A. Knopf, 1994.

Viertel, Salka. *The Kindness of Strangers.* New York: Holt, Rinehart & Winston, 1969.

Weinstein, Allen, and Alexander Vassiliev. *The Haunted Wood: Soviet Espionage in America—The Stalin Era.* New York: Random House, 1999.

Wills, Garry. *John Wayne's America.* paperback ed. New York: Simon & Schuster, 1998.

~

Index

~

About the Author

Robert Mayhew is professor of philosophy at Seton Hall University. He is the author of *Aristotle's Criticism of Plato's Republic* and *The Female in Aristotle's Biology* and of numerous articles on Aristotle. He has translated a play of Aristophanes (*Assembly of Women*) and has edited unpublished material of Ayn Rand's, including *Ayn Rand's Marginalia, The Art of Nonfiction,* and (forthcoming) her Q&A. His present research interests include Plato's *Laws* and ancient Greek conceptions of justice.